D0411133

THE SHOW MUST GO ON

A Century of Club Cricket in the South of England

THE SHOW MUST GO ON

A Century of Club Cricket in the South of England

First published in the UK in 2015 by All Out Cricket Ltd

British Library Cataloguing in Publication Data.
A catalogue record for this book is available from the British Library.

ISBN: 978-1-909811-26-3

Cover image courtesy of Getty Images

Illustrations by Joe Provis

Printed in the UK by Jellyfish Print Solutions

CLUB CRICKET CONFERENCE: 100 YEARS

The Club Cricket Conference (CCC) celebrates its centenary in 2015, having been established 100 years ago to support the survival of cricket clubs in London during the Great War.

Between then and now, the landscape of the amateur game is greatly changed and yet one truth remains: cricket clubs serve their immediate communities and provide an outlet to sport for young and old of all abilities.

In determining how best to mark its centenary, the CCC wanted to recognise the extraordinary social and historic value clubs in southern England, its geographical footprint, have provided over the past 100 years and how, despite the challenges of current times, many clubs continue to provide vital service to cricket and to the social order of their localities.

The CCC has evolved and today, through its founding joint ownership of the National Cricket Conference, it works within the recreational game on a national basis, as well as a regional one, to give voice to the issues that affect the club game. Its cricket programme continues to offer opportunities for club cricketers to play at the highest level of the amateur game and to tour abroad; in its centenary year the CCC will take representative, ladies and veterans teams to Grenada and Barbados.

The CCC continues to represent the interests of amateur club cricket and remains committed to supporting the grassroots game however it can. *The Show Must Go On* is a homage to our wonderful game – its participants and supporters – and to club life, in all its glorious variety.

Simon Prodger
Secretary, Club Cricket Conference

CONTENTS

EDITORS

Ed Kemp is features editor at *All Out Cricket* magazine. He is a former first team captain at his childhood club Fair Oak CC near Southampton, where he proudly dons club maroon to this day

Phil Walker is editor at *All Out Cricket* magazine. He grew up in Essex; more specifically around the outfields, nets and heaving bar tables of Gidea Park & Romford CC. And it's there where you'll still find him every Saturday during the season, except when Glastonbury's on

CONTRIBUTORS

Michael Burns has produced nine cricket films, including the award-winning *A Gentleman Cricketer*, and is the author of a centenary history of Malden Wanderers, where he has been first team captain and president

Stephen Chalke has written 15 books about cricket. His latest, *Summer's Crown*, tells the story of the County Championship. In 1988 he was a founder member of The Journeymen Cricket Club, for whom he played for 25 years. They are one of more than 100 clubs featured in *Gentlemen, Gypsies and Jesters: the wonderful world of wandering cricket*, a book which he co-edited with Anthony Gibson and which raised nearly £50,000 for the Chance to Shine charity

Sahil Dutta is a political economist at Sussex University and writes on cricket for *ESPNcricinfo.com* and *All Out Cricket* magazine. He joined North Middlesex CC as a colt and now struggles on for St Peters CC in Brighton

David Frith is an award-winning writer of 35 books, a former editor of *The Cricketer* and founder of the *Wisden Cricket Monthly*. He has played club cricket for Cheam, East Molesey, Shepperton, Blackheath and Guildford, where he is a vice-president

Will Macpherson is a freelance cricket and rugby writer based in London who works for *ESPNcricinfo.com*, the *Guardian* and *All Out Cricket* magazine. His own cricketing career – all stodgy middle-order batting and apologetic off-breaks – didn't really make it out of his teen years

Peter Mason is a journalist who has written books on the Caribbean and cricket, including a biography of Learie Constantine. He played for Letchworth CC from 1979-1984, Shepherds Bush CC from 1985-2000, and had a season of league cricket in Jamaica with University of West Indies in 1999

Andrew Miller is a former editor of *The Cricketer* and, before that, UK Editor at *ESPNcricinfo.com.* A founder member of the Celeriac XI, he currently plays for The Camel CC in East London. He has been known to open the bowling for the Cricket Writers' Club and counts Mike Gatting and Charlotte Edwards among his luckless victims

Benj Moorehead is a freelance writer who has written for the *Times, Wisden* and *The Spectator.* He worked as an editor at *The Cricketer* magazine between 2008 and 2014, and, years after a brief spell as a north London leg-spin sensation, as the magazine's Village Cup correspondent he travelled far and wide to watch the club game all over the country

Raf Nicholson is a freelance women's cricket journalist who has written for *All Out Cricket* magazine, *ESPNcricinfo.com,* and *Wisden.* While studying history at Oxford University, she played cricket for Merton College. Since retiring to the press box, she has become the world's leading historian of the women's game, spending the past few years working her way through mountains of women's cricket club minutes, as well as interviewing women cricketers past and present for her forthcoming book on the history of women's cricket

David Perrin was a journalist with the BBC, ITV, and Channel Four, working on such programmes as *Panorama, Inside Story, TV Eye,* and *Cutting Edge.* He joined Shepherds Bush CC as a colt and 2nd XI scorer in 1958, and has since been a captain, president, and even stand-in groundsman at the club

Joe Provis is a designer and illustrator at *All Out Cricket* magazine. He lives in rural Herefordshire, where, having seen the disbandment of both of his long-established childhood clubs through falling numbers, he now plies his trade at the picturesque Goodrich CC in the Marches League

Dr Duncan Stone is a historian with an interest in the social and philosophical origins of amateurism and its utility in sport, as well as the links between class, the suburbanisation process and cultural change. He has played cricket in the north and south of England and Australia, but his real claim to fame is bowling a dot ball to Darren Gough during an England net session in New Zealand

Dan Waddell is a journalist, novelist and author of more than a dozen works of non-fiction, the latest being *Field of Shadows: the true story of an English cricket tour of Nazi Germany in 1937.* He captains the amiable scoundrels of Acton CC's 2nd XI where, in between taking painkillers, he tries and fails to pass on sage advice to young players

FOREWORD

by Angus Fraser

"I am a product of club cricket... This game we love is full of good people, men and women who spend large parts of their lives trying to provide opportunities for others to play it"

In my teenage years Stanmore Cricket Club was like a second home to Alastair, my brother, and me. During the summer we would spend a couple of evenings each week on The Common playing in the nets or for the under 13s, 15s or 17s. On other evenings we would mow the outfield, roll the pitches and generally help maintain the ground.

At the weekend we were always at the club ready to make up the numbers should anyone pull out of the 3rd XI, the team my father captained. Then, the 3rd XI used to play on a dodgy square between pitches at Harrow Rugby Club, which was the other side of the ponds, or at Whitchurch Playing Fields a couple of miles down the road. If I wasn't required by the 3rd's I often used to score for the 1st XI.

Playing in the 3rd XI was quite an experience. On several occasions there were only two or three of us under the age of 45. Our job was to run around and collect the ball from the boundary. There were several great characters in the team. Norman Jacobs (Ace), Clive Desmond (Tosser), Ken Andrews (Little Tosser), Les Bowditch, Gordon Williams, Derek Arnell and Reg Hayter to name but a few. They all played cricket because they loved the game. I didn't appreciate it at the time but it was a wonderful environment to grow up in.

Once my cricket began to progress I quickly moved through to the 1st XI, captained by Graham Pauncefort, a legendary figure in Middlesex league cricket. Stanmore CC meant everything to Graham and he did most of the jobs at the ground, with a little help from Alastair, myself and a couple of our mates. Stanmore had a very good side containing Richard Ellis and Andrew Miller, who were on the Middlesex staff, and Andy Needham, who was at Surrey.

Initially I bowled first change behind Arthur Ferry and Ross Chiese, two formidable and gobby fastish bowlers. Ross used to, still does, think he is Dennis Lillee. According to Ross I learnt everything I know about bowling from him. Our spinner was Pete Nichols, the senior pro, a wonderful man. In 1983 we won the Middlesex County Cricket League, the biggest prize in the club's history.

Sunday fixtures were important then, with Graham always reminding us that Stanmore were our opponents' biggest game of the year. The fixtures were mainly in the counties surrounding Middlesex and many pleasant afternoons were spent at Tring, Beaconsfield, Berkhamsted, Dunstable, Letchworth, Hertford and Radlett. Graham loved a singsong in the bar after games and they were occasionally accompanied by silly games like boats, spoons and the three-man lift.

Graham often used to pick up and drop off my brother and me from home. Getting to bed at midnight after having had a couple of pints was okay during the summer holidays but during term time my parents weren't too happy to see their sons being dropped off that late on a Sunday evening. On the occasions one of my parents picked us up the rest of the team used to sing the 'Ovaltineys' song to us as we left.

Through club cricket I have made many good friends, mates that I still see regularly now. Through Graham there were lots of social games to play during a season too. The biggest were matches between the Thames Valley Gentlemen and Stoics at Teddington Cricket Club. Lunch often lasted a couple of hours and the port flowed freely. They were great days that I have extremely fond memories of.

Club cricket has changed, in some cases for the good, others not. Facilities at clubs are, in general, far better now than they used to be. Through the ECB and Lottery funding many clubs possess excellent net facilities and changing rooms and bar areas are far more, let's say, welcoming. Colts sections at many clubs are thriving too, which is just as well because the revenues that these sections bring in underpin most clubs.

The tightening of drink-driving laws has undoubtedly affected club life, as has the influence of a wife, girlfriend or partner. I don't know whether Stanmore CC was unique but we were expected to be available to play on most Saturdays and Sundays. Girlfriends and wives spent many Saturday evenings at the club too. Now, sadly, it is a shower and a quick soft drink after the game for most players, before going out in the evening.

These changes, along with the fact that everybody's time seems so precious now, leaves club cricket with many issues to address. Sadly, it is inevitable that some will cease to exist but, as with pubs, there may at one time have been too many around. The good thing is that new clubs are being created.

The challenges individual clubs face vary but most revolve around making everything about them more attractive. Clubs need to make themselves a more attractive place for people to socialise. They also need to do more to ensure that junior members remain at the club when their time as a colt ends. People expect a lot more now than they used to and clubs need to do their utmost to provide them with what they are looking for. Then, hopefully, fewer games will be called off through lack of players.

To keep youngsters involved the opportunities to play must be increased and 3rd XIs should not be filled with 50-plus-year-olds that bowl 20 overs in a row and occupy the top six batting positions. When work permits my son, Alex, plays for Stanmore 3rd XI and he enjoys it far more when he plays with lads his age and gets a decent chance to bowl.

Club cricket in the UK is unique and it needs to be cherished. Attitudes are vastly different in Australia and New Zealand, where I spent four winters during my playing career. There you get the feeling that clubs exist to provide a service, not to be a social hub of the local community.

Micky Stewart, the former England cricket coach, used to say that the attitude within club cricket would always make it hard for England to consistently compete with Australia. Micky was not being critical but the fundamental difference is that the majority of cricket young men play is serious rather than social.

So should club cricket exist just to produce England cricketers? I do not think so. I believe club cricket in the UK exists to provide 22 people and their families with regular opportunities to play and be involved in this wonderful game. If this environment helps to produce the next Joe Root or Moeen Ali then that is an added bonus.

I am a product of club cricket and, to date, I have been extremely fortunate that cricket has dominated my working life. This game we love is full of good people, men and women who spend large parts of their lives trying to provide opportunities for others to play it. To me they are stars as big as those that play in front of a full house at Lord's.

VII

INTRODUCTION

by Phil Walker

"I fear the threat of apathy to our sport, and I see too much indifference to the reasonable discipline we must all observe if the game is to have any meaning. Club cricket, in the south, anyway, is beginning to suffer from lassitude; it needs a stiff dose of something. But what? And who is to administer it?"
Leo Bennett, The Weekend Cricketer, 1951.

If the title for this book, *The Show Must Go On*, evokes a certain wistfulness, a little vaudevillian nostalgia for an eternal past, then it's barely out of step with our story as told. Yet, far more than whimsy, this title serves as invocation: to us lot – the clubbies and umps, coaches and curators, the tea ladies, treasurers, barmen and board – to play up, play up and play the game, to get it on come hell or surface water. Here's our mantra for the ages, resonating through all those dusty, pencilled scorebooks, and imprinted on the frayed corners of sepia photos, which these days hang above clubhouse bars still alive with post-stumps fables. Because without club cricket's beautiful parade, by turns elegant and elegiac, chaotic and quixotic, there really is no show to put on.

Such entreaties were as pertinent a century ago as they are today. It was in a London hotel on March 15, 1915, that the London Club Cricket Conference was formed, principally to keep some version of club cricket going in wartime. Private cricket grounds needed protecting and looking after, while cricketers from both military and civilian life needed a game to play. "The War itself," wrote former Conference official Leo Bennett in 1951, "was directly responsible for what was then quite a new departure. Several of the leading London clubs thought that the formation of such a conference [was] essential to keep the clubs together, as the War had completely wrecked the general organisation of the game."

That first meeting was convened to discover which clubs intended to remain active during the War, with fixtures then being set up with each other. "In other words," writes Bennett, "the initial ideas were a sort of glorified fixture bureau."

A century on, the Club Cricket Conference (CCC) celebrates its centenary year occupied by familiar themes. While club cricket was once threatened by the horrors of war, today's game feels no less endangered by the mundane yet irrepressible pressures of modern life. A storm is brewing on the outfields of amateur cricket in this country and many of us involved in club cricket can feel the clouds rolling in.

In October 2014, the ECB released the results of a landmark survey, completed by more than 37,000 people. Nationwide, participation numbers have dropped by 64,000 in a single year, down from 908,000 in 2013 to 844,000 in 2014. Five per cent of fixtures were conceded in 2014 because at least one of the teams was unable to field 11 bodies. Moreover, less than a third of those 844,000 regarded themselves as 'core' players, with the best part of the other 600,000 deemed 'occasional' or 'cameo' players.

Taking shelter inside the clubhouse, everyone has an opinion. Overlapping theories get tossed around the conversation. So it's straitened times for time-poor families, and the modern disease of weekend work; it's directionless kids getting too heavy on their consoles, it's niche TV coverage of an erratic national team; it's a *society* thing, an individualistic culture at odds with team games, compounded by a scarcity of volunteers and crumbling bar revenues... and it's cricket, our cricket, rumbling on nevertheless.

To those affiliated to the CCC, and indeed other such organisations concerned with the health and accessibility of the club game, these figures are not so much shocking as clarifying; the amateur game has been riding the jabs and haymakers of modernisation for a century and plenty, and yet here it still stands, a little bruised perhaps, but resolute, unbowed, up for more.

This book is intended to be part social history, part celebration of great feats, great clubs and epic figures, part assessment of how far we've come, and part analysis of where we go next. We've sprinkled through the book portraits of some club institutions, alongside individuals who, through runs, heart, sweat and selflessness, have given more to the game than strictly necessary and for which we all owe deep debts of gratitude. And while it wasn't possible to include by name all the deserving figures of club life, it's their spirit, our spirit, absorbed so deep into the collective, which substantiates and humanises these pages.

Our stories remain broadly southbound, in keeping with the CCC's constituents. The mythic northern leagues have been journalised – and romanticised – elsewhere, so here, if you will, is the story of the other side. But just as the CCC assumes joint ownership of the National Cricket Conference, so this book, too, seeks to peer beyond its horizons, addressing elements common to recreational cricket across these invisible borders. As we look ahead to the future, the issues we face are emphatically nationwide rather than regional.

How typical of cricket lovers like old Leo Bennett to fear their great love's demise, and how typically premature. Leo's fatalistic obituary, penned in the modernistic maelstrom of 1951, has no doubt been written for every decade since. In some ways it's all part of the fun. And it's fun that drew us at *All Out Cricket* to this project in the first place. We've always put club cricket at the heart of what we do, from the time our first magazine dropped in 2004. We're all clubbies here. And today that absorption in the club game feels deeper than ever; the more we work away inside the professional circus, the deeper our love grows for the club game. It's here where cricket truly breathes. Right here and right now. Enjoy the book. Let's never forget we're all in this together.

Phil Walker
Editor, All Out Cricket

PICKING UP THE PIECES

CLUB CRICKET BETWEEN THE WARS

by Andrew Miller

"Cricket's restoration was a vital means of nourishing the soul of a war-shattered nation"

"YOUR COUNTRY NEEDS
YOU"

In June 1915, the Honourable Charles Thomas Mills, MP for Uxbridge and enthusiastic club cricketer, stood on the steps of the pavilion at Cricket Field Lane to deliver his farewell address to a packed crowd of friends and constituents. He was 27 years of age, a Conservative MP since January 1910 when, for two years, he had served as the "Baby of the House", the country's youngest Member of Parliament. Now he was off to fight for King and Country, having engineered a transfer from the West Kent Yeomanry to the Scots Guards in order to be sent overseas more quickly.

Eton-educated, and the heir to a banking dynasty, for Mills – as for so many of his contemporaries – the call to arms was merely the logical progression from his exertions on the field of play. "Games were a training ground for life," wrote Malcolm Tozer in *The Cultural Bond*. "War, with its call to self-sacrifice, to duty and to honour, was seen by many as the realisation of a hope."

"I hope you will be good enough to think of me while I am away," Mills told his audience at Uxbridge. "I hope that you will pray that, above all things, I shall do my duty, very humbly it may be, and bring no disgrace upon you and upon my friends down here."

The stampede for military service was universal. At Havant CC in Hampshire, one former player, John Freeston, recalled in his club's centenary booklet in 1974 the sight of telegrams being brought onto the pitch to inform various players of their call-ups. But most didn't need to be asked twice. On September 19, 1914, Private JW Hankin, latterly of Malden Wanderers CC, wrote from the front line: "If there are any more boys in Malden tell them to come at once or they will miss the fun!"

Inevitably, the loss of innocence was swift and devastating. On October 6, 1915, within four months of his deployment, Mills was struck in the head and killed by a piece of shrapnel during the Battle of Loos. He was one of 11 Uxbridge players who did not return from the war, among them Reggie Schwarz, the South Africa Test cricketer, who survived the conflict but died in the Spanish flu pandemic in November 1918, just seven days after the Armistice had been signed.

Kenneth Hutchings, the scorer of a match-winning century for England against Australia at Melbourne in 1908 and the scourge of windows throughout his home county of Kent, was another who never made it home. His finest hour in club cricket had come with a 45-minute century for Southborough against "Town" at the Nevill Ground in Tunbridge Wells, in which he had lost the ball three times and nearly taken out the pavilion clock. Such carefree pursuits were a world away when, in September 1916, Hutchings was struck by a shell and killed while serving with the 12th Battalion, The King's Regiment, during the Battle of Ginchy.

This backdrop of mechanised slaughter quickly stripped away any notions of glory from the wartime sacrifice, and was exacerbated in many unfortunate cases by the heavy casualties suffered by the so-called Pals' Battalions of locally recruited men – many of whom had inevitably played for the same teams in peace-time. All of which meant that clubs were forced to make hard decisions in the intervening four years. "It is supposed the Farnham Ramblers were engaged with the Germans, which is more important than cricket," read a notice pinned to the gates of Hale Institute in August 1914, after 500 of the town's menfolk had enlisted, to leave the club's playing stock utterly depleted.

By 1916, reported Nigel Turk and Geoffrey Charman in their 1973 history of cricket in Caterham, the Hill and Valley area in Surrey had been "almost denuded of its fit men by the successful recruiting campaigns and the grim casualty list". The town lost over 90 men that year – which was reportedly an improvement on 1915's losses – and the survival of the club was left "in the hands of the middle-aged who had been spared active military service".

Some clubs, such as North Enfield CC, were ground down by the war effort on the home front as much as the front line – the club's pre-eminence in north London cricket counted for nothing when the local Royal Small Arms Factory at Enfield Lock and the Royal Gunpowder Mills at Waltham Abbey were forced into overtime production, leaving "no time for sport or indeed any other pleasurable activities". On May 30, 1919 it was proposed that "the club be disbanded and all assets sold", and though the spirit of North Enfield CC lived on in the endeavours of a new outfit, St Michael's, the sense of starting from scratch was absolute.

Other teams were determined to plough on through regardless, seeing the continuation of the status quo as a vital contribution to the nation's morale – "Consideration should be given to the importance of the preservation of a normal attitude towards recreation," read an editorial in the *Surrey Comet* as Malden Wanderers' committee considered whether to wind up the club. Instead its fortunes were placed in the hands of the "old crocks", as were those of their fellow Surrey outfit, Old Cranleighans. "Teams became harder to raise and the old and the crippled were press-ganged into playing," wrote Martin Williamson for his club's centenary in 1990, but, he added, there were instances of levity nonetheless: "In 1917, W Crewe was so keen for a game he landed his bi-plane on St Andrew's and the local police kept guard over it while he sauntered off to the common."

More prosaic matters impacted on the post-war rebirth of many of the country's clubs, however. By the simple fact of their flat, open nature, cricket fields made ideal training grounds for army units, or failing that, auxiliary premises for livestock grazing and crop production, all of which made such venues utterly unsuitable for any level of cricket in the war's immediate aftermath.

Bromley CC, for example, endured a "regrettable interlude" in 1916, wrote JA Parker for the club's 150th anniversary in 1970, when the club's tireless groundsman, Walter Seale, enlisted in the Royal Artillery and left the ground to become a hayfield. Parker recalled being roused at 6am one morning to find his garden full of sheep while another committee member complained of damage caused to his fence by a herd of bullocks.

Moreover, four years of inaction left almost every club in the land facing penury. Treasurers' reports from the final years of the war all hit upon a variation on the same theme; Malden's finances, to name but one example, were described as "hopeless". And yet, the stirrings of a true community spirit would help to rouse many of these beleaguered clubs, with acts of charity coming in varying shapes and sizes.

In Kent, Meopham CC's revival epitomised the sense that cricket's restoration was a vital means of nourishing the soul of a war-shattered nation. A concert on May

3, 1919 "aroused so much enthusiasm that many people had to be locked out of the village hall", wrote William Gunyon in the club's history. The event raised £15, enough money to restore the overgrown field and run fixtures nearly every week – including, for the first time, the occasional 2nd XI game. Later in the season the club was even able to commission a pavilion at a total cost of £70.

Back at Uxbridge, CT Mills' home club, the post-war urgency was made all the more acute by the impending lapse, in September 1918, of the lease for the ground. A swift decision was driven through by Charles Stevens, the club secretary, to purchase the venue as a memorial to all those who had lost their lives in the conflict and the response, once again, was overwhelming.

"Dear sirs," read one letter to the committee. "Our Daddy sent Jack and I some money from Palestine and we thought we would like to give some of it to the cricket-field purchase fund, as we have spent many happy hours in it, so we enclose 5 /-. Yours truly, Marjorie and Jack Hinckley."

"Commemorate forever their unselfish pluck and endurance on the battlefields of France," wrote Henry Grove, another of Uxbridge's generous benefactors, while Captain V Richards RE concurred: "Dedicate it to the memory of those who once played on its turf but who have now finished the game of life so gloriously – true sportsmen to the end."

Alice Lady Hillingdon, Mills' grieving mother, was understandably moved by the reaction. "I think it is a very nice idea as personally I should so dislike the ground to be used for any other purpose than that for which we have always known it," she wrote. "I still see our Charlie being assisted by you to the wickets when he was barely nine years old, and also all those other brave boys each coached by you."

Chichester Priory Park CC in Sussex took a similar route back to functionality. In 1917, the club raised £207-10s-0d from an appeal but it was the decision of the land-owner, the Duke of Richmond, to present the park as a war memorial that secured its future. The City Council took over the running of the club from the Priory Park Society, who surrendered the remaining nine years of its 21-year lease on the understanding that the rights of the sports clubs who used the grounds would be maintained.

• •

However, for better and for worse, the social characteristics of many clubs were unrecognisable upon the resumption of regular cricket. Some, such as Cockfosters CC in north London, stumbled blindly into this brave new world, with what had been a pre-war golden age for the club rapidly fading to sepia. Until 1914, their 1st XI had been one of the mightiest in Middlesex, but now it was so decimated by casualties that there is no record of them having played any games in 1919. By 1920 the club was reduced to advertising for fixtures: "June to August: Medium Strength".

Of those pre-war Cockfosters players who survived the hostilities, many never played for the club again, including the locally renowned Etheridge brothers, the best of whom – Sydney Graver, or SG – had finished third in the Minor Counties averages for Hertfordshire after playing in all eight fixtures in 1914. With SG recovering from being badly gassed in the trenches, the brothers transferred their allegiance to Barnet CC, partially no doubt on account of the death of their father and former club secretary, FB Etheridge, in 1916. Another powerful Cockfosters clan, the Micklems, also left the area, never to be traced amid the post-war upheaval.

Wandering sides such as the Old Whitgiftians found it equally hard to pick up the threads of normality, with neither a regular home ground to act as a focal point nor any reliable means of contacting the school's old boys to offer fixtures. In a tale common to many such clubs, it took the perseverance of one man to get the momentum going once again, with Theo Groom sending out a circular to 570 boys who had left since 1914, and refusing to give up despite receiving only half a dozen replies. A similar situation almost did for Farningham, in Kent. Its ground was briefly annexed by the local tennis club when a meeting to revive the cricket team attracted only three members.

Other clubs were far more successful in their relaunches although it helped, in many cases, to have a local benefactor on which to lean. Bidborough CC in Kent, for instance, enjoyed the use of a ground on the Great Boundes estate, owned by one Mrs Harland, whose love of cricket was so great that it was claimed (via her chauffeur) many years later, when the estate was sold for development: "She'd have given you that ground in perpetuity, if only you had asked."

Either way, there was an absence of existential angst for Bidborough in the immediate aftermath of the war, when the club announced a full fixture card for 1919, with 21 games, culminating in their annual September showpiece, Married v Single. After that match, between 20 and 30 retired to the local hostelry, the Hare and Hounds, whose landlord had been the club treasurer prior to the war, and "with the cloth removed a very pleasant evening was spent in toast and song."

A similar strengthening of the ties between cricket and the brewing industry helped to revive Farnham's fortunes, with a £20 cash injection – £10 each from two local beer-makers, Farnham United Breweries Ltd and Watney, Combe, Reid and Co Ltd – proving sufficient to save the club from bankruptcy. There was a neat historical symmetry in the deal as well: at the time of the club's establishment back in 1782, hops cultivation had been the town's central industry, even though the beverage had caused the club to be banished from its home in the local park in the 1840s, when the bishop took offence at the opening of a beer tent.

Mayfield CC, in Sussex, received similar largesse from its local brewers, Messrs Taplin and Sons of Brighton, who charged a nominal rent after purchasing the Wellbrook Ground in 1925 and "maintained a public-spirited and beneficent interest in the Club". And Dorking CC was another that had reason to be grateful for the lucrative thirst that its existence had so clearly created among its players. The publican at the Red Lion saw to it that the club's ground rent was paid throughout the war so that cricket could resume without delay in May 1919.

In the absence of such a convenient arrangement, Norwood CC took an alternative step, selling its club and grounds jointly as a sports venue for the employees of two banks, Eagle Star and British Dominions Insurance Co Ltd, and Cox and Co. With 200 local members also accepted in the deal, the club was able to continue playing under its original name before being bought back by Croydon Council in 1932.

But, as Kenneth J Cole, Dorking's historian, notes: "the pattern of club cricket was already altering in the wake of the social and economic changes brought about by the war". With leisure time at a premium, the club gradually phased out its mid-week fixture as Saturdays took over as the main match days, and though strong traces of the club scene's pre-war class distinction remained in place, new realities were taking hold everywhere.

"As most of us were war veterans there was a wonderful camaraderie in those early years," wrote LC Jenkins, who played for Bromley after the war. "Loyalty to the club and cricket was one hundredfold, and no one ever cried off if they could help it. But generous declarations were a rarity, you had to bowl the other side out. The fixture card still carried a stern injunction – 'The Nets will be up for practice from five o'clock when there is no match.' And when you were short you played your 'groundman' or semi-professional."

Many other clubs ensured a similar measure of discipline was adhered to, often through the presence of an on-field patriarch. Meopham CC, for instance, were guided by the experience of Robert Arnold, aka "The Major" – a solicitor by trade but an Army riding instructor for the first two years of the war before being posted to France in 1916. At the age of 56, he remained the club's driving force into the 1920s, and according to the club history, was rarely shy of the odd subversive tactic – such as neglecting to inform the visiting captain of Meopham's boundary regulations or, on one occasion, marching the opposition out of a local tea shop to resume play after the interval.

Outwood, in Surrey, was another club that resumed its cricket at a low ebb but refused to be downbeat. "Almost all of the old playing members had left the neighbourhood," read a newspaper report in April 1919, "some having given their lives in the war, but it is hoped that even at the risk of losing every match, a team will be gathered together to play the game for its own sake, and to make use of the charming ground on the common."

The man who did most to epitomise that hope for Outwood was Major JRE Cunliffe, the club captain from 1921 to 1923, who made a habit of arriving at the ground on horseback dressed in white kid gloves, tended to restrict his scoring to fours and sixes, and once apologised for running a teammate out with the immortal words: "Sorry old boy, I dropped my monocle."

For some clubs, however, the chance to do things differently was grasped with both hands. Banstead's meeting on April 5, 1919 instigated "a revolutionary rush", according to John Wilcox's history, *Playing on the Green*, as the club was hauled back into existence "with the vigour of young men whose terrible war experiences had given them a mandate for change".

Fundamental set-backs, such as the disappearance of the mower and the death of the groundsman's horse, couldn't hold back the tide of change at Banstead. A subscription of five shillings was put in place and, for the first time in its history, women were allowed inside the pavilion. An ex-soldier, George "Stitch" Muggeridge, devoted his entire 28 days of demob leave to getting the ground back into shape (with the school's horse borrowed in exchange for the roller and clad in leather shoes to avoid damaging the wicket) and Stitch would maintain that devotion well into his eighth decade, retiring with more wickets than any Banstead player before or since.

Perhaps Banstead's most notable innovation, however, was the introduction of a new "parish residents only" membership rule, a decision that ended, at a stroke, one of the most long-standing gripes that had existed about the pre-war make-up of the club.

For many years, the club's 1st XI had been the preserve of masters and pupils from the nearby Rosehill School, whose undoubted talents with bat and ball were secondary to the fact that they formed, as Wilcox put it, "a rather exclusive upper-class ring which was hard to break into." Under that status quo, the villagers had habitually been condemned to the 2nd XI but the parishioners' rule transformed the club's social mobility.

Among the men who benefitted from this new order was a self-made entrepreneur named Vic Stevens, who would go on to become one of the club's most generous benefactors and would later be responsible for installing the pavilion clock. His finest hour on the field came in 1936 when he added 300 for the first wicket against the jazz-hatters of Butterflies: "I doubt whether anything he ever did later gave him the delight he derived from putting those Old Etonians/Harrovians to the sword that day," wrote Wilcox.

By breaking down its social boundaries, Banstead found itself ideally placed to thrive in the inter-war boom years, as the branch line to Epsom Downs was electrified and the town experienced its first wave of commuter residents, many of whom had the sort of disposable income that would prove rather handy to a hub of the town's social scene. A new ground was purchased for the club by one of its members, Charles Garton, who died before they had relocated in 1932, but who had prudently been made a vice-president to encourage such largesse to be executed through his will.

The transformation in many clubs was notable, even within a generation. Writing in 1970 for Brighton Brunswick CC's centenary brochure, the president, AK Wilson, recalled how his club's facilities had "altered out of recognition" by the mid-1920s. "When I started playing the present Secretary's office had to accommodate the professionals of both sides (all are Cricketers today)," he wrote. "The amateurs used the main pavilion and, apart from some lavatory basins we all shared one rusty bath, a gas geyser (rarely working) and a cold shower."

An investment in facilities was, for many clubs, the fundamental means to self-improvement. Purley had retained a modest income during its fallow war years by selling the cricket field for £12 for haystacking (the club sensibly resisted the lure of 10 guineas for bullock grazing, and the accompanying damage to the pitch that would have caused). Then, in 1924, it bought for £3,650 the freehold for the sports club's original eight acres, plus an extra acre for the laying of six tennis courts.

The outlay unleashed the social potential of the club and by the 1920s the confluence of tennis, hockey, bowls and cricket had created a rich "off-field" scene, epitomised by the so-called Flannel Dances that formed a high point of the summer months.

"If members do not wish to dance all the while on these occasions, and find that a stroll in the moonlight is beneficial to them, I suggest that they arm themselves with a strong knife each, and in the course of their journeyings remove some of the weeds from the cricket ground," wrote the secretary in a mischievous entry to the *Club News*. "At the same time, I might point out that this weeding is not absolutely necessary behind the sight screens."

Banstead's pavilion on the eve of war in 1938. Photo courtesy of Banstead History Research Group

"If one tired of cricket for a minute or two," added the local paper, "there was always the spectacle of mighty men and charming maidens qualifying for the tennis championships at Wimbledon and further afield one could watch the ancients at the more soothing game of bowls."

That jingoistic sense of purpose of the pre-war years may have been eroded by the horrors of the trenches, but in many ways, the character of the club cricket scene not only endured but was calcified in the years that followed.

After all, most of the problems that beset the club scene back then – a shortage of decent players, a surfeit of the reluctant and inept; an over-reliance on the goodwill of the few and a chronic lack of funds – were not so fundamentally removed from what most match managers encounter to this day.

Ultimately the recreational game remains fuelled by escapism. The reasons for abandoning one's day-to-day worries – even to replace them with a first-ball duck and a rash of dropped catches – remain as valid in peacetime as they were so essential during and after the war. Which is why, when the clouds started to gather once again in the summer of 1939, the sport was able to retain that innate belief that the show would go on, no matter what.

• • •

CLUB INSTITUTIONS
Guildford CC
by David Frith

In 1988, with the 50th anniversary of County Championship cricket at Guildford fast approaching, I put together a magazine style book called *Guildford Jubilee.* Surviving players from that inaugural 1938 match came down to see Surrey play Hampshire again, and club and civic celebrations made it a memorable summer.

In 2013, a quarter-century having sped by, it was now time to commemorate 75 years of big cricket at the Woodbridge Road ground. The first need was to update the county matches, taking in sensations such as Alistair Brown's 203 against Hampshire in a 40-over match in 1997, Darren Bicknell's 228 not out against Nottinghamshire in 1995, his brother Martin's 16 wickets against Leicestershire in 2000, and Justin Langer's ground record of 342 for Somerset in 2006 (the eighth highest score ever in the history of the County Championship).

Because it was now urgently beckoning to be done, this time I also gathered everything I could find on the history of cricket in Guildford generally. Some colourful characters emerged, among them Sir Harry Waechter, who gave the ground to the borough in safe keeping for sport; MP Denzil Onslow, who dreaded Guildford Cricket Club committee meetings because everybody wanted to discuss politics with him (he also believed that cricket should be changed as little as possible, bless him); and club patron the Duke of Sutherland, who, stated Dame Barbara Cartland, "may well have been" the father of her daughter Raine.

But in scanning the broad history of the area, to my astonishment I came to realise that a greater quantity of significant cricket development attached itself to Guildford and its immediate surrounds than to any other part of England. The true 'Cradle of Cricket' was here.

By chance, I was recently invited down to Hampshire to speak at Hambledon Cricket Club's lunch, held in the cosy and evocative Bat and Ball Inn, across the road from the historic expanse of Broadhalfpenny Down. With some trepidation, I broke the news to the gathering that the true cradle of cricket was actually Guildford. Hambledon was fortunate to have a fine chronicler in John Nyren. Had Guildford had someone similar then this town would have been recognised long ago as cricket's 'cradle', or something similar. Happily, the diners seemed to take it in good humour, though it is perfectly possible that many thought I was merely joking.

With the publication of my 2013 book *Guildford's Cricket Story* during the Surrey v Warwickshire match at Woodbridge Road that season, the claim became official. To date, there has been no counter-argument.

The claim is based on the following:

Oldest surviving reference
In 1558, John Derrick, a Surrey coroner aged around 59, testified in a dispute over some land at the top of what is now North Street, Guildford that he "did runne and play there at Creckett and other Plaies" with his friends about 50 years earlier. This document, recently transferred from Guildford's Muniment Room to the Surrey History Centre in Woking, remains the earliest surviving example of the word cricket, albeit with its late medieval spelling.

The middle stump
Edward 'Lumpy' Stevens, the crack bowler of his time, was traditionally allowed to select his own pitch, one which favoured his nifty underhand deliveries. With only two stumps then being used, with a longish 'bail', he beat the bat so often, only to fail to knock either stump down as the ball whizzed between them. Evolution now stepped in as the sensible inclusion of a middle stump was finally adopted. Lumpy, the instigator of this progressive move, came from Send, just outside Guildford.

Pads and spikes

From Ash, on the western border of Guildford, came Bob Robinson, a tall and burly left-hander born in 1765, who had an innovative mind. Fed up with having his shins skinned and bruised, he devised leg protection. In that innocent age the only material available was timber slats. 'Long Bob' went to the crease with this novel protection, saving himself from further injury but causing much laughter as the ball crashed noisily into the slatting. Embarrassment got the better of him, and he abandoned his invention. A few years later improved protection was devised, and the game took another step forward. Not that this was Robinson's only nod to cricket's progress. He was also the first to wear spikes on his boots. The problem here was that the spikes were so long that they churned up the turf, and were soon banned.

'Test match'

Who first coined the expression 'test match', a term now uttered around the globe millions of times every week? It was William Josiah Sumner Hammersley, known as 'Will'. Like Robinson, he was born in Ash. The well-educated Hammersley abandoned his wife and four children and took off to Australia, where he played, wrote and served briefly as Melbourne Cricket Club secretary. Most significantly he became established as a journalist, and when the first English touring team, under HH Stephenson, landed in Melbourne late in 1861, Hammersley referred to the principal matches on their programme as 'test matches'. Years passed before the term entered regular usage and aspired to a capital T, but today, of course, it is a standard term in everyday cricket language.

First women's match

The first ever cricket match between female teams was recorded on January 26, 1745 at Gosden Common, on the southwestern side of Guildford. It must have been rather chilly when Eleven Maids of Bramley, dressed in white with blue ribbons in their hair, lost to Eleven Maids of Hambleton (red ribbons) 119 notches to 127.

First match agreement (laws)

In 1727 the earliest known set of 'rules and conditions' (ie early versions of the Laws of Cricket) was drawn up between the 2nd Duke of Richmond and Mr Alan Brodrick before their teams contested home and away matches that summer. Brodrick was from Pepperharowe. And – you've guessed it – that area is around three miles south-west of what was then the small town of Guildford.

Formal big-time cricket came to the centre of town in 1938, when Surrey played Hampshire in the County Championship. Since then some startling performances have been witnessed by large and keen crowds as Guildford continues to survive the sad cull of county outmatches.

Meanwhile, I'll be leaving it to someone else some way in the future to write the centenary history of county cricket in Guildford. By then the reality of this area's unique place in the history of the game should have become firmly accepted.

• • •

CLUB INSTITUTIONS

Malden Wanderers CC

by Michael Burns

The life of a Wanderer

When Malden Wanderers was founded in 1879 as Malden Victoria Cricket Club, New Malden was a frequently flooded village of fewer than 2,000 inhabitants. The toffs lived up on Coombe Hill, while the villagers were gathered in terraced cottages around the newly built railway station. The club's name was changed to Malden Wanderers in 1886 after the team had to use several fields around the village before settling on a permanent ground behind the old police station (now a pub), and next to the smoky Norbiton Pottery. The club quickly became one of the centres of New Malden village life, with large crowds attending its weekend games. Annual events included a mid-summer cricket week, and an autumn dinner that attracted the great and good from the worlds of cricket, politics and entertainment. In 1920, with very little notice, a ruthless landlord evicted the club from its by now well-established ground, forcing the Wanderers to move again, this time to its present location in Cambridge Avenue. This picturesque ground, with a golf course on one side, and a country lane on the other, was ready for play in 1921. In 1928 the current pavilion was opened in a grand ceremony by former Surrey captain HDG (Shrimp) Leveson-Gower.

Sadly, in 1932 it was discovered that the club's secretary Charlie Kirk had absconded with £1,000, forcing the club to sell off part of the outfield for housing. This spoilt what had been an almost perfect ground. Nevertheless, in 2005 Malden Wanderers was chosen by *The Wisden Cricketer* magazine as one of the 12 most beautiful grounds in England. Thanks to recent grants and bequests, the 1920s pavilion has been extensively renovated and boasts facilities fit for a 21st Century independent cricket club playing in the Surrey Championship.

Major players

Voted the second most handsome man in New Malden, the 6ft 6in **Archibald Rough** was a founder member of the club, and its first captain, playing with great all-round skill from 1879 until 1915.

Captain **Jimmy Walker** came out of the Great War determined to make Malden Wanderers one of the leading London club sides. He created a new ground from a farm field in Cambridge Avenue; designed and supervised the building of the pavilion, and captained the Ist XI for 16 years – a team that in the 1930s was as good as any in the south of England. One of Jimmy's greatest honours was to be made president of the Club Cricket Conference.

Fast bowler **Vic Ransom** was capped by Hampshire after topping their bowling averages in 1947. In 1950 he came back to Malden to play for his local club where in 1937, as an 18-year-old, he had taken 103 wickets. He also took over running the family

butcher's shop where he could be seen serving prime cuts in his MCC sweater. In 1954 and 1955 he captained Surrey 2nd XI to victory in the Minor County Championship.

John Cope was the outstanding Malden Wanderers cricketer in the second half of the 20th century. A fine allrounder who played for Devon, he was asked to be the West of Scotland professional after bowling them out on a club tour. In the 1960s John was a leading light in the formation of the highly controversial Surrey Championship, with Malden Wanderers becoming one of its founder members.

Schoolteacher **Giles Puckle**, an outstanding Surrey youth cricketer and a mean left-arm spinner in the Underwood tradition, is the captain who has been driving the club forward in the 21st Century. He has twice won the first division of the Surrey Championship, in 2000 and 2007.

Star names

Several cricketers who started at Malden Wanderers went on to bigger and better things. John Edrich and Geoff Arnold were two of Surrey and England's finest post-war cricketers. When Sir Len Hutton moved to New Malden his two sons played for the club, with Richard Hutton following his father into the Yorkshire and England teams. In the 1970s a colts section was formed and three of its earliest members Neil Kendrick, Mark Feltham and Alec Stewart became first-class cricketers. Surrey and England legend Stewart learned of his first international call-up while playing at Malden Wanderers.

• • •

A LEAGUE-FREE ZONE?

CRICKET, COMPETITION AND THE CLUB CRICKET CONFERENCE

by Duncan Stone

"League cricket, in my view, is ideally suited to the northerner. His character, outlook on life, and temperament differ widely from those of his southern counterpart"

VII

"From the 1880s onwards English cricket experienced a subtle change, with the blending of the professionals from the industrial north and the amateurs from the genteel south."

Cricket in 20th-century England was always divided in some way – most significantly by the class-based peculiarities of the amateur/professional distinction – but, as the above quote from a display at the Bradman Museum in Australia implies, there were also very distinct regional divisions. These entailed a hard-nosed, 'professional' and 'competitive' north, and a 'genteel' amateur south where 'friendly' cricket was preferred. But while it is true that league structures were resisted in the south, is it really the case that the region saw no competitive cricket before the late Sixties? And if not, why the misconception? More importantly, why did progress towards the league structure we know today take so long? The answer to all these questions has more than a little to do with the Club Cricket Conference (CCC).

It is no accident that amateur cricket in the south is known as 'club' and the predominantly amateur cricket of the north as 'league'. Each title reflects not only the style of cricket practised, and the ideological basis of each, but the established social histories of cricket in each region. These social histories have been predominantly written by a succession of authors, such as Robert Lyttelton (Eton and Cambridge), Allen Steel (Marlborough and Cambridge) and Harry Altham (Repton and Oxford), who presented (and belonged to) the establishment view of cricket; a view based largely on amateurism and class supremacy. As Major Rowland Bowen, one of the few cricket historians to buck this trend, noted in his 1970 book *Cricket*, these histories have recorded the cricket "played by a certain, comparatively narrow section of the population of these islands [Britain] and even then indeed only one part of these islands [England]." Not only is there a distinctly 'southern' bias within the game's history – Yorkshire being regarded by one sports sociologist as a "subculture [of professionalism] in a wider climate of amateurism" – the repeated focus upon public school, varsity, county and Test cricket has, as EP Thompson outlined, ignored the vast majority of the population: the working classes. Many writers (and of course cricket supporters) have since fallen for – utilised even – the crude regional stereotypes created by these histories.

Inherent in the vast majority of cricket's historiography has been the systematic exclusion of league cricket. The book that Bowen regards as "easily the best", is Altham's *A History of Cricket* (later republished and co-authored with EW 'Jim' Swanton), which – despite two chapters on amateur cricket – only ever alludes to league cricket that, even in the north, was almost entirely amateur. Subsequent authors, such as Sir Derek Birley, have revealed how cricket's 'bible', *Wisden*, which regarded the Lancashire and Yorkshire leagues as a "menace", did not publish more than the most cursory of details regarding the northern leagues. The Midland and northern leagues, and what Birley suggested was their "vulgar competitive manner", is portrayed as a particularly northern phenomenon with close links to urban environments and industry. The "sheer unredeemed snobbery" of the southern cricket elites towards such competitive, commercialised and 'professionalised' undertakings implied, as far as he and the broader historiography suggests, that leagues in the south, prior to 1968, simply did not exist. This mistake repeated that made by the league cricket historian John Kay, following the inaugural season of the Surrey Clubs' Championship. Kay stated, incorrectly, that the Streatham-born former England batsman Raman Subba Row's "bold experiment" (establishing the new league in Surrey) was the "beginning of league cricket in territory previously totally opposed to such a move". These cherry-picked social histories resulted in regionalised and class-based narratives for the sport as a whole that have had important repercussions on the relative regional identities of cricketers of the north and south. And yet it is Birley, in his relatively recent (1998) award-winning book *A Social History of English Cricket*, who, despite acknowledging the significance of Subba Row's league – which he regarded as the "most significant social change… of the South to the vulgar practice of the North" – dedicates just 144 words to the subject. It is regrettable that such a historical myopia has been allowed to remain untreated for almost a century; for what has been regarded as a league-free zone has a rich history of competitions, some with surprising patrons.

Cricket in the south

The distinct image and cultural meaning of cricket in the south is, in part, a consequence of the game's strict control by the CCC, for this influence went well beyond the elite coterie of clubs under its initial administrative control. However, prior to the establishment of the Conference in 1915, cup competitions and leagues were significant features of southern cricket from the early 1880s. Indeed, up to this point there is very good evidence that cricket throughout England shared a broadly universal 'competitive' culture.

Competition, the intrinsic basis of sport, was appreciated and embodied by aristocrat and village cricketer alike, and many clubs took their cricket very seriously indeed. At Oxted CC players were required to be available for practice every day except match days with "three days' notice of non-availability [being] mandatory." Such demands upon time were possibly beyond the ordinary villager however and the *Westerham Herald* reported in 1890 how the club's chairman was bemoaning the villagers' lack of interest in the club, despite having established the club for their benefit. The club's subsequent decision to draft in players from other locations had, however, transgressed one of the most important elements of cricket at this time: local identity. So important was this local 'patriotism', when these players were drafted in to play "the Oxted people did not want new blood, and said, 'we don't want your London Cockneys down here.'"

Prior to 1914 therefore – a time before the widespread 'suburbanisation' of small rural villages such as Oxted by the middle-classes – the opinions of ordinary 'villagers' were regarded as important by many local elites. Almost every club, village or otherwise, benefitted from the support of men and women of high social, religious, military or political status. A good example is a report in the *Woking News* of a concert held by Ripley CC in 1896:

> Mr. C. H. Combe M.P. took five seats; the Hon. Mrs. Stewart Wortley took six seats. The Misses Freeland also took tickets. All the reserved seat tickets were disposed of. Amongst those present we noticed the Rev. Hamilton Vernon, Mr. and Mrs. Aubery Wilson, Mr. and Mrs. Evans and others of the elite of the village.

One patron who had enormous influence within cricket and politics was Sir Richard Webster, 1st Viscount Alverstone QC. President of Surrey CCC from 1895 until his death in 1915, he was also the president of Cranleigh CC and clearly a lover of competition. Following on from the Surrey Challenge Cup, established by the Surrey club in 1880, Alverstone, who was also the attorney general for England, assisted in the foundation of the (West Surrey) Village Cup in 1896. Indicative of the large number of clubs in a relatively small and sparsely populated area, 17 clubs were eligible for the competition. However, in its inaugural season only eight had entered. These were Abinger, Albury, Bramley, Cranleigh, Holmbury St Mary, Shalford, Shamley Green and Shere. The competition's secretary, the Rev. AW Leach of Shamley Green, noted, according to the *Woking Mail*, that: "the competition had done a great deal to excite interest in cricket and he was told by those who knew that it had done so, and had made the village teams much more anxious to win." The winners that first year were Alverstone's club Cranleigh, and at the club dinner he stated that "he was quite satisfied that it would promote wholesome healthy rivalry and would tend to lift and raise the standard of cricket in the villages." The *Woking Mail* then reported how "the newly won village cup… was brought in to great ovation."

A swathe of competitions, and no doubt similar celebrations, were soon manifest throughout the south of England. Some of the most noteworthy of these competitions were the Oxfordshire Cup in 1890, which still operates today as the Airey Cup; the City of London Championship in 1892; a London Daily Newspaper League founded in 1895, in which the *Times, Daily Telegraph* and *Daily Mail* participated; the Postal Cricket League of 1897; the Reading and District, Hastings and District, and the East Grinstead Leagues of 1899, and, in 1901, the I'Anson Cricket League, which operates in and around Farnham and claims to be the oldest village league in the world. By the outbreak of the First World War, competitions, such as the South London Cricket League, which operated four divisions, and competition itself, had become the staple diet of many cricketers and the game's followers. Although it is likely that friendly matches were still very common, the significant point is that many of the social elites, such as Edwin Ash, co-founder of the strictly amateur Rugby Football Union, who also established a Cricket Challenge Shield for the elementary schools of Richmond in 1892, had no obvious problem with competition *per se*.

In fact, cups and leagues were participated in (and rejected) by members of all classes, the *Woking News* reporting in 1898 that Alverstone's Village Cup Competi-

WG Grace was on the first committee of the Club Cricketers' Charity Fund

tion had alienated some players of the Chilworth Gunpowder CC, who preferred to play for their villages instead. Moreover, although almost every cricketer would have been an amateur in the sense that they played for free, most of the better subscribed clubs (even in the south) employed a professional who would also act as a groundsman and it would appear that other 'independent' professionals existed at this time.

Professionalism, which historians have cited as the main reason for class conflict in British sport, was not however the key factor for such a schism in southern club cricket. Levels of "excessive competition" had been questioned as early as 1894 by the traditionalist the Rev. RS Holmes. Holmes, a Yorkshireman, "was amazed at the extent of gambling" he witnessed at a local league match, and he thus made an early association between league cricket, large working-class crowds and gambling, which was to be used by (largely southern) anti-league lobbyists well into the 1950s and 1960s. Indeed in his book *The Weekend Cricketer* (1951) – an ostensibly balanced examination of competitive cricket – then-CCC committee man ACL 'Leo' Bennett writes that:

> League cricket, in my view, is ideally suited to the northerner. His character, outlook on life, and temperament differ widely from those of his southern counterpart; he loves a gamble; he likes a game to be invested with a keen, competitive atmosphere; he wants the result to be a practical kind of triumph – something, for instance, that may make his favourite team League champions.

Although Holmes' extreme opinions were, in his time, the minority view, they gained support and clearly achieved longevity. Certainly, by 1910, some attitudes among the cricketing elites were either changing or particular individuals were becoming more vocal. Not only was the payment of professionals in London club cricket being questioned in the pages of *Cricket*, but developments in society generally – and the English County Championship specifically – had led a number of the cricketing elites to question the unintended social repercussions of competition. These concerns were given a forum with the establishment of the Club Cricketers Charity Fund (CCCF).

• •

'Some suitable gentlemen of good social standing and influence'

The foundation of the CCCF in 1910 – the organisation which was to form the ideological template for the CCC – reflected the social and ideological 'establishment' of the late Victorian and early Edwardian period. The founder, a journalist called EAC Thompson, and the first president HDG Leveson-Gower, invited the elite cricket clubs of London to become members and, according to a November 1910 minute book, "some suitable gentlemen of good social standing and influence" to become vice presidents. By 1912, the Fund's vice presidents included Leveson-Gower, PF 'Plum' Warner, Lords' Harris, Hawke and Southwark, AE Stoddart, GL Jessop, the Hon. Alfred Lyttelton MP and WG Grace – a veritable who's who of the cricket establishment.

The range of interests these men – universally public school educated – shared across a variety of social, political and cultural pursuits was significant. But it was in their roles as senior members of the MCC, the CCCF (CCC) and as journalists or authors that they have proved most influential, for their opinions on 'first-class' cricket, and the game's social distinctions, became the basis of cricket's orthodox history. It was the Fund's first Official Handbook of 1911, however, that clearly spelt out the ideological parameters that were to colour cricket in the south of England, as Bowen noted, "right down until almost our own time". Essays were contributed by Grace, Hawke and Harris. While Grace ironically bemoaned, yet again, that county cricket was becoming "too much of a business", Hawke stated that those who conducted their 'business' outside cricket – the amateurs – were "better men and generally better players than the unhappy folk who, at the end of every cricket season know not which way to turn directly their savings are gone". It fell then to Lord Harris to rubber stamp both the values and "value" of amateurism in his essay by stating that to play cricket, or other amateur sport, "keenly, honourably, generously [and] self-sacrificingly is a moral lesson in itself".

This dialogue reached its zenith (or is it nadir?) in a pseudo-editorial by the cricket author HV Dorey in the Fund's Official Handbook of 1913. Entitled 'Curse of the Championship', Dorey let loose a tirade against competitive cricket, and the "blighting and killing effect of the tournament, league, or championship system". He bemoaned the fact that although county cricket was no longer the game of the village green cricket remained, despite this, "the sport for the amateur, or the man who played for the love of the most glorious game the world has ever seen". Dorey regarded the rise of competition, and its bedfellows, the working-class professional and the paying customer, as the death knell of cricket. The future, he argued, if the county game remained unchecked, would be cricket as a Saturday game operating like the "Football League, with its motley teams of paid players and all its attendant evils". But Dorey went further: "The knife [he stated] has to be applied first of all to the professional. He must be cut away from the cricket system". Although he conversely then argued that professionals were necessary as coaches and ground bowlers (indentured servants) to the counties and the affluent members or subscribers of elite clubs – men who Dorey regarded as the "backbone of cricket, as in everything else." Yet Dorey was yet to twist the knife. "Must he [the professional] be left to starve?" Society, he continued, had "only one answer – they must suffer for the sake of posterity". Amateurism's philosophical mask was beginning to slip as men like Lord Harris, and Dorey, thought it was up to the professionals to make the sacrifices frequently advocated by those playing cricket as amateurs.

These essays represent both the ideological foundations upon which the Conference was to build its approach to club cricket in the south and the increasing status insecurity of the social elites. As early as 1892, *The Globe* had commented on this issue and the rising status of the professional cricketer. The news that the Surrey professional George Lohmann was to "winter abroad", on medical advice, had been advertised in the "personal paragraphs which immediately succeed the Court Circular in the *Times*". The article then proclaimed: "What ampler or more significant recognition of the social importance of the professional cricketer could be wished for?" and concluded that: "The exclusive privileges of the aristocracy of birth are a thing of the past. The average man takes quite as much interest in the fortunes and movements of the aristocracy of sport". Although somewhat tongue-in-cheek, this appraisal of the announcement did appear to catch the zeitgeist witnessed at many cricket club dinners in the 1890s and early 1900s. However, by 1913, *The Field* was reporting on how it was not just the working-class professional's status that was on the rise, but how the amateur cricketer's status, in a reaction to the game's popular commercialisation, was in decline. It stated:

> In the present stage of evolution games have been both democratized and universalized. As soon as the patronage of the public was assured it was inevitable that some games should be exploited on business principles. This result has had its good influences. There is one interesting effect of public patronage generally, which shows how public games react upon social life; that is, that not the professional only, but the amateur also, have become in a sense 'the servants of the public'.

The meritocratic developments that arose from modern, commercialised sport were obviously unacceptable to a number of upper and middle-class amateurs. Whereas such groups in the north needed to consider the demands of their (much more numerous) working-class neighbours, those in the south now sought to stifle such outcomes by establishing an exclusive, 'amateur plus', version of the game. This was to stand apart from the competitive cricket played in the north, and by less socially exclusive clubs in the south, and represented the beginning of the end of a cricket which had very often epitomised egalitarian community relations.

A product of the public school curriculum, and the 'ethos' such schools encouraged, 'amateurism' had been firmly embedded in the middle and upper-class consciousness by the late-Victorian period in all aspects of cultural life. The tenets of the amateur ethos cited by Lord Harris were omnipresent values in novels, poetry and at the dispatch box, pulpit and cricket dinner alike. The small group of influential men who were to set a new cultural course for cricket in the south, were both the product and promoters of these values. Although many had played competitive cricket at public school, university, county and even in Test matches – the most competitive level the game could offer – league and cup cricket was to be outlawed by these men in 1916. Yet this was an unsustainable position and the rule in question – what eventually became 'Rule 4' – was somewhat archaic at its very inception, with exemptions and compromises being made almost immediately.

• •

Decisions, decisions

Following a meeting called by EAC Thompson "by request of some clubs" at the Charterhouse Hotel in London, on March 15, 1915 the Fund was re-formed into the London Club Cricket Conference (LCCC). Unlike its predecessor, the LCCC was not established to raise funds for hospital charities, but to keep club cricket in wartime London going, protect and preserve private grounds and provide cricketers, both civilian and military, with opportunities to play. Most significantly, the Conference's strict adherence to its inherited orthodox amateur ethos and practices appears to have instigated the constitutionalisation of class exclusiveness following the outbreak of the First World War.

This was brought about by two committee decisions of the Conference in 1916, which set both the short and long-term trajectory of this organisation and 'club' cricket in the south of England. The first decision that was to have such far-reaching ramifications was made at the very first general meeting on March 22, 1916, which was presided over by Sir Home Gordon. Gordon, along with hon. secretary Thompson and committee members elected that evening, decided that they alone, as the first committee, were "empowered to frame and agree upon the objects and code of Rules to govern the Conference." Mirroring the educational and social composition of the Fund, the social make-up of this first Conference committee was, although not as well known nationally, certainly of like mind.

The second decision, which would create an elitist version of amateur cricket and set the image and context of 'club' cricket in the south apart from the north of England, was taken at the first committee meeting not two weeks later. Having decided amongst themselves that they would decide the ideological direction of the Conference, this group then passed a set of rules that would, over time, "enforce" a

Former Conference official and author of a book about club cricket, Leo Bennett

collective ideology; the most significant of these rules being 'Conditions of Membership' (originally Rule 5):

> 5. It shall be an indispensable condition that this London Club Cricket Conference shall neither recognise, approve of, nor promote any Cup or League system, and no club connected with a Cup or League competition, or playing a man as a professional, except the groundsman, shall be qualified to attend any meeting of the Conference. Any club subsequently joining a Cup or league competition, or playing a professional other than a groundsman, shall, ipso facto, cease to become a member of the Conference.

These conditions of membership represented a divisionary ideology between the so-called 'club cricket', played by the members of elite clubs, and other amateur cricket played throughout the south of England by the members of less socially exclusive clubs – whether in a league or not. This was not, as might reasonably be assumed, an unintended consequence of the rule, for Thompson, from the outset, as he had previously at the CCCF, wished the Conference to recruit membership from the better resourced and more exclusive London clubs. This exclusiveness persisted until clubs deemed to be 'village' clubs were finally invited to join the Conference in 1936.

In light of such restrictive conditions of membership, why did 'village', works or working-class clubs want to join a Conference that clearly promoted a socially and culturally different version of amateur cricket? From the outset, the CCC operated a fixtures bureau which, despite existing to arrange matches in emergencies, very quickly, after 1918, proved to be both the CCC's major selling point and source of power. Member clubs thus gained a sense of belonging (although the elite clubs would have still formed a small clique and maintained their exclusive fixture lists) and a service well worth the subscription, in return for the sacrifice of certain freedoms.

• •

Constitutional compromise

Despite an increasing number of clubs appearing content to make such concessions, because 'competitive' cups and leagues had been present in London and the south from the early 1880s, it was no surprise, even among Conference member clubs, that an overt desire for structured, unambiguous competitiveness was never far away. Only a matter of months after the Armistice, the Conference had to make its first decisions regarding so-called 'competition' cricket. While 'City' clubs were denied membership of the Conference due to their participation in a cup competition, Thompson reported that the "Hospital clubs [original benefactors of the CCCF], who had for years competed in the [London] Hospital Cup Competition… shall be… exempt from Rule 5'. However, he continued, "no other exceptions shall be made in future"; a decision immediately compromising the legitimacy of the rule.

What was becoming clear to the Conference, despite its restrictive conditions of membership, was that as more clubs re-established themselves or were inaugurated following the First World War, membership was going to increase dramatically. But, in a move to regulate the status and behaviour of any new clubs, the AGM of February 1920 added a significant caveat to the conditions of membership.

> 5. Nor shall any player, or member of an affiliated club, institute, or take part in any league, cup or prize competition within the boundaries of 'The Conference.' Any player or member of an affiliated club so offending, shall be dealt with as the council shall deem fit. All clubs affiliated to 'The Conference' and the members thereof, shall accept this rule as final and binding upon them.

This additional stipulation, although designed to control member clubs and negate any confusion regarding competition or professionalism, failed. This was due both to the inconsistency of the rule's construction (professionals were still allowed to play for teams if also acting as a groundsman) and the manner of its application. It is clear from the minute books that compromise for some and strict adherence to this rule for others led, as in 1919, to institutional hypocrisy. Having allowed the hospitals and others to compete in their "in-house" competitions, others such as Steinway Athletic CC, who had joined the Music Trades League, were removed from the Register of Clubs, and their subscription returned. Punishment enough one may think; but other member clubs who had fixtures against Steinway were then "notified that they must cancel their fixtures with the offending club forthwith". It was somewhat bizarre therefore that the executive council went on to state at the same meeting that "a club under the Rules of the Conference could play what club it desired".

Steinway Athletic's excommunication would have further repercussions in the September of that year. A team called WGW Eshelby XI's close association with Steinway Athletic CC also resulted in their "removal through [a] transgression of Rule 5". Official pariah status was then also given to Eshelby's XI and, as if suffering from a contagion, further Conference clubs were officially warned "not to exchange fixtures… as the two teams would appear to be closely connected" (both clubs were readmitted in the October, a public point having been made).

As for Rule 4, which in 1920 had, perhaps for the first and only time in sports history, constitutionally advanced the amateur ideal of "play for play's sake", its existence was short-lived and it was deleted from the rules at the AGM of 1921. Consequently, Rule 5 now became Rule 4.

• •

Commercial competitions

The AGM in February 1922 saw a tightening of the new Rule 4, with the Hospital Cup exemption being removed, and this forced the hospital clubs to resign from the Conference having (one must assume) refused to give up their competition. Although finally appearing decisive regarding the issue of the hospital clubs, the Conference executive was less so on other issues, particularly professionalism, which it tended to ignore. For example, Cheam CC, having played the Surrey professional Lowe, contacted the Conference after he had "invoiced" the club for "playing assistance". Despite the Cheam club having broken Conference rules, the council committee decided this was not a disciplinary matter, but that it should be settled between the Cheam and Surrey clubs. This oversight regarding professionalism in club cricket is peculiar, but it may explain the long-held historical assumption that professionalism did not exist in southern club cricket. Another reason for such inaction may have been the challenge of commercially sponsored competitions during the 1920s.

By 1925 the first newspaper-sponsored prize competition had affected the Conference, with *The Star* advertising its competition, using the Conference's name without permission. It remains unclear as to the format of this competition, but the editor was informed, via a very stiff letter with quasi-legal undertones, that *The Star*'s Prize Competition was, under Rule 4 of the Conference, "illegal and consequently must be banned."

The Star ignored this and the 1920s was a period where newspapers, such as the *The Weekly Press* in Guildford during 1927, were actively sponsoring leagues and cups

League activist Arthur Gilligan during his days as England captain. Photo by Getty Images

across the region. Although the *The Weekly Press* competition was populated predominantly by works and church sides, members of numerous Conference cricket clubs breached Rule 4 by accepting prize bats. But "as the players had in every instance either returned or refused to accept the prize bats", the clubs were not, on this occasion, reprimanded.

Consequently, in a reaction to the increasing number of newspaper competitions, October 1926 saw Rule 4 amended further, with the following paragraphs added:

> Inter-departmental league or cup competitions, wholly confined to bona fide permanent members of the staffs of their own business firms shall be approved, but clubs affiliated shall not take part in any recognised outside business house league, cup, or prize competition.
>
> A prize competition shall be deemed to be one in which a club, or any of its members, may enter for prizes, either in money or in kind offered from outside sources for playing skill at cricket.

This change appeared to reverse the Hospital Cup decision in an attempt to keep controversies – if not contradictions – to a minimum (the Conference had reinstated its own inter-county tournament, with a Lord's final, in 1925). This 'sticking-plaster' appears to have worked until 1929, when a further five clubs breached Rule 4 by taking part in newspaper competitions. Four of the five players had either returned their prize bat or their club had prevented the winner from accepting it. However, in the case of the fifth, People's Palace CC, the member had refused to return his prize. The club, likely threatened with expulsion, had then forced the player to resign. This he duly did, much to the committee's pleasure, who wrote to congratulate the club on "their firm attitude towards their late member." They were, however, reminded to "take greater heed [of the rules] in the future."

Prize bats and newspaper competitions aside, the years up to the outbreak of the Second World War, in cricketing and political terms, were full of "menace" for the Conference's various committees. Competitions were being established across the south and reports of leagues in Dorking in Surrey, Bognor in Sussex and Gillingham in Kent were reported. Other commercial concerns were becoming involved, and in an incident that further highlights both the implicit power and influence of the Conference, one such concern, Bentalls Department Store of Kingston in Surrey, cancelled its 1935 competition after correspondence from the Conference. But it was the ever increasing number of newspaper competitions that created the most anguish for the Conference, with *The Star* a serial offender.

• •

Comply or die?

Change, if the social and political events of the immediate post-war period were a guide, appeared to be on the horizon, but the Conference stood firm. Other competitions and associations were being formed throughout the south (as they were in the Midlands and the north), such as the Brighton and Hove Cricket Association in 1941; the Sussex Cricket Association in 1943; the Flora Doris Cup (Guildford) in 1946; the Surrey Association of Cricket Clubs in 1947; and the Association of Kent Cricket Clubs in 1949. All of these associations advocated the promotion of youth and a move towards competitive cricket, but resistance from those in charge at the CCC and certain 'senior' clubs, remained strong. Much of this conflict was generational and the post-war period saw ever more calls from the players for competitive cricket, only for it to be stifled by the retired players frequently populating the club's committees. Indeed, at Malden Wanderers CC's annual supper in 1960, the club captain Jimmy Walker's speech, which had advocated a move towards league cricket, was immediately rebuffed in the club chairman's speech.

Indicative of the power held by the older members of the cricket community was the desire among the newer associations to become affiliated with the Conference, but this was to come at a price. Both the Brighton and the Sussex Associations were forced to delete clauses within their constitutions advocating the promotion of any competitive cricket before they were allowed to join. The Conference was clearly used to getting its own way and when, in 1949, the Surrey association circularised its member clubs about competitive cricket, the Conference expressed "surprise" that they had not been consulted. Other proposals to form leagues in Essex and Sussex occurred that same year, and forced a reaction from the Conference. While the Surrey proposal floundered, the Essex proposal was "crushed" when the senior clubs were threatened with expulsion from the Conference. And yet, the ex-England captain Arthur Gilligan's Sussex proposal succeeded – despite the senior clubs' withdrawal following further threats of excommunication. In a classic 're-negotiation', reflective of the class, status and power relationships involved, Gilligan's league went ahead with working men's clubs.

Gilligan was at pains to state that there were plenty of working men's clubs in Sussex, "who care less than nothing for the CCC" and that, as the new associations had no doubt suspected, "it is a mistake to suppose all youngsters worth developing are attached to Conference clubs". Conversely, and perhaps unsurprisingly, Gilligan's league was decried by Bennett who thought it a lesser undertaking without the senior clubs who had capitulated to the Conference's demands. Importantly, Gilligan and his member clubs had shown that there was a future for competitive cricket and that non-compliance to the Conference's rules did not mean the end of cricket. Despite this, the Conference – with its powerful men, and perhaps most importantly, its unrivalled fixtures service – retained an enormous influence over club and village cricket in the south until the modern world in which it operated could no longer be ignored.

• •

The unstoppable tide

By the time Gilligan's league had completed its second full season Bennett was still "acting for the defence". Although a relative moderate, Bennett's position within the CCC obliged him to defend the continued opposition to leagues during a debate at a meeting of the Cricket Society in November 1951. A report of the debate, which discussed the motion 'That in the opinion of this House, League Cricket should be played in the South of England', appeared in the *Society News Letter* and it is worth citing at length:

> Judging by the speeches from the Platform, the arguments seemed very much in favour of the Opposition [led by Bennett]; but when the Debate was opened to the House by our Chairman (who kept an exemplary control of proceedings throughout), a surprisingly large number of people wished to speak. Mr. L. H. Phillips, taking a neutral view, gave a sound exposition on the virtues of League Cricket in the North; but several other members attacked Club Cricket and produced strong emotional grievances which appeared, like greyhounds in the slips, to have been straining upon the start for several years. The complaints were mostly those of the spectator rather than the player, and were concerned with unpunctuality, long tea intervals and too much light-heartedness generally, which was often (the speakers claimed) focussed in the direction of the Club bar.

As Peter Goodall had suggested in the *Evening Standard* in 1949, it would appear that the Conference had indeed stifled 'free speech', and those who seized the opportunity to speak provided the CCC's Bennett, who had "come under heavy fire", with a warning: "Discipline was sadly lacking in Club Cricket, and unless the Club Cricket Conference did something about it, League Cricket would have to 'take over'." Characteristically, Bennett made a robust defence by claiming that the CCC was not an organisation with disciplinary control, but an 'advisory council with a voluntary membership'. Bennett may well have defeated the motion by nine votes to eight (with several members abstaining), but such a defence seemed to contradict the events of 1949.

If the surviving records are accurate, debates of this type appeared to die down for the rest of the decade until the innovations of the 1960s finally made the Conference's anachronistic position untenable. Cricket, despite the positive effects of the abolition of the amateur/professional distinction and the establishment of the Gillette Cup, was, under threat from the alternative attractions of "television and cars", and the social repercussions' of the birth control pill and the breathalyzer.

And yet, despite all of the changes going on around them, the Conference failed to understand the modern world. Good old-fashioned Victorian hypocrisy and prejudices persisted, and these were thrust under the spotlight when Raman Subba Row, Norman Parks and their associates sought to establish the Surrey Clubs' Championship (SCC) with the blessing of the Conference in 1966. The committee's predictable rejection of the proposed SCC would not have been so problematic had they not already agreed to another competition being allowed, and one with distinctly commercial origins at that.

The Kemp Cup was a limited-over knock-out competition based upon the Gillette Cup, and it involved a number of Conference clubs, including Wimbledon CC and Honor Oak CC, who were forceful opponents of league cricket at Conference meetings. Objections were understandably raised by AWA Leigh, of Highgate CC, as to the Conference's approval of the Kemp competition on commercial grounds, while DA Lynn of Banstead CC questioned why this competition was deemed acceptable when the Surrey League was not. Once again, the chairman defended the decisions on the basis that the Kemp Cup – a commercialised knock-out competition – did not affect long-standing friendly Saturday fixtures and was thus allowed under the amended (1950) Rule 4. The Conference were running out of excuses, as the preservation of Saturday fixtures against carefully selected opposition now formed the sole basis for any objections to leagues.

Such hypocrisy was not lost on Subba Row and his associates, after the Conference made clear their threat of expulsion to any club joining the new league in a statement which read: "The Club Cricket Conference executive council has ruled that all the 17 members who compete in the new Surrey Cricket Championship Association will be contravening Rule 4." This was countered strongly by the SCC Association in their statement:

> While it is not for our association to tell the Conference how to conduct its own affairs, we cannot allow its statement to pass without saying it seems extraordinary in our view that its council has found our championship to be against its rules when it has just approved a sponsored knock-out competition [the Kemp Cup]. There appears to be some fine distinction between playing ordinary club cricket for points and playing limited-overs cricket for a commercial pot. We can only repeat that our members have not the slightest wish to leave the Club Cricket Conference, whose name is even included in our rules. If we were forced to do so, we would have no option but to protect our own interests and a second conference would start to emerge – with all the duplication of work involved. We ourselves would regard this as a necessary evil, but surely for the Conference it could be the thin end of a catastrophic wedge.

The Conference had clearly lost its way. It had, as an organisation, forgotten the reasons why the first committee had consciously rejected any form of competitive cricket, and desperately clung to its ideological foundations in order to preserve the invented tradition of 'friendly' cricket as much as to maintain its own power. By the late Sixties, the drive to create a more cohesive cricket structure – based upon leagues – amongst many of the region's biggest clubs, was unstoppable. Even back in 1951, Bennett had described the competition question as "the issue of the day" and it was perhaps only due to the influence of a few key decision-makers on the Conference committee that such a move was delayed for decades.

But before long – while it wouldn't wholeheartedly endorse the change and would remain somewhat sniffy – the Conference, thanks in no small part to the intervention of committee member John Slack, would accept that the tide of change was inexorable. The annual report of 1970, under the heading 'League Cricket', witnessed the executive council report that: "Several groups of clubs held meetings and decided to start leagues" in Kent, Surrey, Essex and Middlesex. The members of these leagues were not to be expelled, as in the past, but were to be "shown as an additional item in the Handbook in future." It was also noted that the Conference would offer assistance to "clubs whose fixtures have been affected by the institution of leagues."

In the years to come, as it became clear the leagues were the way forward, and the sky had failed to fall in after their introduction, so the Conference view of competition would be loosened, until it eventually threw all its weight behind the new structures. But its sometimes reactionary history, aided and abetted for decades by a broadly sympathetic cricket media, had had a profound impact on the long-term perception of southern cricket and its supposed differences from the game in the north. Over 60 years without any official league cricket has left its mark, and cricket in the south still has a meaning all of its own, but the game has, for the most part, returned to its cultural origins.

• • •

VII

CLUB LEGENDS

Vic Loveless: New Forest game-changer

by Benj Moorehead

The birth of competitive league cricket was a painful process right across the south of England, but its path was particularly thorny in that rural enclave in the west of Hampshire which is really a world all its own: the New Forest. The resident commoners whose heritage stretched back centuries, and who enjoyed special privileges bestowed upon them by local law, liked things just as they were. They enjoyed the confinements of their daily lives.

The cricket clubs were no different, concerned only with playing in their immediate surrounds, and fiercely protective over their independence. Each looked after their own. 'League cricket' was a dirty phrase, seen as a preoccupation of the north, or else of the urbane. Certainly it had no place among the ponies and meadows of the New Forest. Most horrifying of all was the thought of being hostage to a prescribed fixture list rather than arranging your own matches against trusted, congenial opponents.

It would be a formidable challenge to break down these divisions and bring the clubs together under one flag – but then Vic Loveless was a formidable presence in New Forest cricket in the 1960s and '70s.

Loveless was a descendent of one of the Tolpuddle Martyrs, the men banished to Australia in the first half of the 19th century after they were found guilty of establishing an agricultural trade union. Perhaps it was in the genes.

In many ways he was an establishment figure. Loveless had served in the Royal Marines during the Second World War, and lived by military principles. He wouldn't tolerate any 'nonsense' with his cricket – sledging was denounced in vehement terms. Tall and upright with a thin moustache, he was dressed smartly whatever the occasion, and wore a signature flat cap. To some he is an enigma, to others a lovable rogue. "You aren't always sure whether Vic is joking or not," says one old friend. "He is rather idiosyncratic, but I have always found him a charming and delightful companion."

Loveless grew up in Totton, a village just beyond the eastern tip of the New Forest, and played for the local club, Calmore, for whom he was a steady allrounder for many years. After the war his ambitions began to shift beyond the boundary as he sensed the change rippling through society and cricket in the 1960s. He recognised that people were after cooperation on a broader scale. Loveless may not have been alone in acknowledging the change in mood – but he was the only one prepared to take on the parochial attitudes prevailing in the New Forest.

He began by enlisting the support of clubs local to Calmore, then he threw the net wider to include the bigger fish – Lymington, Beaulieu, Sway, Brockenhurst, New Milton. After the death of Sydney Watt, a noted local cricketing personality, a number of Forest clubs came together in 1964 to create an evening knockout competition in his memory. Loveless was struck by the opportunities that a wider association of clubs might bring.

In October 1965 he called for a meeting at Lyndhurst, where the New Forest Club Cricket Association (NFCCA) was established. A constitution was approved and officers elected. There was a hat-trick of Vics at the helm: Vic Doggrell (Calmore CC), the treasurer; Vic Trippick (Bartley CC), the secretary; and Loveless himself, the chairman. These three ran the show, but Loveless was the driving force. Trippick was an ardent socialist, Loveless a determined Conservative, and the two would often be found sparring over politics. When it came to cricket, however, the divisions fell away.

The very idea of a unitary body representing cricket sat uneasily with many clubs throughout the region – indeed Loveless had to contend with a lot of resistance through the 1960s and '70s. But as an authoritative and charismatic public speaker, he won local support for his vision to establish bonds across the Forest for the first time.

Cricket leagues were springing up either side of the New Forest throughout the period. In the west the Bournemouth League began to attract a number of the more ambitious Forest clubs. The Southern League had also enlisted a number of teams from the area, while the Hampshire League had a bias towards the east of the county. Still, though, there was no form of competitive cricket which bound the New Forest.

In 1974 the miracle came to be, when the New Forest Cricket League was founded under the auspices of the NFCCA. At long last Loveless had convinced his fellow Foresters to create something that was all their own. By the end of the decade nearly every club had signed up to it. Knockout competitions followed – the Stone Cup for junior sides, the President's Cup for the seniors. The New Forest League sailed along merrily, not necessarily producing the highest standard of cricket in the county, but invigorating New Forest cricket with a new competitive edge.

Its final season was in 2000. English cricket, back in the doldrums, was streamlining the amateur game in an attempt to fast-track the best cricketers in the country. The ECB – under the guidance of its first chairman, Lord MacLaurin – mapped out a new pyramid system for club cricket, with new premier leagues supported by 'feeder' divisions. Thus the NFCL was amalgamated into the Hampshire League, which in turn fed into the Southern Premier League at the top of the tree.

Loveless carried on playing until he suffered a stroke at the age of 69. He established the Calmore Wanderers Club, which played friendlies and was open to players either under 14 or over 40 – until, ironically, the club folded because all its traditional opponents had defected to league cricket. Later he wrote a book on cricket in the New Forest, and into his 90s remained a distinctive figure on the boundary edge with his imposing frame, flat cap, and military blazer and tie.

•••

Loveless: man of the forest. Photo courtesy of Simon Rowley

VII

CLUB LEGENDS
David Goldsmith: Park lifer
by Benj Moorehead

David Goldsmith – 'Goldie' to everyone – was adored wherever he went as a cricketer between 1960 and 2006, not just in his domain of Essex and east London, but right across the shires where he played Minor Counties for Buckinghamshire in the 1980s. Teammates and opponents could not but fall for his cheeky charm, good humour and warm spirit. He was in the best tradition of wicketkeepers; teasing and chuckling with batsmen all afternoon while sweeping up nimbly behind the stumps with a rare grace and skill. Born in Romford in 1947, Goldsmith's roots went down in Gallows Corner, home of Gidea Park CC – or Gidea Park & Romford CC as it became after the two clubs merged in 1970 – where he played for nearly half a century. In that time he saw the landscape of club cricket transform, from the 'social' cricket of the 1960s he grew up with, to the beginning of a new era with the arrival of Essex Cricket League in 1972.

Goldsmith on starting out in cricket

The only way my mother could get rid of me and my elder brother on a weekend was to send us off to the cricket at Gidea Park. My brother was the scorer and I opened up the little trap doors to put the numbers up. There was a big two-story scorebox at Gallows Corner dedicated to Ken Farnes, the England fast bowler who played for Gidea Park. You went up a big long ladder to reach the top. I took over the scoring when my brother started to play for the first team. As a scorer you have to watch every ball – that was a great way to learn how to play.

On socialising with the opposition

The other place I learnt my cricket was in the bar afterwards. All 11 of the opposition stayed afterwards for a beer or two. I can remember standing in the bar and looking up at all these big older guys and listening to people's interpretations of the game. You can listen to your own team talking about the game but it's much better to get both points of view. The camaraderie with the opposition has waned very slowly over the years, like a long sunset. With drink-driving of course, people don't really stay for a beer any more, and by the 1990s only the opposition captain and whoever he was giving a lift to would have a drink after the game. The rest were already on their way home.

On kit etiquette

Today bats are soft-rolled, pick up well, and have a lot of meat on them. We used a lighter bat – about 2lb 4oz – and it was hard-rolled, which meant it lasted longer – two or three seasons if you were lucky. That's what you wanted because you couldn't afford another bat. And you daren't ask anyone else to borrow one. I left my bat at home once and I asked our opener, who was in his 30s, if I could use his.

Goldie behind the stumps in '95

He just looked at me in disgust and walked away. You didn't borrow anybody's gear. You had your own bat but everything else came out of a kit bag in the middle of the dressing room, which had three pairs of pads, three pairs of gloves and a multitude of things you didn't really want to know about. Of course the youngest in the team was the one that had to lug it from the car to the changing room.

On club cricket in the 1960s

Before the advent of league cricket, the weekend games were the most enjoyable of all: 235-8 declared plays 236-9, for instance. And the beauty of club life in my time was that everybody generally got a game. To a certain extent these games, which weren't limited-overs, were manufactured. The thinking was: "The only way we're going to get them out is to toss the ball up – tempt them into chasing our total so we can take a few wickets." That went out of the game with limited-overs league cricket. You'd have a slow left-armer bowling it flat and slightly quicker, with six on the leg-side and three on the off. League cricket stifled creativity. There were a set of rules, and you abided by them. Some people thrived on it. There was a lovely guy called Tim Smith who was a tall, slow left-armer for Saffron Walden. When he floated it up it didn't turn and you could hit him. But he came into his own in league cricket because he had a superb arm ball, and he went on to play a lot of limited-overs representative cricket.

On the appeal of amateur cricket

A lot of the players had high-powered jobs and club cricket on the weekend was their relaxation. My first captain in the Gidea Park first team was a solicitor. At No.3 you had someone who worked very high up the chain in the Ford motor company. There was another player who worked for British Petroleum. Their release was not to drive to the coast to or dash off to Majorca for a long weekend, it was to play club cricket. Get some fresh air, hang out with mates, and forget about work. But you were obliged to play league cricket because it was important. In the 1960s and early 1970s it was a case of: "Do you want to play?" There was no pressure. And often they did play because there was no pressure. Why have pressure at the weekend when you've had pressure all week?

On the rivalry between Romford and Gidea Park

In the 1960s the fixture on Bank Holiday Monday in May and August was always Romford versus Gidea Park. It was like West Ham against Millwall, which was quite unusual because the game was generally played in a more convivial way back then. I remember when I was 17 coming in at No.7 or No.8, and my skipper, Derek Brazier – 'Chopper' – was at the other end. The Romford bowler came in and beamed me first ball, and it hit me on the shoulder and went for four leg-byes over the top of the keeper! Chopper did two things: he shouted down the wicket to congratulate me for the four leg-byes, and then turned round to give the bowler awful grief for bowling me a beamer. I also remember Romford's opening pair, Kenny Wallace and Jack Clifford, walking to the wicket on a bright sunny morning – it always seems that it was sunnier in those days – and Kenny had Vaseline over both eyebrows because he considered he'd be out there for a long time. Those derbies were probably the most enjoyable cricket I played. It hadn't gone the way of the leagues yet – it was still a 'normal' game. But you had to play hard to win it, and you had to play attacking cricket. It wasn't a case of 50 overs and who scores the most wins.

On the merger between Gidea Park and Romford in 1970

There were two teams at Gallows Corner, Romford and Gidea Park, but only one bar and not enough revenue to support both clubs. Romford were by far the stronger team in the 1950s and '60s but the situation had reversed by the time of the amalgamation in 1970. That's why it's called Gidea Park & Romford, and not Romford & Gidea Park! Gidea Park were the ones who pushed for the merger, and there was quite a bit of animosity about it. We lost a large proportion of the Romford players, who walked away because they saw the amalgamation as taking away their identity.

On life before mobile phones

We had a taxi driver who used to get the tea lady to take his taxi bookings while he was fielding. So the club phone line was blocked up with people ordering taxis. My wife did once get through and asked to speak to me. The tea lady told her I was batting, at which point she said, "Don't worry, I'll hang on".

On Sunday cricket

The Sunday XI was if anything stronger than the Saturday XI, on the basis that you went out of the county to play your cricket – into Kent, north London, Surrey. Up until the 1980s we'd have some wonderful fixtures on Sundays, and in those days you would bring the wife and kids with you. Some of the grounds where we used to play were superb. Gore Court down in Sittingbourne, which sat in a beautiful bowl with banks going around the ground and a lovely old thatched pavilion at mid-on. The Bat & Ball Ground at Gravesend. Brondesbury, where the Gattings played. Enfield, Maidstone, Winchmore Hill… you can reel them off. And you'd meet up with long lost friends.

On Conference cricket

In the 1970s, when I was in my mid-20s, I went into a retail business with a partner who I met through Gidea Park. We opened up kitchen showrooms and the key working day of the week was Saturday – so I couldn't play in the new league matches. Instead I played in those wonderful fixtures on Sundays, and then in mid-week for the Club Cricket Conference, which was my way of getting my second game of cricket of the week. I remember as a boy one match when I was the Gidea Park scorer and the Romford players LCS Jerman and Eric Palmer were doing a lap of the boundary and walked past the scorebox wearing their Conference jumpers. And I thought: 'I'd love to have one of those one day'. As luck would have it I got one.

On league cricket

I came into league cricket in 1980. It felt different. Batsmen didn't walk. They'd nick it to first slip and still wait for the umpire to give them out. There was a lot more animosity. I wasn't for it because I enjoyed the game in a different way. As a wicketkeeper I had a lot of fun behind the stumps, with lots of chat and mucking around. In league cricket I'd have a chat with the batsman and he wouldn't talk back! But I would say the majority of the players wanted league cricket because they saw it as a way to prove their team was the best. Tom Ford was the skipper at the club when Gidea Park became a founding member of the Essex Cricket League in 1972, and he was a massive competitor. Dear old Tom. He worked in the Essex May Market and was one of those guys who was competing every day of his life – no more so than on a cricket field. When I was having a laugh with someone on the field he'd say to me, "Stop buggering about!"

On overseas players and professionals

Gidea Park & Romford weren't really advocates of paying someone to play. Typically overseas players would be put up by someone, and they didn't have to pay their match or subscription fee, but would coach the kids in the nets on a weekday evening. In Essex overseas players didn't really arrive until the early 1980s. They were mainly South Africans and Australians and the odd Kiwi; now it's often Indians and Pakistanis. We once had an Australian called Paul Lacey. It took us two weeks to work out that he wasn't as good as his CV said. But do you know, that boy was the best overseas player we ever had – from the point of view of integration. He was great with people, talking to everybody. He was probably 10 years too late; if he'd come when we were playing social cricket he would have gone down a storm.

• • •

VII

CLUB LEGENDS
Eddie Poulter: Fives master
by Ed Kemp

Paper will tell you Eddie Poulter was president of Fives & Heronians Cricket Club. What it won't do is explain everything he did for them. The East End boy dug trenches and laid pipes in the club's infancy (just Fives at this point), spent 10 years pressing to see them admitted to the Essex League in their adolescence; and saw them win that league in their prime. Having become a stockbroker at the age of 14 – straight out of school – he has been captain, fixtures secretary and president at Fives & Heronians – as well as president of the Club Cricket Conference. Eddie has given the better part of his life to the grassroots game: in his own words "everything else has taken second spot".

Poulter on starting young

I come from a big family from the East End, Hackney Wick. There were 12 of us at one stage, and there's still six left. They go from 80 to almost 92. Cricket-wise I was brought up in a wonderful club called Eton Manor; it was a boys club that was formed by Old Etonians; very affluent bank managers, merchant bank managers and stockbrokers. The reason it was so wonderful I always put down the fact the club committee was actually formed of the boys. We ran the club, with one senior adult as chairman. I was privileged, at 16 years old, to be elected onto that committee. And I think due to that training I had from a very early age, I just took to administration and running clubs, and organising people. I'm 84 now, and I only just stopped doing that.

On building a club

Fives was an old boys' club, formed from the fifth form of Leyton County High School. We played on a rugby ground, way out in Epping. There was only one car in the club so we would have to take buses or the tube to get there.

In the mid '60s a chap named Bill Humphrey went to an auction with a view to buying a house in Chigwell. It was a big house at the beginning of the lane that went down to the ground. The house was of no interest to him, and in the end the auctioneers split the house, the contents, and the field behind the house. He ended up buying the field for £2,000 – it was called The Paddock because there were horses on it. That's what we named the ground from then on, and it's still called that today. There was a lot to do though, it didn't have gates on it or anything, and horses were galloping out of the field and down the lane into another field. It was so difficult at first, the 20 members of the club would go over there, dig trenches and lay pipes from the main road. There was no electricity or water so it was really hard work. Our secretary at the time, who was a surveyor, was having 1,000 bricks delivered for under the drains and under the pavilion. I remember getting a phone call on a Sunday morning, and maybe half a dozen of us had to go over there and unload the lorry.

On coming together and the battle for acceptance

We had to amalgamate. I talked to a number of clubs, and in the end, in 1971, we joined with another old boys' club, Old Heronians. This proved very successful because we gained a connection with Wanstead County High, and were getting good players straight from school. We were going from strength to strength, but all our games were friendlies. The next step was joining the Essex League, a process which was to last 10 years in all.

There were other small leagues forming, but we were quite well known among the big clubs because as Fives and as Old Heronians (before the amalgamation), both clubs had played friendlies against their second or third teams. We needed a 97 per cent vote from the teams in the league. I was in charge of the fixtures at that time so I concentrated on organising matches against all the league sides. I wanted to show them what we had to offer; show them the ground, and show them our hospitality. We also had to attend all kinds of functions all over the county.

What helped us a great deal was the unfortunate plight of the Metropolitan Police. They were one of the clubs in the Essex League. This was in the early and mid '70s, when all the riots were going on. They were continually dropping out on a Friday night, unable to play their game the following day. The league couldn't put up with this. There were 19 clubs at the time, they decided the Met couldn't keep their place so it went down to 18. They were then looking for two clubs to be elected. We had already applied three times, and we just struck lucky that they were looking for two clubs, and Fives & Heronians were one of them. This was in 1982. By '98 we won the Essex League; the Essex Premier League title followed a year later – we had great players like Mel Hussain in our ranks. That year I also became president of the Conference.

On a life in the game

Eton Manor was phenomenal; it was so unique. At Fives and Heronians we had a lovely ground and a great set of people. We knew if we worked hard we would attract better players, and that's exactly what happened. We would beat big clubs, like Finchley and Enfield, they didn't know much about us; but they sure did afterwards. The growth of the club wasn't down to just me, it happened thanks to all the senior members. We would never have won the league without the sheer effort we put into creating the ground, amalgamating, and then being accepted.

• • •

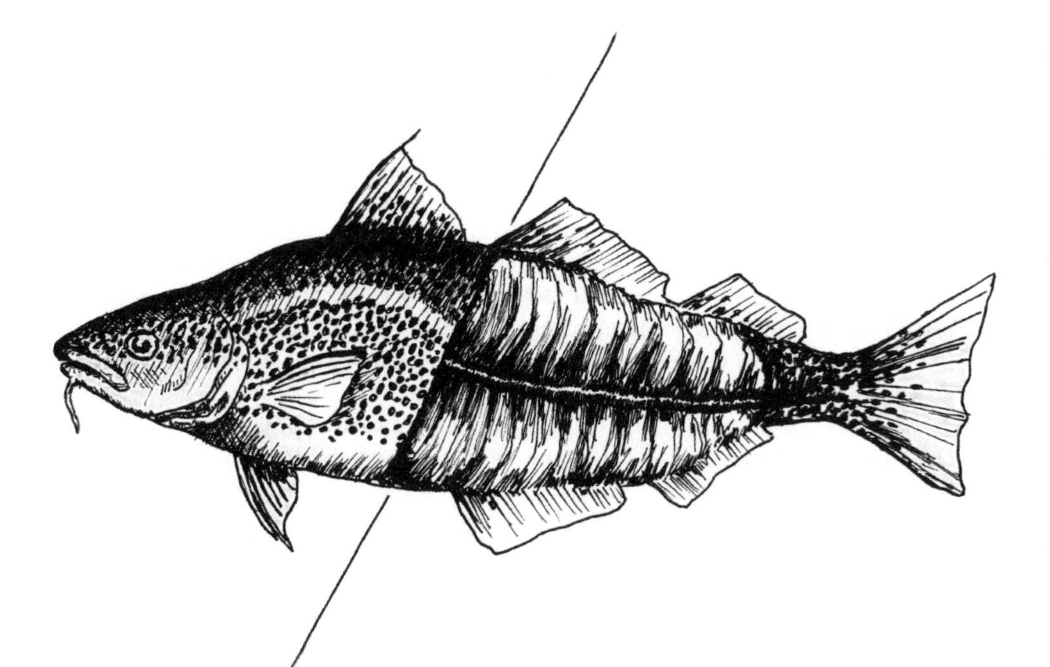

ACROSS THE GREAT DIVIDE

IMPRESSIONS OF CLUB CRICKET BOTH NORTH AND SOUTH

by Dan Waddell

"Rumours of southern cricket's softness had been wildly overstated"

VII

Whisper this very quietly: Yorkshiremen, even those unfortunate ones exiled in the south like me, are not short of opinions or bereft of certainty. We say what we like and we like what we say. So: fish and chips up north are better than in the south, so is the ale and the same goes for the people. I once heard a fellow Tyke opine that Yorkshire dogs are better than their southern counterparts "because they're less uptight."

Add sport to the list too, cricket in particular. We play it harder and we play it better, especially in the leagues. The Yorkshire leagues, even the ones in (deep breath) Lancashire, boast a legion of legends who didn't play first-class cricket, but are nonetheless celebrated for it. Former Bowling Old Lane supremo Jack Hill, a man who didn't just think cricket was better in his day, *he bloody well knew it was*, used to extol the virtues of Spen Victoria seamer Percy Jackson. "He played for more than 30 year and he never bowled a half volley. Not even in t'nets!"

The view was that if Percy had been brought up in Surrey, God help him, he'd have played first-class cricket and captained England because those namby-pamby southerners wouldn't have known how to handle him. But because he played in the Bradford League, the hardest, toughest league in the land, he was merely a good bowler who was unlucky to miss out.

I too used to cleave to such opinions. In fact I still believe southern fish and chips are an abomination (you leave the skin on? And fry it in oil not beef dripping? Are you mad?) I grew up playing Bradford League cricket and was a talented schoolboy cricketer. However, the glossy badges stitched to my jumpers and caps might as well have been target signs, earning me derision rather than respect.

And that was just from my teammates. I was 15 in the first full season I played in the first team of my club in Pudsey. Every week, home or away, the senior pro threw my kit out of the dressing room window because wherever I chose to get changed was the place he'd been changing "for 25 years." He did this even when we played at a club who had built brand new changing rooms that winter.

It was often a relief to be on the pitch. Not for long though. In one match I got some runs, sweeping a veteran spinner to distraction.

"Keep f***ing playing it," he said. So I did.

"Who the f*** told you you could bat?" he said. I knew better than to reply. I started to go down the wicket.

"You're not f***ing good enough to charge me, son," he said after I patted one back.

"F*** off back to the f***ing hutch you f***ing little p***k," he harrumphed when I was out for 70-odd.

After the match, the spinner came up to me in the bar. I expected a bracing analysis of every flaw in my technique and prepared myself with a nervous glug of bitter-shandy.

"I run the Yorkshire Academy. I want you to come along on Monday."

I nodded, almost speechless.

"You'll have to stop playing that f***ing sweep shot though."

The Bradford League wasn't so much the school of hard knocks, as the Institute of Shut Up and Gerron Wi' It. A few lads would make their way up from the south (and it was always up – both geographically and morally.) Some did well, but all remarked on the fiercely competitive way matches were played and marvelled at the large crowds some matches attracted. I formed the impression that southern league cricket was genteel, sterile and played in front of one man and his dog.

Fast-forward several years and I'm making my debut for Acton in the Middlesex County League. There's not even a man or an uptight southern dog watching. It seems like my fears that southern league cricket will be thin gruel in comparison to the hot meat of the Bradford League are to be founded. But then the match starts…

The opposition bowler sledges me for a perfectly played leg-glance; cover-point chunters incessantly about my inability to score any of my first 20 runs in front of square; I'm given a send-off when I chip one to mid-wicket; our captain edges us close to victory, thriving on the fielders' antipathy; there is genuine needle between the two teams. With 10 runs needed and one wicket left, a fight almost breaks out over some perceived slight. We scrape home in dramatic style and drink long into the night.

I don't stop smiling for days.

The next week, batting helmetless, I am bounced, called 'granddad' and made to look a mug on a sporting pitch. A local derby against Shepherds Bush a few weeks later is played in such a heated atmosphere it makes Pudsey St Lawrence v Pudsey Congs look like one of the inter-house matches they play in posh schools. It turns out that rumours of southern cricket's softness had been wildly overstated. This is league cricket as red in tooth and claw as any I played up north.

There are differences. The wickets in the Middlesex league are far better batting pitches than the damp seamers you often encounter in the north. I'm delighted to say from a personal point of view that I see far less of the nagging, parsimonious seamer that prospers up on those sappy pitches, but would be cannon fodder on the roads of Teddington and Richmond.

Young players seem to be given more respect, though this might be as much to do with recent child protection legislation as a sign that southern cricket is more civilised. Certainly, some of the older hands I play alongside share the pain of my stories about having my kit ejected from a window every week, while simultaneously wondering if it didn't help keep big heads in check, as we watch talented young peacocks preening about in sponsored gear as if they own the place.

The only dissimilarity that really disturbs me is that too many players are in a rush to get away after the game. Part of the joy of playing the game in the north was to lean on a bar with the opposition afterwards and relive the game in minute detail. Such in-depth post mortems have gone out of fashion now, but again this might be a sign of changing times rather than different cultures. And while the Saturday night delights of Bradford had little to commend them, London offers the young far more attractions, and had I grown up in London, I dare say I might have been more keen to prop up the bar of a chi-chi winebar and chat with comely women than spend an hour discussing whether a leg-slip is a luxury or a necessity with portly spinners.

These are trifling differences though. Far more significant is what unites league cricketers of the north and south, even though they'd rather not admit it. The desire to win, to compete as hard as you can, can be found in both. The real division lies between league and friendly cricket. For league cricketers both north and south, the idea of playing with a bunch of jazzhats, with no points to play for, is no more appealing than a trip round Debenhams on a Saturday afternoon with the wife.

CLUB LEGENDS
Alan Burridge: North-South Superman
by Benj Moorehead

Captains preparing to bat first against Watford Town in the 1970s would invariably ask their opposite number: "Is Budgie playing?" And if the answer was 'yes', they would know not to consider making a declaration. Such was the fearsome reputation of Alan Burridge, the great left-hander from the north-east whose big-hitting in the middle order broke windows and roof tiles up and down the country in a spectacular career that began in Sunderland in the 1950s and ended in Hertfordshire some 40 years later. His father, Fred, had grown up in the south and was on the groundstaff at Lord's before moving up to Sunderland where he played in the Lancashire Leagues. Alan thus grew up in the tough, competitive environment of cup and league cricket in the north-east, where he played Minor Counties for Durham as well as for an array of clubs who competed in the Durham Senior Cricket League, including his beloved Sunderland. He moved south when he was appointed Head of Leisure at Watford Borough Council in 1974, the same year that the Hertfordshire Cricket League came into being. Watford Town were only too pleased to welcome a player seasoned in the competitive environment of the north, and with the help of his runs the club won its first league title in 1980. In 1975 he was a member of the Hertfordshire side which won the Minor County Championship for the first time in nearly 40 years. And, as if all this wasn't enough, he played football for Gateshead and rugby for Sunderland and Watford. Alan Burridge was a sportsman supreme who transcended the north-south divide.

Burridge on cricket in Durham in the 1960s

In the north-east we had Yorkshire and Lancashire as neighbours, so you couldn't afford to be anything other than totally competitive. The standard was very, very high, and there was an intensity to the cricket. We used to play cup ties on a Wednesday, Friday and Sunday; nets were compulsory on Tuesday and Thursday evenings; and then we played a league match on Saturday against top players. Sunderland were one of the best sides around up there. We had six Durham players, and all the

teams had top-class pros who would run the nets and the coaching. Alec Coxon was the professional at Sunderland – he was a Yorkshireman, and a tough bugger. Whitburn had Lance Gibbs. These days some sides are paying the players – it's outrageous! That won't help raise the standard unless the person is a professional who throws his weight behind the club.

On hitting the ball a long way

I used to pop the ball out the ground a fair amount. My father gave me one-to-one coaching from a young age and even as a youngster I could always hit the ball a long way. And I had a good eye. I once scored 186 not out in two hours in a league match for Horden Colliery Welfare. Many years later I was at Lord's when Durham played against Hampshire in the 50-over final in 2007. This bloke came up to me. "You're Budgie, aren't you? You scored 186". It turns out he had been the treasurer of Horden and he remembered how many fours and sixes I'd hit – 24 fours and eight sixes – and that I had left holes in the football stand behind the cricket ground. He was speaking in a very loud voice. Everyone was looking at me and I felt a little bit embarrassed. Then he said: "But you weren't as good as Derick Parry [later a West Indian Test cricketer]. He was hitting them over the football stand and into the centre circle!" I said, "Thank you very much."

On coming down south

When I came down to play for Watford Town in Hertfordshire I was coming towards the end of my career, and league cricket was just beginning in the south. I couldn't really understand why people would be against league cricket. It was a much more determined, positive attitude to playing on a Saturday. And we still had friendlies on Sundays. Perhaps there wasn't quite the same intensity as there was in Durham. I don't remember so many ex-professionals while I was in Hertfordshire – that had made a huge difference when I was playing in the north. Nets were optional. And there weren't nearly so many cup ties. But the Hertfordshire League was still very competitive. Teams like Hertford, Berkhamsted and St Albans were all clubs who were on a mission. At Watford we had Vince Ferrigno as captain, and he was very keen to do well. He recruited some good players: Terry Finn – father of Steven – Stuart Ambrose, Andy Needham, Ian Beven. In fact there was a family of Ferrignos – one was the captain, one was the secretary, one was the chairman. They really looked after Watford Town and made it a very social and pleasant club.

On the Club Cricket Conference

One Sunday I happened to be batting for Watford Town against Hounslow. There was an Australian bloke called Greg Ritchie, who became a Test cricketer, standing at short-leg and another fella called Robin Syrett and they were screaming: "Get this northerner out!" The aeroplanes at Hounslow were flying about 50 feet above you and I thought, 'What the hell is all this?" And I got a bit angry, so I hit them for a big hundred. After the game Robin came to me and said, "Would you like to come for a trial for the Club Cricket Conference?" He told me they were going on a tour to New Zealand, Hong Kong, Singapore and Australia that winter. So I went to this trial and a fella bowled me some medium-pace and I smacked him for 80-odd and got on the tour. I was 42 years old. I got a hundred in the first game at Auckland – I was hitting the roof of a church in the next field. We had a great time. It was the best tour I have ever been on.

On nearly playing county cricket

My one regret is that I didn't go full-time as a county cricketer and see how well I could do. But I had a career as a manager in the leisure business. I nearly signed up for Derbyshire. I played a match against them for the Minor Counties in the Benson & Hedges Cup in 1972, and I smashed the ball out of sight. I made 76 but I ran out of partners and we lost narrowly. The next thing Brian Bolus was asking me to play one-day cricket for Derbyshire. I got permission to get off work on a Sunday and play in the John Player League. I started filling out the forms and when I put my age down as 36, they said, "What's all this? We didn't realise you were so old. We'll never get it through." So it never happened.

On school cricket

The biggest change in my time was in the school system. The grammar schools all had good facilities and plenty of PE teachers. Now they do not seem to be concentrating on sport as much as they should. I was a lecturer in physical education, and in those days we had all these specialist physical education colleges such as Carnegie and Loughborough and Manley. The Carnegie motto was: 'A healthy body, a healthy mind.' Now there are fewer specialist PE teachers and less time given to sport in schools. Most of our cricketers come from public schools – that's because they spend a bit of time on sport. So there is a bigger onus on clubs to try and attract players because the schools are not producing. The clubs are trying but it's not easy. The other problem is that we have become a bit of a 'watching nation'. Kids don't take part – they watch it on their computer screens. They have so many distractions that we didn't have. We just wanted to play sport.

On the establishment of ECB premier leagues in 1999

I think the change to a premier league system in club cricket was misguided, because the leagues are extended too widely. You have a situation whereby Harlow have to travel all the way to Windsor on a Saturday. They have to leave at eight in the morning and don't get back until midnight. It's happening in the north-east as well, where a side from Northumberland would have to travel all the way to Middlesbrough. It's a major problem. I know of umpires who have decided to pack it in because of the long journeys. At Sunderland in the 1960s we mostly played against clubs who were nearby geographically. So there were local derbies and there was a great deal of competitive humour between the players and the crowd, because they knew each other. I remember an innings I played against Durham City, which was always a big game with a big crowd. I hit the ball as hard as I could and it got as far as mid-off. I hit it again and it was still no good, so I called for another bat. Next ball I was caught at mid-off. The Durham pavilion was raised and so I had to walk up the stairs through the crowd, and one little wag says: "Why, my Budgie got more bats than runs."

•••

CLUB LEGENDS

Jack Hyams: North London leviathan

By Benj Moorehead

Some have called him the Bradman of club cricket, for his sheer weight of runs. Boycott might be a more apt comparison, because of his unrelenting faith in himself. But to compare Jack Hyams to any cricketer would be unfair, for he surpassed them all.

In 1934, aged 14, Hyams made his first hundred, for Kingsbury Town in north-west London. He made his last some 60 years later, for Brondesbury, a few miles down the Edgware Road. He played competitively into his 90s, still able to run between the wickets – at least when they were his runs. Even in 2012, the year he died aged 92, Hyams had bought a bat for the new season.

In between he represented nearly 50 clubs, most of them dotted around his patch of north London, but also extending up to Birmingham and Bradford. It is estimated that he scored nearly 130,000 runs and 171 hundreds.

These are the towering numbers one is confronted with when considering the great Jack Hyams. They are so extraordinary that the mind struggles to make sense of them. Here's another one to suck on: he played competitive cricket in nine decades, scoring hundreds in seven of them.

Dorian Gray would envy Jack Hyams; lean, short, nimble, a keen swimmer and cyclist, he always looked 20 years younger than he was. Into his 70s batsmen would hesitate over a second run if they saw him field the ball on the boundary, and bowlers knew what a prize his wicket was. On tour in his 80s he was as hard to budge from the dancefloor as from the crease. "When you saw him at breakfast you sometimes wondered whether he had been to bed," recalls Michael Blumberg, a teammate and friend for many years. No wonder the Barmy Army made him their life president.

Hyams once revealed his secret: "I've got a good wife who looks after my diet and I don't drink much and I don't smoke. Well, I gave up when I was 70 but I smoked 60 a day up until then."

There was a little more to it than that. For one thing, he had talent. In his teens shortly before the outbreak of World War Two, Hyams was offered professional contracts in football and cricket. But his father, a member of Fred Karno's circus who shared a stage with Charlie Chaplin, was appalled by the terms, and told his son to forget it. Instead Hyams became a PE instructor, which is how he made his living, although his greatest currency was runs.

He was ferociously determined, taking the Boycott view that an opening batsman served his team best by being selfish. 'I live for this game, so I want to be out in the middle all the time' was his motto. He would not be rushed, sweating out his runs, grinding down the opposition. He was a handsome driver of the ball, then later a crafty nudger and glancer into the gaps – anchored by a barn-door defence. He

The hundred man: Jack Hyams

carried his bat regularly – managing the feat against a Sussex colts attack at Hove at the age of 84.

His craving for hundreds only increased with age. Hyams was very proud of his achievements, wouldn't sell himself short, and as the seasons rolled by he began to keep a meticulous record of every run he made, every landmark passed. The way he reached his final hundred – in 1996, at the age of 76 – is revealing. Hyams, now playing for Brondesbury, had made 98 when rain forced the players off. Match abandoned. But Jack Hyams wanted his hundred. And so, under a downpour, the Edmonton players were frog-marched back onto the outfield so that he could score the two runs he needed. This he did – after blocking out nearly an over.

Hyams loved a bit of needle with his cricket. He was once asked about facing West Indies' Wes Hall: "Fast bowlers have never worried me. I've always liked them." He thrived off the contest and so, unlike many a southerner, the arrival of league cricket in the 1970s came naturally to him. He'd had a taste for it during a post-war spell in the Bradford League, where he had found himself among kindred spirits in the hard-edged cricket of the north. Winning mattered. "An American friend once asked me how I can watch cricket for five days for a draw," Hyams once recalled. "He's right. It's like paying to watch a film and leaving half way through." He welcomed the cut and thrust of one-day international cricket, and then Twenty20.

As witnessed by that soggy scene at Brondesbury, Jack Hyams was a master opportunist. While serving for the RAF in Scotland to protect the North Atlantic convoys, he took to eating with the Italian POWs because the food was much better, and threw a couple of them into his football side to ensure it could not be beaten. In Bradford after the war, Hyams used his father's stage name, Sinclair, to conceal his amateur status while turning out for the professionals of Bradford Park Avenue Football Club, with whom he enjoyed a famous success in 1948 when Arsenal were beaten in the FA Cup. Two decades later he lied about his age in order to ensure a smooth passage into West Bromwich Dartmouth CC. There were a number of grumbles when it was discovered that he was in fact 49 – not 39 – but they ceased the moment Hyams swooped on the ball in the deep and ran out a batsman with a direct hit.

Just occasionally his steadfastness counted against him. In 1966 Hyams was suspended by Cockfosters, the north London club, for slow scoring after carrying his bat for 30 runs. It was the fashion of an era which yearned for 'brighter cricket'; a year earlier the England selectors had dropped Ken Barrington for the same reason, and Boycott was to suffer the same fate in 1967. Hyams took umbrage and left Cockfosters immediately, having scored well over 20,000 runs for the club to which he was wedded more than any other. A new start at Barnet lasted half a season after Hyams fell out with the captain, but there followed a happy decade at Mill Hill.

A few years after his 50th birthday Hyams called time on his playing days. But he was lured from retirement in 1975 by an invitation to open the batting with Reg Simpson, once of England and Nottinghamshire, for the Forty Club. Hyams made 116 and he was off again, signing for Finchley in 1978, and then a cathartic reunion with Cockfosters in 1981.

Two years later, after refusing to wear a helmet against a Clive Lloyd XI at The Oval, he told a journalist: "I can give myself another five years, in the lower XIs and touring teams. I can do it." This was an extremely rare case of Jack Hyams underestimating himself; he played for another 27 years.

• • •

HARD GRAFT

THE STORY OF WORKS-BASED CRICKET

by Will Macpherson

"Their motive was the same: to play cricket and have fun away from the work sphere"

VII

Folk who work together have played cricket together for far longer than the last 100 years, in the south of England and beyond. Cricket clubs have taken the names of workplaces, workplaces have spawned cricket clubs and workmates have become teammates since the middle of the 19th Century at least. Out of 100 clubs in an alphabetical listing of CCC-affiliated institutions in 1915, 15 were workplace clubs – a sizeable number that is indicative of the rest of the scene.

These clubs have come in all shapes and sizes, from all corners of the working world, with vastly differing levels of involvement from the workplaces whose names they have taken and often unrecognisable gulfs in quality – both of facilities and the cricket played. There are those from vast, international companies with five figures' worth of employees in London and the wider south alone, and thus the resources to lay on large sports clubs at private grounds and the manpower to put out many teams, host competitive intra-company competitions and be a force on the local cricket scene. At the other end of the spectrum are small clubs made up of people who both work and play cricket together, often without any involvement from their employer whatsoever, but merely the brainchild and responsibility of a pair of co-workers, scratching around on a summer-to-summer or even week-to-week basis for the funds, the kit and the grounds to play a game of cricket.

Yet defining 'works cricket' is difficult, and never more so than now. Of course, huge, paternalistic companies putting out four, five, maybe six XIs on various days of the week at their plush, private grounds and with exclusive fixture lists bear little to no resemblance to small, wandering sides made up of a few friends who work together, struggling for 11 or perhaps just touring annually. All they share are the fact that the same people who work together also play cricket together; origin, organisation, raison d'être and modus operandi diverge wildly. Creating a simple definition of works cricket as cricket played by those who work together is all very well, but in 2015, no formal works club in the south is entirely made up of workers from a single company and some works clubs haven't been in that position for 50, 60, even 70 years; there are those that never even were and those who carry a workplace's name but no longer have a single employee in their ranks. While casual, inter-city, weeknight, short-form competitions such as Last Man Stands are home to many workplace sides, fully-fledged works clubs are not the force they once were. Workplace clubs have had to diversify, to accept associate members and, in almost every case, open their doors entirely to survive. The attempts of many to open up, to branch out beyond the office, ultimately failed and the pavilion doors were closed for good.

It is important to state the obvious and bear in mind the nature of the corporate beast. Works clubs aren't just cricket clubs, they are cricket clubs attached to workplaces or corporations. There is more than merely cricket, or even recreation, at work. Works clubs are and always have been at the mercy of the company whose name they take and the industries they serve and therefore changes can have disastrous consequences – be that a cut in funding, relocation, or closure. In some instances, changes further above board at government level – privatisation or nationalisation – can filter down and hurt individual workplaces and the cricket clubs attached to them. Naturally, old industries can become redundant and as they close, new ones emerge.

It is also pertinent to address shifting workplace culture and wider socio-economic trends and how such changes have affected the viability and vitality of works cricket teams. In the latter sense, *all* works cricket clubs suffer the same threats as any sports team as ever-increasing entertainment opportunities and changes in the family sphere and weekend culture impinge on their ability to attract and keep players. In terms of the former, white collar industries have, by all cricketing accounts anyway, seen a change in office culture that has resulted in a lengthening of working hours and a greater focus on work not play, which has resulted in a hit on participation. On a micro level, small clubs can be floored by a seemingly irrelevant change such as adjustments to shift patterns and less flexibility in taking annual leave.

Despite all of this, the works game is still alive and, while those feet aren't kicking the way they once were, still shuffling along – just to a rather different beat. Through clubs' diversification and the tireless efforts of a number of committed individuals, the works game isn't ready to retire just yet.

• •

They say you can choose your friends but you can't choose your family. True. But we generally spend more time with colleagues than either of those two groups, and broadly speaking, we can't choose our co-workers either. Love them or loathe them, they're the folk you're likely spending at least 40 hours a week with, cooped up in a stuffy office or sweaty factory and you've got to make do. The chances of a group of people thrown together with only their line of work in common all getting on smoothly are slim. As is guaranteed in families and highly likely in friendship groups – even though you've chosen to spend time with them – there are going to be conflicts.

Yet in an enlightened society, it's seen as important that colleagues get on, that they're happy in their work and don't consider their workplace one of doom and drudgery. In the 21st Century, between 'touching base', 'moving forward', 'idea showers' and 'creating synergy', we're told that the 'workplace environment' and 'team bonding' are crucial. These days, in the UK, that ordinarily involves eating pizza and getting drunk together or, if the boss is feeling particularly adventurous, an afternoon in a kayak or firing paint-balls at one another.

But workplace satisfaction, for all its hackneyed jargonry, isn't a new concept. The idea was first *researched* in the USA at the turn of the 20th Century, as an outgrowth of the Industrial Revolution and as production lines were first used. As the pace of production rose, employees tired more quickly and errors crept up. At first, research into "Industrial-Organisational (I-O) Psychology" (pioneered by Hugo Münsterberg) centred around making employees more efficient. But as it became clear that happy employees work more productively, it focused on their well-being too. I-O Psychology is behind team bonding trips, training days, satisfaction forms, performance appraisal and other such joys. Since its advent, the role of management has morphed from a simple case of organisation and direction-driving to keeping employees happy, too. Which is where the pizza, booze and paint-balls come in: companies providing for their employees in order to make them happier and, as a result, more productive.

Providing for employees was the motivation behind the earliest works cricket clubs, which come from various corners of industry. Take, for instance, the cricket club at the Reading Biscuit Factory. In *Bats, Balls and Biscuits: A Brief History of Cricket at Reading Biscuit Factory*, Martin Bishop chronicles the link between the town of Reading, the game of cricket and one of the area's key trades: the biscuit industry. In the 19th and the first half of the 20th Century, Reading was also famed for the brewing of beer (at Simonds Brewery) and the growing of bulbs (at Sutton Seeds) but, while biscuits are no longer made in the town, it was an industry so synonymous with the area that Reading FC were, for over a century, nicknamed 'The Biscuitmen' (not 'The Royals') and the place itself was known as Biscuit Town.

The town's link with baked confectionery came through Huntley & Palmer's, which was founded in 1822 and had a giant factory in the town at the junction of Gas Works Road and King's Road. By 1900, they were the biggest biscuit manufacturers in the world, a key employer in the town with over 5,000 workers (10 per cent of the local population) and a crucial plank of the town's identity. The company organised excursions for its staff from the early 1850s, while the earliest mention of cricket and the factory, according to Bishop, came in 1855 and the club was finally fully formalised in 1899, with four teams and a junior section. The aim of setting up such excursions and of forming such a club, he writes, was to provide leisure-time opportunities for staff.

The life of this club displays neatly the challenges faced by the typical works cricket club. In the century after the first reference of cricket at the company in 1855, when Huntley & Palmer's were the globe's grandest biscuit producers, the company's cricket section flourished concurrently and, indeed, "the level of cricketing activity at the Biscuit Factory represented by far the highest level of participation of any club in the town or, in fact, Berkshire". The club's Kensington Road ground and facilities drew green eyes from all over the town and the club was able to field five XIs on a Saturday, another on a Sunday, a junior XI, ladies teams and host an inter-departmental competition. There was a wider sports club, with the bowling team often joining the cricketers on their travels. The company was providing facilities, serious practice, membership at affordable rates, sports days and looking after its employees through sport.

Reading, biscuits and cricket's first snag came in 1914 with the outbreak of the Great War as the company, not just the cricket, reeled. The 1914 season was cut short by war and there would be no cricket until six months after the armistice in May 1919. Over 1,800 of the 5,000 factory workers would serve and 145 didn't return. The club picked itself up after the war and continued to be central to the game in Berkshire, with the depth of the club displayed by the continuing intra-company competition and ladies teams, before struggling on after the Second World War. An influx of West Indians in the area helped the club in the 1950s but with subsidiary factories of ABM opening in France in 1923 and in Huyton, Liverpool in 1955 to go with the

The Biscuits' old pavilion at Kensington Road

Reading and Bermondsey branches, the company came under pressure. As the 1960s arrived, Jacob's biscuits joined ABM and by the end of the decade the company had been reorganised as Associated Biscuits Ltd. From there, nails started to be driven into the company's coffin. The proud history of biscuit production in the area ceased with the closure of the Huntley & Palmer's factory in Reading in 1976, as well as the others in Huyton in '83 and Bermondsey in '85. Associated Biscuits was first sold to American multinational Nabisco in '82, then to the French food group BSN/Danone seven years on. The final crumbs of the Reading biscuit industry were swept away when Jacob's moved their head office back to Liverpool in 1996.

The cricket club, like the famous factory, had wound down in the 1970s and while the belated arrival of league cricket in the area in that decade saw them pop around different competitions – as a club associated with the former factory – for some time, there was no real sense of connection as there had been when the company thrived. The wars caused hiatuses but, more crucially, also tightened the purse strings and tested manpower. As the company had thrived, so too the cricket, but ructions at management and suit level affected cricket on the factory floor. The Kensington Road ground that they'd played at for so long and the original field at King's Meadow were lost with the Nabisco sale (gifted to the town), but, writes Bishop, because two members were also involved with Purley Cricket Club, the two merged to form Purley-on-Thames CC, which continues to this day. Many other works clubs would follow a similar path, merging with or being gobbled up by a local club in order to continue playing.

Before moving on from Bishop's book, which reveals as much about the factory and the socio-economic state of Reading and the digestive dynasty's decline as it does about cricket and sport, there's a line in it that is probably worth dwelling upon, qualifying, and exploring. Discussing the number of teams put out by the club from the factory, Bishop writes:

> At times the Reading Biscuit Factory or Huntley & Palmer's Cricket Club were fielding up to five Saturday XIs, a Junior XI, a Sunday XI as well as Ladies teams and inter-departmental teams representing various departments of the business. Although some of this activity would undoubtedly have been of a works standard, the club was able, for much of its history, to field a high-quality XI…

What is meant, then, by "of a works standard"? The words that follow certainly suggest a sense of inferiority and carry a derogatory tone. Yet due to the CCC's avoidance of league cricket until the 1970s and thus the absence of works leagues in the south of England and the varied size and nature of works clubs described in the introduction of this chapter, it's difficult to form a definitive picture of what works-standard cricket could possibly be. Such a standard would be easy to define in the north, where league cricket had raged for so many decades, creating a point of difference between the club game and the works game. Works cricket simply wouldn't get a look in in the powerhouse Lancashire, Bolton or Bradford Leagues, where it was crystal clear who the finest sides were, and who the top players would play for. This was not so in the south.

• •

Whatever its level or standard, works cricket was rolling along just fine all over the country in the first half of the 21st Century, as Jack Williams' book *Cricket and England: A Cultural History of the Inter-War Years* demonstrates. Williams also insinuates that the works game was at the bottom end of the cricketing pyramid, writing that cricket "at the lower levels was not expensive" and that "subscriptions at the more humble levels of cricket cost little", before saying "growing numbers of cricket clubs based on workplaces increased the opportunities of working men to play", adding that "playing cricket for works clubs was usually very cheap." That said, Williams notes elsewhere that church and Sunday school cricket were the "most humble forms of cricket playing" at the time, so there was life even further down the cricketing food chain than the works game.

Much of the inter-war works cricket expansion cited by Williams took place outside of the south, but his examples are telling: between 1922 and 1939, five works teams became 31 in Bolton, two expanded to 21 in Burnley and three to 28 in Halifax. In the same time frame, the Birmingham Works Cricket League expanded from a 20-team league to a 56-team, eight division competition, with the Birmingham Business Houses Cricket Association not far behind with 54 teams across six divisions. In the 1930s in Mansfield, there was a league especially for those who worked in collieries. Williams notes that it was the vast engineering works and collieries that hosted intra-company and inter-departmental competitions. Alongside these developments, Williams reports that by 1939, works cricket was strong in Middlesex, with 95 of 430 CCC clubs in the county workplace teams, and the majority of these were in white collar industries, unlike those in the north.

Perhaps the most telling line of Williams' work, however, is "the standard of cricket facilities provided by works recreation clubs was often very high" in this period. In the south, this was no different. From the Metropolitan Police's four sports clubs at Imber Court, Bushey, Chigwell and Bromley to the spectacular grounds owned by the Bank of England and other City institutions, there are many grand sports grounds backed by workplaces.

One such example is Royal Arsenal Co-operative CC, whose old ground in Footscray Road in south-east London features in Chris Arnot's book *Britain's Lost Cricket Grounds*. The company was founded in 1868 and had a wide range of operations across the south, with a membership of 500,000 and upward of £60m in sales. It was the second largest co-operative in England at its peak. So a pretty big company, and a substantial and important sports club with a healthy cricket section.

Talking me through the club's evolution is Mike Donnelly, a veteran clubman and former Royal Arsenal employee, with pamphlets, medals and memories of the way the club has evolved – it is still going today – since he joined in 1953. Royal Arsenal's sports club had been founded 33 years earlier and was originally based at Church Manor in Plumpstead, before moving to the Footscray Ground recalled so fondly in Arnot's book and by Mike in person. Mike enjoyed long careers in both the cricket and football sections of the club and worked in the wages department of the business. He joined the company at 16, had played cricket for Greenwich as a schoolboy and, because it was "the done thing" at the company, joined the works team as well – playing for his club on Sundays and RACCC on Saturdays. This wasn't an atypical arrangement but soon enough a decision had to be made and he committed to his works team.

When he joined up in the decade after the war, the club was thriving. The club was paternalistic, providing the ground, full-time staff to tend it, impressive additional facilities and cheap membership (four shillings for the season). They provided in other ways too: the company produced a magazine called *Together* for its employees (Mike still has copies), as well as a thorough joining guide for new starters detailing the football and cricket clubs. Everyone involved in those clubs was an employee, and although that would change, they remained extremely strong until the arrival of formalised league cricket in the area in the 1970s, when the cricket section could boast six teams on Saturday, three on Sunday and another midweek. Many would play on all three days.

There was a thriving inter-departmental competition too – The McLeod Cup – which Mike remembers even more fondly than representing the club itself and one senses this competition would have been all the richer in a business as diverse as this. Mike played for one of the two office teams ("everyone wanted to beat us") and there were teams from the bakers, dairies, retail branches, funeral directors and the abattoir ("a rough match – they were literally a blood-thirsty bunch") and the standard was competitive and high. Mike still has the McLeod Cup medal he won in 1958. This, at that time, was their league cricket but an indicator of the club's quality is that when league cricket was formalised in the area in the 1970s, the 1st XI won the first ever Kent Metropolitan League.

PAGE 8

SPORTS ASSOCIATION

The object of the Sports Association is to provide facilit
for indoor and outdoor games and social gatherings
employees.
The large area covered by the Society's trading activit
enables the Association to be divided into regional grou
each of which have active sections for sporting and soc
functions. This is done to reduce the travelling difficult
which would result from one central sports ground
headquarters.
Membership is open to all bona fide employees
the Society on a voluntary basis. The ann
subscription of 4s. is payable in two equal amou
deducted from your half-yearly bonus.
Facilities are provided at a well-equipped Spo

Together, the RACS staff magazine

RACCC's social life also flourished, with the Footscray Road ground's beautiful pavilion at the heart of that, with a dancehall, bar, billiards and snooker room. The club had a family atmosphere, welcoming wives and children and was the social backbone of the lives of many of its members. There were tours too – great family affairs – with bus-loads ferried off to the Isle of Wight and Devon.

Now, a tour to Brighton still happens but bears little resemblance to the former glories Mike describes. The Footscray Road ground was lost in the 1990s and the pavilion was the victim of an arson attack when it became derelict. The field is overgrown shrubland, completely unrecognisable from the well-tended square that once stood there. From 10 XIs across the week, it has now become a struggle to field two on a Saturday and one in friendlies on Sunday. Oh, and none of those who play are employees of Royal Arsenal Co-operative because it doesn't exist anymore, sucked up in 1985 by the Co-operative Wholesale Society (CWS).

So what changed, for club and company? Naturally, the two go hand in hand, although the transformation came on the cricket side first and Mike has a few ideas as to why. In that post-war period, when Mike joined up, becoming a member of the sports club was very much in the natural chain of events when joining the company. Why? "Simply put," he says, "Britain remained very run-down in that decade after the war. In truth, there wasn't that much else to do, in terms of entertainment opportunities and people certainly weren't flush with money. From what I can remember, it was play sport or go to the movies. Any men with the remotest interest in sport played as adults – and played a lot – which I'm not sure is true today; people seem to be busier." Due to the nature of the club, with that pavilion and its wonderful facilities, the sports club provided all the socialising its members could need, with dances, tours, trips to Margate and more.

Mike cites the 1960s as a decade of shift. It wasn't a case of people leaving the club altogether, but folk certainly trimmed the amount they played and the club was hit on all fronts. By the '60s people had more money and more options for spending it. More wives and girlfriends worked, meaning men were expected to play a greater role at home, and family and weekend time became of greater importance. In terms of entertainment opportunities, people had cars, started to go on more holidays and televisions appeared in households: it wasn't easy to fit all this, a family, work, a social life and three games of cricket every week into the schedule. All of this filtered down, and joining the company *and* the cricket club concurrently was no longer *de rigeur.* As a result, the club opened its doors, first to so-called associate members – those with a direct link to the club and company: dads, brothers, sons, cousins, mates, ex-employees – and eventually to all-comers as the club became completely open. Mike, who served on the committee throughout these changes, says there was no watershed moment, but a long-term erosion of the club's relevance and role and a requirement to adapt in order to – at first – thrive and eventually, survive.

Concurrently, the company (and most other co-operatives) suffered. The retail market was changing, supermarkets had muscled their way in, and co-ops weren't quick to adapt as their sheer scale and democratic structure made them cumbersome. Membership plummeted, reserves dwindled and dividend payments declined markedly. The company expanded for a century after its 1868 founding but the two-decade downward curve experienced in the 1970s reached a peak in 1985, when it avoided liquidation by 'transferring its engagements' to the national CWS – now simply the Co-operative. By 1994, all regional co-ops had been overtaken by the CWS.

For the cricket club, though, there was more pain to come yet as its most valuable asset was taken away. When the CWS took over, there was some inevitable penny-pushing and book-checking. The club, ground and all its staff were still being funded by the company, but had just one player left in any of its XIs who still both worked for the company and played for the club. Unsurprisingly, that funding went and the Footscray Road ground was sold, leading to its undignified demise. It lies on green belt land so can't be built on, although Lloyd's Leisure have tried their best only to be blocked by Greenwich Borough Council. With the help of the Marathon Trust and National Playing Field Association, the club struggled on, moving to the Metrogas Ground just round the corner in New Eltham. Mike is naturally delighted that the club lives on and he remains heavily involved, but says the Footscray Road ground was irreplaceable and the lifeblood of the club. "Everybody involved remembers how good it was," he recalls. Alongside Mike, there are still a few folk kicking around from the club's halcyon days, on the board, in the scorebox and out in the middle as umpires.

One of the remarkable things about RACCC is a list of opponents Mike draws out to show me and the sheer number of them that are works clubs. Peak Freans – the Bermondsey biscuit folk – are among 30-odd on the list, as well as all sorts of recognisable names of clubs that no longer exist, such as Sydenham Gas, Siemens, Harvey's, Henleys and Hayes Wharf. There are clubs that are still going, such as Lloyd's Register and Unilever, and those who never made it close to the 21st Century.

A look at the list is a stark reminder of how quickly businesses and corporations change. That I've never heard of many of these companies reflects how few corporations, businesses and services we use on a day-to-day basis now have existed for long periods and that the shift in culture that hamstrung RACCC would prevent any of these new companies starting teams today. There is simply too much going on to imagine employees sitting around a table at Amazon, Virgin or Vodafone or whatever the next trendy start-up mobile app is and deciding that what their brave new world needs is for their employees to play cricket together for eight hours every Saturday. A friendly knockabout through a city-based competition like Last Man Stands or a quick Twenty20 on a Wednesday evening between mates perhaps, but full-scale, multi-team, club-style cricket on a weekend? Not a chance. This change kicked off as people became more prosperous in the 1960s and 70s, but the world has moved on too much.

• •

While many of the companies on Mike's list have faded into obscurity or liquidation, one of the things that really does stick out is the presence of recognisable financial institutions that we use in our day-to-day lives. Indeed, three of the biggest four banks in the UK today: HSBC, Barclays and NatWest (RBS).

NatWest and Barclays' official cricket clubs folded some years ago, but HSBC are still going strong, and a pair of impressive histories have been written on the club by David Roberts. His first book – with a foreword from Alec Bedser – was published in 1970 (at this stage the club was Midland Bank CC) and documents the club's first century of existence. It deals in the opening chapter's very first section with the many complicated mergers and amalgamations that came to make Midland Bank and eventually HSBC, displaying the challenges works clubs can face. Through many adjustments, however, HSBC CC continues to thrive today, having appeared under a number of guises since its founding as London Joint Stock Bank CC in 1870. The club plays at HSBC's marvellous sports ground at New Beckenham and suffered heavy losses in World War II, losing 11 players and its pavilion, which was "almost completely gutted" when a "V2 rocket plunged to earth a few yards from it". The club played on at the same site, with groundsman Jenner's ability to prepare "perfect pitches" undeterred by the maimed pavilion, which was naturally replaced. The site of the ground lies adjacent to the club's original ground – The Three Banks Ground – home also to The National Provincial Bank of England and the Union Bank of London and Smith's, which is now the Royal Bank of Scotland Sports Ground.

Today, as honorary club secretary Kevin Dare tells me, the club remains strong. It maintains four Saturday sides (all playing in leagues), two Sunday sides, one of which is in a league, and a thriving colts section that started 15 years ago and has around 100 kids involved. The late 1970s and 80s – as in so many other cases – saw the club peak, with eight Saturday sides and as many as five on a Sunday. Dare reckons this made the club the biggest in England at the time. Only in recent years have membership stipulations relaxed, as former employees are able to retain their membership when they have left the bank, and now the club can invite non-employees to join. "Numbers are strictly controlled and membership is reconfirmed annually," says Dare, who believes these changes, alongside the inevitable move to league cricket, are the greatest adjustments in his time at the club.

Bank of England CC remains strong, and works-driven, to this day. Their club doyen, Barry Hoffmann, explains some changes in the near 60 years he has been a member. In terms of changes to the make-up of the club, Barry reports that there's no obvious slump in the club's history and, considering their incredible facilities, that's little wonder. He concedes, however, that the club – and the Bank – is different these days. The Bank itself has shrunk in size – from 9,000 in London when Barry joined to perhaps a ninth of that size today – and the culture of the City has certainly shifted. He believes that the social side of the club was better in times gone by and that the atmosphere shifted marginally when the club joined leagues in the 1970s. Works cricket, after all, was designed as an escape from work and due to the nature of life working in the City now, that escape is perhaps more difficult. Barry believes the club's laid-back and unstuffy nature reflects that. The number of teams the club has fielded hasn't veered wildly or declined massively like many other works clubs; in its infancy in the 1920s and '30s, there were four, by the 1980s, it boasted six and now is back at four.

"There was an expectation of contribution beyond the office when I joined," he says. "On my first day I was seen by someone at the Bank and they asked me what I played. I said football and cricket and that was that, I joined the club." All of which sounds rather like the first day at one of the public schools or top universities which many of the Bank's employees would likely have attended. An effort is still made to recruit inside the Bank but it doesn't bear resemblance to the conscription-style efforts of Barry's early days. Hoffmann and Mike Donnelly are in agreement on the post-war period, believing that the late-1940s and early '50s were when got people into social activities such as sport, simply because there wasn't much else going on. It was the done thing if one had the remotest interest in sport to join up.

It seems occasionally, the cricket club acted as a handy diplomatic and business tool for the Bank too. In terms of tours, the first team would tootle off to Sussex, with the county's 2nd XI and top club sides on the schedule, while the second team would head for Kent, where they still have a fixture that has been running biannually for 85 years. Inevitably, those tours, which like RACCC's, involved wives, partners and all sorts of frivolity, have been downsized to suit the modern day, shrinking from a standard six-day trip to a shorter three-day affair.

More impressive, however, are the overseas tours. The first came as the club thrived in 1982 and was to Barbados. Barry remembers it with the widest smile yet ("One of the finest fortnights..." – I don't press him further), as the club were hosted by the Central Bank of Barbados, who wined and dined them in some style, and played them in a match at Kensington Oval, which the Bank of England actually won (their only victory on tour). Such a success was the tour that they vowed to head overseas every five years, with the Australian Reserve Bank playing host in 1987, a trip to New Zealand (and Fiji) in 1992 and South Africa – where they played fledgling future stars AB de Villiers and JP Duminy and were hosted at times by current internationals Gary Kirsten and Jacques Kallis – in 2003. The touring party would be about 30 people (including wives) and it was all about fun and fostering good relations with their overseas banking and cricketing counterparts. The Bajans came and visited the Bank of England in London, too, with – reportedly – their rather different pace of life getting them into some trouble as they all overslept on the morning of the governor's welcoming event!

Barry's impression is that wider City culture has changed. There are certainly longer working hours now, and less time for play, but another sea-change too. The Bank isn't helped by the lack of "one-club men" which is an ever-diminishing phenomenon. When Barry joined the Bank, you'd expect to be in it for the long haul, whereas now new starters might not look so far ahead and moving companies is more common. Combine such ambition with today's hard-working culture and it's not hard to see how the sporting set-up has shifted and, to an extent, simply been put to one side.

• •

Hoffmann had mentioned that while the Bank of England's Sunday side used to play against Surrey villages (with some extremely long-standing fixtures still going), the club would play against government departments and other London institutions – the Treasury, Lords, Commons and so on – on weeknights. A little research on the London lot throws up information on two clubs that seem unique: Commonwealth Offices CC and Australia House CC.

To find out more about the former, I speak to David Narain, a jolly civil servant with with a Caribbean lilt, which is a pretty good indicator of the nature of his club. Commonwealth Offices CC was actually born out of these mid-week, inter-departmental evening fixtures as the teams from the government offices met to play. Involved in these fixtures were the ministries of Justice, Work and Pensions, Health, Transport and many others, while the Foreign Office's team were named Commonwealth 1920 CC after the year in which they formed. But after such games, which were convivial affairs (all about that escape from work), the increasingly large Caribbean contingent (the team from the Royal Mail in particular had a strong West Indian influence) would usually meet for a beer and a natter. One such chat went further, and a decision was made to play together on weekends as Commonwealth Offices CC, throwing all manner of characters – not just those of Caribbean origin, it should be noted – under one umbrella.

Narain, who hails from Guyana, joined the club when he came to England to work as a civil servant in 1985 and succeeded a long-standing English captain five years later. The club plays on Saturdays in the Surrey Cricket League and on Sundays in friendlies all over Surrey and even a little further afield. This is impressive given the player base, which is as small as 15, with many having to double up and play both days, and with more than half still working in the offices from which the club was spawned. David knows nothing of whether the club received cash from their offices back in the day, but they certainly don't now and one imagines – given the collective, thrown-together nature of it all – that they never would have done; indeed, who would they have received it from? The inter-departmental cricket is still going, David says, but not with any of the same gusto or clout that it once did, and some of the Commonwealth Offices folk will still dabble on occasion. These days, as the club's administrator-in-chief, it's increasingly difficult to mobilise the players, especially the youngsters, says David, as they all lead such busy lives, are distracted easily and have plenty going on beyond the boundary.

It's a mighty multi-cultural club, with players from all over the Caribbean – Trinidad, Jamaica, Barbados, Guyana and more – as well as other corners of the cricketing world such as Sri Lanka, India, South Africa and, of course, England. Their ethos fits the way the club came into being and the places they represent, with David saying that they "play with passion, with pride and to enjoy the cricket and respect the opposition, regardless of their ability or ours on any given day." Again, given how it was born, it's no surprise that the club is immensely social, with that beer at stumps every bit as important a part of the day as the game itself. Their friendly fixture list hasn't changed and the fact that they keep being invited back to places is a huge source of pride for the club and for David, who says their flagship fixture comes against another works club – although no ordinary one: the Royal Household's side at Windsor.

Australia House CC, another unique club with plenty of peculiarities, say exactly the same: that their annual trip to Windsor is the year's highlight. To learn more about this club, I speak to Lieutenant Colonel Michael Buldo, who is nearing the end of a stint at the Australian High Commission in London and is the vice-captain and coordinator of Australia House Cricket Club. He's friendly and vivacious, keen to impart interesting stories and quick to tell of how wonderfully his club has been hosted at various plush works grounds.

The club was formed in 1922 by the staff of the Australian High Commission and the make-up of the team is extremely fluid. You don't have to work at the High Commission to play (many of the small gang of staff do though), but you do need to be an Aussie – be that an ex-pat, on your holidays or a cricketer over for a summer in the English leagues keen for an extra game. Much of the team's backbone does come from the small staff of the High Commission, however. It was formed by and for the staff of the High Commission with the culture and traditions all about Australian endeavour in the UK. It aims to maintain the connection of Australians with their London base and foster engagement with the British government, business and people. The club looks to maintain the High

Commission's connections in the UK and has a number of long-standing fixtures against works clubs, including the Bank, The Foreign and Commonwealth Office and the Royal Household, as well as the Honourable Artillery Company and the Metropolitan Police. Away from the works sphere, the club plays a fixture against Sutton Veny, a village in Wiltshire, which is the resting place of 144 Australians who lost their lives in WW1.

Buldo sees it not only as a thinly veiled diplomatic and social tool used to foster good relations but as a focal point for the many Australians in the UK, too. The staff of Australia House has shrunk markedly – it used to push 2,000, he says, but is now down in the 200s, with approximately one quarter of them Australian. Appropriately, the club has its own 'baggy green' and its honorary president is one DK Lillee. Perhaps most charmingly of all, there is a fireman from rural New South Wales who uses all his annual leave to come and play for the club every second summer!

Buldo mentions the Metropolitan Police Sports Club, one of the more famous clubs on the works circuit. As mentioned earlier, the Met provided four sports clubs around Greater London: Imber Court, Chigwell, Bushey and Bromley. Greg Keene of Met Police Bushey CC says that the relationship between sport and the Met has changed almost beyond recognition in recent decades. Once, those grounds were all owned by the Metropolitan Police Authority (MPA). Now they've all been sold off on long-term private leases to commercial limited companies. There remains a link – and discounted rates for members of the Met – but it's an adjusted scene. Once, such was the club's status – and it was such a great source of pride in the force – that officers would be able to get time off to play any sport for the Met. Now, shifts are so inflexible that Greg says he takes as many as 10 days of his annual leave to play for MPBCC. It is not an accommodating environment and, unsurprisingly, most aren't prepared to sacrifice as much. Once, the Met Police sports clubs were family and heavily social affairs with vast player bases across the four sites, funded by the MPA; now it's the polar opposite. Once, the Met's sports clubs had a policy of recruitment akin to the Bank of England's; now, while they still send out flyers and look to recruit folk from the force, they would do well to pick up a couple a year. The majority of Met Police Bushey players no longer work for the force and one senses they may even be considering the state of the club's name. The Met's priorities have simply shifted away from the social and the sporting. Bushey has an affiliation with the force but is completely open.

Strangely though, it's not all bad. Bushey, which was founded by an enthusiastic officer from the force's main works team out of Imber Court, manages three teams despite battling a small player base and membership, and the 1st XI enjoyed nine promotions in 11 years in the Hertfordshire League in the early part of this century. As established, grand clubs in the area struggle, the battles MPBCC fight to survive are extreme – a lack of funding, the player base, draconian shift schedules and limited annual leave – but the club seems to be rumbling on just fine. Greg puts the works game's struggles rather nicely when he says "rest space needs valuing"; there has, of course, been a shift in the way people spend their downtime since the works game's peak half a century ago. Attitudes of employers have changed, but employees view and value their precious holiday and time off in a very different way too.

There are a number of clear comparisons to be drawn between Met Police Bushey and a rare club to have formed completely from scratch in recent years: North Bucks Ambulance CC. This is a club that shows the struggles faced by works cricket in the 21st Century in microcosm. One could go further and argue it shows the battles faced by any recreational club.

I speak to Dan Holliday, who founded the club in 2003 for paramedics in the North Buckinghamshire region. With most guys not having played since school, "we were so bad we weren't even all the gear, no idea," he jokes, "we were so much worse than that." The club started out by playing a couple of seasons of friendly fixtures before joining a league with clubs of a similar standard, which he describes as "sort of third team level at a decent club", and of a similar mindset, which was laid-back and centred around enjoyment. They lost a lot at first, before getting a bit better. For a few years they were a wandering side before getting a ground from the council, which in the end proved to be a curse, as the club's budget was so shoestring that Dan and a couple of others had to act as groundsmen, a role in which they had no background, experience or any real desire to fill.

Life in a league was hard work, and not just because Dan had to tend the track. On a macro level, the league was beset by petty bureaucracy, with big clubs – who could absorb extortionate fees that new ones couldn't – not all that welcoming, and numerous barriers to entry. For instance, if a game was washed out, the club still had to pay for the ground and teas, a fee of £65 that a club with a wide player base could just swallow, but Dan found himself increasingly footing the bill, which – unsurprisingly – grates. On a micro level, the club's struggles were akin to Met Police Bushey's, with a player base of no more than 30 shift workers across a pair of ambulance stations proving very difficult to coordinate and mobilise. The club was open but it still proved tricky; with shift workers, an evening or weekend fixture is not guaranteed to be any more convenient than one that starts at 5am on a Monday. When the club started in 2003, most of the players were in their late-20s or early-30s, but a decade on with families having expanded, that free time had become more valuable and fielding 11 was more difficult than ever. Unsurprisingly, after a decade, Dan and his teammates decided to knock the club on the head at the end of the 2013 season, although he hasn't ruled out giving it another shot. His club's story serves as a happy reminder that those who work together are still keen to start cricket clubs together, but also a frustrating nudge to the struggles they must face to do so.

• •

While North Bucks Ambulance CC is evidence that works clubs are still starting up, there are plenty of others with long histories that are playing on, even if – like Mike Donnelly's Royal Arsenal CC – the companies to which they were attached have long been gobbled up by bigger companies and conglomerates, resulting in a change of name.

Take for instance NPL Teddington CC, a club that came together at the turn of this century as an amalgamation of the non-works Lensbury CC and works-based NPL

Cricket Club in south-west London. Talking me through the history of NPLCC, NPL Sports Club and NPL Teddington CC member Tony Hartland describes the merger as "a salvation", which saw the number of teams expanded.

The National Physical Laboratory was founded as a government research laboratory in 1900 and is based at Bushy House (where William IV learned of his ascension to the throne 68 years earlier) in Teddington. The lab grew from just 20 people to a workforce of about 200 by the time Tony joined in 1963, most of whom were scientific civil servants. As with many government-funded projects, the NPL was attached to various departments, ministries and sections over the years: the DSIR (Department of Scientific and Industrial Research) from 1917 until 1965; then the Ministry of Technology; then the Department of Trade and Industry until, in 1995, it was taken over by the outsourcing company Serco, becoming NPL Management Ltd in the process, with a staff of about 650. At the turn of 2015, NPL Management Ltd became part of the Universities of Strathclyde and Surrey.

How was the sports club, which was formed just five years after the company was founded in 1900, forced to merge with a local club at a time when the company that it represented had never had a larger workforce? The fact that it did suggests that in the late 20th and early 21st Century, larger, stronger workforces did not necessarily produce larger, stronger works cricket clubs.

Bushy Park Football Club was founded in 1905 and became NPL Sports Club seven years later when the cricket club was founded. It would later incorporate tennis, hockey, bowls, table-tennis, archery and volleyball sections too, and Tony understands that in the early days, while the club was self-funded, with contributions in kind from the NPL (for example, the director of NPL has always been the president of NPLSC), all members were NPL staff, although soon enough workers at the Admiralty Research Laboratory (ARL), separated from NPL only by a fence, would join up too.

Until approximately the time Tony joined, the cricket section had just one square, but a second was created in order to accommodate a 3rd XI, which duly thrived. As with all clubs, in order to survive, the 1950s and 1960s saw, according to Tony, "a gradual influx" of outsiders, with about half of his Sunday XI in the 1960s working for the company. Subs were the same for internal and external players and Tony has no memory of limits or quotas on who could or couldn't play. One of his chief memories was how highly qualified its members were, and the distinguished careers they were enjoying: he reckons approximately half the 1st XIs on Saturday and Sunday had PhD.s in either physics or chemistry.

As the '70s rolled around, the number of players joining from NPL dropped, although numbers remained good and, Tony believes, were unaffected by the laboratory's fortunes. Now, the merged NPL Teddington plays in the Thames Valley League on Saturdays, while Sunday cricket has all but disappeared and there are perhaps four players across the club with any association to the NPL. Both of these trends, Tony believes, began with the advent of league cricket in the area in the 1970s. In the 1960s, it was perfectly normal for seven or eight of the players to have played on Saturday to turn out on the Sunday, too. So, a typical pattern: post-war strength; gradual opening up and slowing; company upheaval; unstoppable slimming; club merger helps survival.

Another works club displaying many other typical works qualities is Allenbury's of Ware, Hertfordshire, fromed from pharmaceutical company Allen & Hanbury's. The company had been founded in 1715 before being taken over by the conglomerate GlaxoSmithKline (GSK) – another employer with an active sports section – in the 1970s. Inter-departmental cricket at GSK was very busy, not based purely on department but with subsidiary companies based all over the country involved, too. The clubs would play for a trophy sponsored by financial services company Johnson Fry and would have fixtures all over the UK, right up to Montrose and Barnard Castle. This level of travel for a game of inter-departmental cricket is certainly a thing of the past!

Brian Stephenson joined in 1971 and says that now, unlike NPL, the club is not fully open. He says the club, besides the inter-departmental competition, played friendly cricket around East Hertfordshire, before joining the Hertfordshire League in the mid-'70s. It is, was and always has been a family club based around Ware, with those families united in the strength of Allen & Hanbury's and the number of people it employs. The company remains the marketing wing of GSK and the club requires members to have a close link to the organisation: a family member, partner or former employee. Finally, and perhaps most typically of all, Brian believes the club's social side has dwindled.

On the topic of sociability of these works teams, it seems apt to acknowledge the most casual of works teams, whether that's a group of doctors playing together fortnightly through summer without a formal fixture list, fixed membership or any form of registration, or touring, general collectives who might not even work directly together but are united by profession and meet once a year or for sporadic fixtures throughout the summer. In the latter group are the recently-founded Accountants XI, London Theatres CC and Authors XI. On the same note, I speak to Roger Jones of Roving Reporters CC, who were founded by a collection of journalists in 1974, after a few years as a successful football branch, including having John Motson as a member. They enjoyed 25 years as a wandering club, with a set of highly sociable fixtures. They've never entered a league – as so many works clubs have – and have opened out to include family members and close friends. They still tour annually.

Perhaps the most perfect joining of all works and social cricket came with 54th OCA CC, whose original players had served together in the Home Guard as the 54th East Surrey Division in Wimbledon during the Second World War. The regiment had such a wonderful time together during the war that they started up again as a social club (the 54th Old Comrades Association) in Wimbledon when the conflict was over and formed a cricket club – more Pike than Mainwaring, Jones or Fraser, presumably – and, according to member Terry Cunningham (who joined in 1968), have records dating back to their first ever game in 1953. They played all over south and west London over the years: Wandsworth, New Malden, Raynes Park, but always

Glaxo Group News, September 1976

News from A H

Cup win crowns Cricket Section's 75th season

ALLENBURYS' Sports & Social Club's Cricket Section at Ware have retained the Hertfordshire Group II championship – an appropriate crown for the Section's 75th anniversary season.

Allenburys were already Group II champions when they entertained Boxmoor in a Group II fixture on September 12, beating them by nine wickets. The team, with skipper Barry Price holding the cup, posed for this picture before the match. Photo by courtesy of the 'Hertfordshire Mercury'.

The league competition, which Allenburys won last year when they took part for the first time, consists of a series of weekend matches.

Of the 12 Group II matches played during the past season Allenburys won nine, drew two and lost 1. Their performance earned them a total of 58 points, an average of 4.83 points per match.

Among the individual performances, Bruce Darvell headed the batting averages with 67.50, scoring 270 runs in five innings, including a top score of 91. Barry Price made 211 runs in eight innings (top score 96) to gain an average of 35.16, Brian Stephenson made 230 runs in ten innings (top score 68) to return an average of 28.75, and Peter Walker notched 271 runs in 12 innings (top score 62), with an average of 27.10.

Lion's share of the bowling was taken by Jack Wilson who took 30 wickets for 313 in 164 overs (an average of 10.43). Other leading bowlers were: Tony Perry (105 overs, 231 runs, 26 wickets, average 8.88), Bruce Darvell (77 overs, 183 runs, 19 wickets, average 9.05), Brian Stephenson (61 overs, 121 runs, 15 wickets, average 8.06) and Don Bick (63 overs, 140 runs, 12 wickets,

there were full tributes to one who had contributed so much to the establishment of the Ware Club.

Three years later Mr A. Salmons repeated his 1928 achievement by taking all ten wickets in the match against Wyddial for only 19 runs, and the following season Mr F. Hitch and Mr F. Wallis both scored centuries.

In 1937, after a number of years of sharing the trophies, Ware won both their matches against Bethnal Green.

Between 1940-45 fewer matches were played because of the war and the departure of a number of members for active service. Local fixtures during that time included matches against teams from the RAF, Army units and the Home Guard.

The Ware section had one of their finest seasons in 1947, winning 15 out of 17 matches and drawing one.

In 1953 there was a record partnership of 137 for the ninth wicket set by Mr E. Beans and Mr F. Wallis.

Another landmark in the Section's history was reached in 1963 with the move to the new sports ground at Harris Lane.

More recently, the Ware Section won the Group's Australia Cup competition in 1973. In the same year they organised the Allenburys Evening League competition which is

which Allenburys regularly take part. They won it in 1952 (its first year), scoring over 150 runs in each of their matches, and also gained it in 1955 and 1956. In the past five years, during which the event has become much more competitive, Allenburys have reached the semi-finals three times.

The Club's present skipper is Barry Price, serving his seventh consecutive term. He is a good tactician who has played a major role in welding the side together. Other stalwarts include Club secretary Bruce Darvell, former Hertfordshire county off spinner, who has served the team for 19 years. A very stylish bat, he has had an excellent season this year.

Another long-serving player is Jack Wilson, still the Section's leading pace bowler, who regularly takes over 50 wickets each season.

Of the comparative newcomers, Brian Stephenson joined the team in 1971, having previously played for the Lincolnshire Under 23 side. In 1974 he scored over 1,000 runs for an average of 55 and in 1975 again topped that figure, averaging 65. He is also a more than useful medium pace bowler.

Another consistent batsman is vice-captain Peter Walker who in 1975 hit three centuries. His score of 150 out of

An article from the Allen & Hanbury's internal paper from 1976

headed back to their old base at Hadden Hall in Wimbledon for their drinks afterwards. They played on Sunday and the side thrown together was handy, and naturally had to branch out to be sustained, but played – almost without exception – on dire pitches. As you'd expect of a club born out of Dad's Army, they never entered a league and played to win, but not at all costs.

Sadly, however, slowly but surely, the social club was taken over by newcomers suspicious of – and with little time for – the cricket club, and their Hadden Hall base was sold in 2013.

• •

This chapter has featured plenty of works clubs, some who've spent their time playing against other works clubs, others who've never come up against one. When they have played against each other, it's been in friendlies or if they've just happened to have fallen into the same league. There is, however, tucked away in eastern Kent, an example of a group of works clubs who formed, and indeed still exist, to solely play works cricket against other works teams: the Thanet Works Cricket League. There are various works leagues in the Midlands or the North, from those mentioned in Birmingham and in the collieries of Mansfield, to Sheffield and elsewhere.

John Websper, who was involved in founding the league in 1967 and still plays his part to this day, doesn't remember why the league started out but remembers how.

That was in the pub, as a group of mates who worked in various different industries decided to start teams and compete in a league. John worked in oil, another in local government, one chap in a bakery and another at the council. "Fortunately," he says, "there were several better administrators than cricketers!"

There were 13 teams to start, a figure which had dropped to six by 2014, but at the league's peak it had four divisions, with the top two containing 12 teams each and about 40 teams in total. There were teams from the police (unsurprisingly strong), the postmen, Thanet Press, Baxters Sausages, Pierce Signs (innovators in the use of neon) and many more. In recent times, there have been a couple of local sides, but still teams from Thanet Dairies, Cummins Power Generations and the Sparkies (an electricians' collective). A picture of quite how 'works' the league was at its peak is provided by the fact that there was a minor brouhaha over whether the local Territorial Army should be allowed to enter a team: were they truly a works team in the purest sense?

The rapid growth was simply down to word of mouth, John says, and the league was full of guys who'd played the game at school but, due to the lack of organised club cricket in the area, hadn't since. Over time, inevitably and as elsewhere, rules relaxed and family and friends were able to represent clubs. These days it is completely open. There were offshoots – a cup competition, a single wicket competition, the Thanet Indoor League and a local umpires association, for instance – and, says John, despite the existence of the Association of Kent Cricket Clubs, the Thanet League became the strongest association in the area. There were raucous dinners and many Kent county benefits happened through the league as it thrived through its competitive spirit, good discipline and high standard. This was basic recreational cricket drawn not along the lines of location, but employment.

The league peaked with the arrival of the 1980s but the years of Margaret Thatcher saw its decline, and John and I are only half joshing when we say she played her own personal role. Websper believes that decline was, in part, down to the government, as utilities were privatised and shifted elsewhere, with South East Electric and Gas depots and showrooms among those moving on. It was also in part down to bad luck, with a number of companies moving elsewhere and simply disappearing in the area. Herein lies the nature and dangers of works cricket: while these clubs weren't necessarily financially linked or dependent on their companies and industries, they were utterly at their disposal.

• •

The overall picture painted of works cricket by those who were and are still involved is a vast, varied tapestry, with each corner unrecognisable from the last. In purely cricketing terms, there are those who played on pitches never fit for purpose, and those whose company employed multiple full-time groundsmen to tend their lush, plush, multi-sport facilities; those who never came across another workplace club, and those who played them weekly in large works networks or leagues; those with access to large, sponsored intra-mural competitions and those managing to meet once a year for a tour; those founded, funded, organised and provided for by their workplaces and those who were the brainchild of a couple of employees keen to become mates, rubbing two pennies together each week to field a side. On a corporate level, there are those used as a diplomatic tool by their companies and those whose companies weren't even aware of their existence; those now without a single employee and those fully represented; those who felt rumbles and ructions when changes were made at government level and those affected by nothing but the hand they were dealt by a particular summer's weather.

There are commonalities, however. While the processes and causes of coming together as a club diverge wildly, the raison d'être is the same. The Reading Biscuit Factory, way back in the mid-19th Century sought to provide leisure time opportunities for its staff; when North Bucks Ambulance CC formed in 2003, staff were seeking leisure time opportunities for themselves. The cause may have been different but the motive was the same: to play cricket and have fun away from the work sphere. Sadly, cricket appears to be on the decline as the preferred mode of having fun outside of working hours.

Right at the heart of the picture is that decline, which every club shares, whether they can claim to be fully open or not. While HSBC and Allenbury's may identify themselves as closed clubs, the reality is that works cricket in its traditional form no longer exists in the south, and hasn't for perhaps half a century. Yet due to the efforts and industry of a number of committed folk, works cricket lives on proudly, having adapted and diversified to reflect the changing landscape.

With many clubs founded around 1920, the wider works scene in the south enjoyed a 20-year high from 1950, with the state of society and certain industries invariably linked to the works game's peaks and troughs. There are over-arching themes that affected the game, such as a fast-moving, developing economy in the second decade after the Second World War meaning people, with greater disposable income, looked to spend their leisure time in different ways. Yet each club must be viewed individually, too. Seismic shifts in the culture of one industry needn't impact on another, whether it be seemingly minor cultural changes in the City of London, absolute overhaul of co-operatives or the closing of a biscuit factory.

The works movement may have faded and contracted as societal, socio-economic and individual threats have taken their toll over the last half-century, but it rolls on, grafting away, adapting to the environment, be that by opening its doors or scaling commitments back. The growth of the short, low-input, works-friendly Last Man Stands format shows there's life in the industrious, sociable, wizened old dog yet and – contrary to cliche – it's teaching itself new tricks in order to stave off retirement. You can keep your pizzas and your paint-balls; maybe put those beers on ice, though.

• • •

CLUB INSTITUTIONS
Bank of England CC

I'm greeted in the bar of the Bank of England Sports Centre in Roehampton by the beaming smile of Barry Hoffmann, who over the next two hours will talk me through the cricket club's past and present in wonderful detail. Sat by the window of the bar, we look out over the first team cricket square, surveying the vast facilities the Bank boasts. There are people all around, popping in for a bite of lunch, for a meeting, for a workout or a game of squash and the place is buzzing. Even now, when the Bank of England's sports club has fought battles that other clubs have had to endure too, there are five football teams, two rugby, three men's hockey, two ladies' hockey, a netball team and sides in tennis, badminton and squash to go with the four cricket teams.

The Bank of England sports club looks remarkably similar in 2015 to the way it did 30, 40, even 50 years ago. It's different in the sense that it is a semi-open club, whose commercial members – there are 1,200 of them – pay top dollar to use the outstanding facilities, which extend away from the lush grass of the perfectly-manicured playing fields and includes the Lawn Tennis Association courts next door, an all-weather astro hockey pitch, a superb gym and all sorts of other high-standard sports facilities. It's expensive but extremely plush, and you'll do well to find better more centrally than its Zone 3 location in the capital. Unsurprisingly, given the range and quality of those facilities, the ground has played host to a few handy sides over the years, whether that's the England rugby team – or some of their touring opponents – for training, the England football team ahead of fixtures at Wembley or the Surrey 2nd XI in representative matches.

Like so many works clubs, the Bank's representative teams have been forced to open up to non-employees in recent years, and some have quotas on the number of guest players allowed to turn out for them. Barry reports that the rugby section is completely open, half of the first and second teams of the cricket club are made up of Bank employees and "almost all" of the third and fourth teams are Bank folk. In addition to the four teams, they host between 80 and 90 colts on Friday evenings throughout the summer, between the ages of eight and 17. Some are the children of Bank employees, others are just children from Roehampton, Barnes and the surrounding areas.

Barry indulges me in a history of the club too. The Bank of England bought the land the club now sits on in 1908, when it was a rather decrepit old stately home. They duly pulled the house down and set about building the club, its pavilion, wonderful facilities and a rather grand red-brick building which now houses, among other tenants, the International Tennis Federation.

Perhaps more interesting is the effect that the culture of the City and its institutions and the leadership of the Bank have had on the cricket club. Much, according to Barry, is down to the Bank's governor and his personal leanings. A series of governors enthusiastic about sport, and cricket in particular, has helped – Robin Leigh Pemberton, Sir Edward "Eddie" George and, of course, Sir Mervyn King (a well-known cricket buff who co-founded the charity Chance to Shine) – and makes the club's annual Governor's Match the showpiece event of the year. The current governor Mark Carney, a Canadian, last year put a choice to the employees as to which sports they'd like played at the club's sports day and the people spoke, choosing a game of football, tug-of-war, rounders and a three-legged race among other events, with cricket nowhere to be seen.

League cricket rolled in to Surrey in the 1970s and, as the Club Cricket Conference had been, the Bank of England club was resistant to the winds of change. The club had fixtures that were 40 years old and was keen to honour them, rather than start over in a new league. Eventually they had to join one, but instead of joining the Surrey Championship, the club entered the Surrey Cricketers League, which was started by Esher CC and lasted 10 years. The league allowed a similar network of teams to play one another – just in the newly fashionable (in this part of the country, at least) league system. The Cricketers League was eventually taken over by the Surrey Championship, but Barry identifies that decade as the most enjoyable he had playing the game. Competitive but laid-back, he says, which fitted that escape-from-work ethos that the club carried. The Surrey Championship was all a little too serious at this stage, he felt. They would go on to win the Surrey Championship not long after joining, and indeed were the only side in the league without a paid professional in their ranks at the time. Now, Barry says, the first and second teams are serious, competitive, hard outfits after a win, while the thirds and fourths are Corinthian in spirit.

The Bank of England is not just an institution in the City; it's an institution on the cricket field, too.

• • •

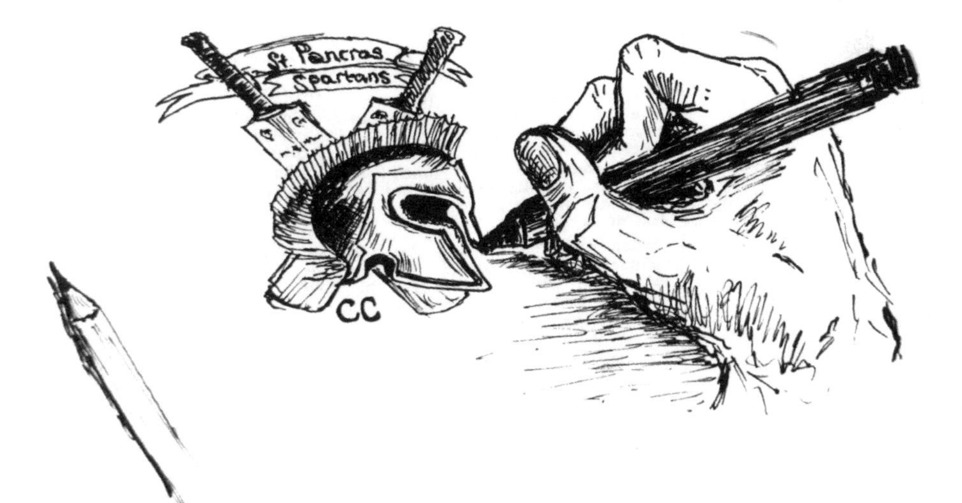

THE CLUB THAT WASN'T THERE

LES WILLIAMSON, THE ST PANCRAS SPARTANS AND CLUB CRICKET IN THE PRESS

by David Perrin

"The paper was the target of a hoax known only to its perpetrators and a circle of friends for 40 years"

The game was then virtually over and the visitors, at 83 for six, gained a grand victory with 10 minutes to spare. Curtis took four for 31.

★

HOOLEY THE HUMORIST WAS A HERO

Against Southampton Police on Sunday, St. Pancras Spartans groaned when they lost the toss. Police opened on an easy-paced wicket and went in to lunch confident in the knowledge that 62 runs were on the board without the loss of a wicket.

Then rain fell. When play was resumed, Stephens and L. Williamson found the pitch suited their spinners and from a commanding position, the local side were skittled out for 83.

Spartans decided that aggression was the only policy on such a wicket and reversed the batting order so that Hooley found himself batting in the unaccustomed position of number eleven. The plan only partly paid dividends for when he did go to the wicket to face the last ball of the day, five runs were *still wanted for victory.*

Hooley was humoured by the situation. He carefully took guard, patted down a suspect piece of turf, glanced around and settled down. The last ball was hurled down—and Hooley calmly hit it out of the ground *for six!*

★

OLD CAMDENIANS LOSE

Old Camdenians 2nd XI lost by 64 runs to Old Finchleians at Woodside Park on Sunday. Batting first, the home team totalled 162 (Simpson 4 for 35) and on a badly cut up wicket, Old Camdenians were dismissed for 98 (Simpson 38, Cornelius 20).

new champ

British Drug Houses m *of becoming Division One* pions in the Finsbury and League by defeating F Albion (18). Albion coul joint champions if they remaining games.

Responsible for Parkhu score were D. Willis (six and Stewart Squires (t two). B.D.H. soon hit t sary runs for the loss of or

Copthall completed a Division "double" over Athletic winning again wickets.

Caxton prospects looke grim when the score stood for five at one stage but b by the tail-enders raised to 35. Bill Pannell took six and Johnnie Whetton 10.

Mathews supplied early for Copthall by taking with his first ball and Chi back another batsman befo had been scored. Again it to the later batsmen to su runs and Mathews finished for 16.

★

Boys' Brigade c

Members of the 115th I Boys' Brigade Con attached to Holloway C gational Church, and t *Middlesex Company,* will for their annual car Angmering, near Wor Sussex, to-morrow (Sat week. Capt. V. Warren, Company, will be in c with Capt. A. McDonald, adjutant.

For club cricketers, scoring a fifty or bagging five wickets has brought with it – besides a call to buy the teams a jug of beer – the chance of a mention in a match report in the local newspaper, or even a headline. That piece – *Jones Top Scores Against Town* or *Dawson Skittles Saints* – would be something for the scrapbook, or mum and dad, or for teammates to rib you about. In the homes of club players there must be tens of thousands of fading, fraying cuttings filed or tucked away or just forgotten. Now, in the days of countless television channels, the National Club T20 final is shown on TV, and a club cricketer from one end of the country can be seen by people at the other.

For most of the century of club cricket commemorated in this volume, however, the sports columns of the local Gazette, Chronicle, or Observer were the one small field of fame available. They may only have been speed-read by other cricketers in the area, and just as quickly turned into wrapping at the chippy, (and there was a downside: Park Fall Short or Bedford Fails Again) but they were some recognition, and a reminder later, of all those hours, and years, spent playing the game. They were also – because they were after all in a newspaper – proof of your mighty playing deeds, or at least something to show your partner that you were where you said you were on a Saturday or Sunday. Or were they?

If what appeared in a certain weekly newspaper in the 1950s is a guide, you would be wise not to believe everything you see in print. The paper was the target of a hoax known only to its perpetrators and a circle of friends for 40 years. Today, in a world of instant internet checks and club websites, the deception would be far harder, if not impossible. Many may even doubt that it did happen. They, and readers of a certain sophistication suspecting that this account is some sort of postmodern fiction about a fiction, may rest assured. It can be attested – yes, in print – that the prank took place and also that it captured so much about the club cricket of 60 years ago. Rich in comic detail, it was essentially simple. A man and his pals invented a cricket club and for two years got fictitious results and news about it into a local paper. They called their team the St Pancras Spartans. Here is the true story of the club that wasn't there.

• •

The man behind it all, Les Williamson, turns out to be as interesting, and funny, as his hoax. A lad of modest origins from inner north London, he went to Cambridge, where he won a soccer blue and performed in the famous Footlights club. In the very era of TV's *Mad Men*, he became a successful ad-man behind award-winning campaigns, such as Esso Blue paraffin and Fox's Glacier Mints, which made a mark on posters across the country and on ITV in its early days.

The first I knew of his past bout of fakery was from a renowned after-dinner speaker, Peter Ray, of Wembley CC and later Richmond CC, who insisted that Les was a far better speaker than he. In the 1990s I twice heard Les speak, met him twice, and had two letters from him. When first he was due to speak at my club he had had to pull out at the last minute and sent a long and highly sincere letter of apology. When he did speak, the next year, it was, in the view of a usually critical character who has attended cricket dinners by the score every year for decades, the finest after-dinner performance he has seen. His tales – of the club pads which needed whitening every spring to mask the initials of visiting teams or of the squatter who occupied a cricket pavilion over winter and re-decorated it to his wild tastes – harked back to an earlier era and spirit of club cricket. In one set-piece he would casually work into his speech all 14 lines of the Wordsworth poem *Upon Westminster Bridge* which begins: 'Earth has not anything to show more fair.' Another featured an enthusiastic left-handed batsman who taught himself to bat from a coaching manual which he failed to realise was for right-handers. Wielding a tiny bat, Les would tie his hands and legs into knots as he demonstrated the chap's unique method of dealing with the bouncer or the half-volley. "He took guard, alert, hands at the ready, crossed on the bat-handle. Down came the ball. Forward to the pitch went his back foot." As the tangled absurdity of the stroke-play grew, so did the bafflement of this keen student of the game as to why he was scoring no runs.

As a finale Les would get everyone to their feet to sing, to the tune of *La Marseillaise*, the verse from Sir Henry Newbolt's poem *Vitai Lampada* which begins: 'There's a breathless hush in the Close tonight. Ten to make and the match to win' and ends: 'Play up, Play Up, and Play the Game.' At my club, at nearly one in the morning, with everything having overrun as was traditional, pavilion windows and doors thrown open to a mid-winter night, Les drew a hundred diners, many grumpy at the lateness until he rose to speak, into so full-throated a rendering of 'Play Up, Play up, and Play the Game' that we felt we were re-pledging ourselves to some fundamental principle of cricket.

When I last saw Les, at another club's dinner in 1995, three years before he died, it emerged that he had published his own account of the hoax, and he promised to send it to me. In the post came photocopies of three newspaper cuttings from the 1950s and a draft of an article which appeared in *Cricket Lore* in 1992. Billed by the magazine's editor as 'confessing' 40 years on, Les wrote:

> The St Pancras Spartans Cricket Club began as a football team.
>
> It sprang from a report in a local paper. I cannot remember the details but it was so fantastic that my brother-in-law, who was living with us at the time as people tended to do just after the war, said that if you made a report full of the most improbable incidents and sent it in, the paper would publish it.
>
> The following week I duly made up a report and sent it in recording that Williamson L. scored six goals in a six-all draw between St John's Ambulance Brigade (Kentish Town branch) and the Home and Colonial All-Stars. The local paper published this and three or four more of our fictitious and fabulous reports before the end of the season. Then we decided to invent a cricket team for the summer and we called it the St Pancras Spartans.

Just like his imaginary footballers, Les's concocted cricketers would pull off barely believable feats and take on opponents with suspiciously unlikely names. For example, the Home and Colonial All-stars faced by the footballers was a play on a then chain of staid counter-service grocers. Today's equivalent ploy would be to portray a branch of Waitrose as a football powerhouse. When summer followed winter in 1951, the reports to the newspaper on Spartan cricket were, as Les explained in *Cricket Lore*, a deliberate challenge.

> Throughout the season we tested the gullibility of the Sports' Editor and never found it wanting. When the club bus broke down on the way to a game and the players hitched to the ground on a hearse returning from the local graveyard he drew the line at reporting that. But that was probably on grounds of good taste rather than credibility.

As Les realised, there is nobody so ready to believe as a hack eager for a good line.

The Spartans' stamping-ground of St Pancras, a poor and densely urban London neighbourhood not known for cricket fields, was where Les grew up. His house was untypically large for the area and came with his father's job as manager of a nearby brewery. It had outbuildings, formerly stables, and a courtyard of sorts, where Les would play cricket with friends. At his secondary school, Dame Alice Owen's Grammar in Islington, he was Head Boy, captain of soccer, and captain of cricket. If Les of the Owenians is sounding too much like Roy of the Rovers, the next story may help. In a match against rival school William Ellis, he bowled a young Fred Titmus. It was, though, with a triple bouncer. Les would nonetheless claim credit for the Middlesex and England player's success by having kept it quiet for years that he was vulnerable to such deliveries.

• •

The London in which the Spartans were set in 1951, the year of the Festival of Britain, was one of bombsites, austerity and rationing, but also of a togetherness left from the war. The club cricket in which he set them was still struggling back to its feet after 1945. You'd see batsmen with bullet scars and bowlers with burnt faces. Some players still had their demob coats. Teams had team kit-bags. Whites were often creams, batting gloves green-pimpled, and boots soled in leather with studs hammered in. Team selection was advised of, not by tweet, but in a brown envelope with a half-penny stamp. Matches were nearly all friendlies. If times were tough, hundreds of post-match pavilions would nonetheless echo to singing like war-time messes. It's a world which needs *translation* for most club cricketers of today. Yet it was one in which cricket was part of Britain's mass consciousness, one in which cricket was what kids played in summer in those so recently battered streets, pretending then to be Compton or Hutton or Harvey or Miller.

In *Cricket Lore* in 1992, Les chose not to identify the newspaper concerned. The photocopied cuttings he sent me had, top right, a date and page number and the words 'N London Press.' Starting to research the hoax, I put 'North

London Press,' the likeliest reading of the words, into the British Library newspaper catalogue. When at first it failed to come up, I feared for a moment that the wacky world of Williamson was wackier than I had thought and that he had after all pulled off a spoof about a spoof. But then there it was – *North London Press*, incorporating *The Islington and Holloway Press* and *The St Pancras Gazette*, 1943 to 1971. If you have time, and the wrist, and remain unsure that I am not spoofing you, you too can spool through rolls of microfilm at the Islington Local History Centre and view the very pages of the *Press* which in 1951 and 1952 carried Les's fictions.

The make-believe drew on people and running jokes at his school old boys' club, Old Owens, which was to be Les's club for 50 years. The names of the Spartans – Attrill, Baker, Cowan, Hooley, Hoyle, Hale, Russell, Stephens, Vandermeer, Wright and so on – are his soccer and cricket teammates there in the early '50s. It is they who, along with Les himself and his brother Peter, attain improbable sporting glory or commit laughable blunders in the columns of the *North London Press*. On February 9, 1951, when the theme of the prank was still football, it was Peter's turn to star in a made-up report:

> **HIS 50TH GOAL**
> St Pancras Spartans retained their undefeated record with a 7-2 victory over Bronsgrove United on Saturday. Baker again dominated the centre of the field in the air. P. Williamson capped a sparkling display at centre-forward by heading his fiftieth goal of the season.

In later weeks Peter scores five in a 12-0 win, Russell displays great agility in goal, and Vandermeer concedes both an own goal and a penalty in a draw in far-off Southampton against an RAF team. (One of these reports appears in the *Press* near an item saying that "television's favourite animal, Muffin the Mule" has visited St Pancras.) Abilities shown in a Spartans shirt are invariably the opposite of those of the real-life counterparts. Brother Peter, for example, is said to have been a far from accomplished sportsman. This first – and only – Spartans soccer season ends: Played 25, Won 22, Drew 3. On September 14, after a season of cricket reports, the paper's sports columnist Norseman, from Les's carefully crafted information, reviews an equally successful Spartans cricket season of 24 wins in 26 matches:

> The brothers Williamson enjoyed a personal triumph, each scoring over 1,000 runs for an average in the middle forties... Top of the bowling too go the names Williamson P. and L., who, between them, took 135 wickets at a cost of less than four runs apiece.

It is interesting that, though far from sporting equals in real life, in the imaginary world of the Spartans the brothers do most of the batting, bowling, and catching, performing cricket heroics together in the sun.

Of a core group of perpetrators, one who went on to be a judge and was the only one alive in 2015 recalled for me how he, Les, and brother Peter would hold what were effectively script meetings to plot the next implausible adventure or bizarre character. At that time, in 1951, Les was waiting to start at Cambridge. The young friends sharing the joke were at university or on national service or starting careers, and what brought them together, when vacation or leave allowed, was playing for Old Owens. The group based the Spartans' enthusiastic founder and later president, Harry Susser (who figures, as we shall see, in the weirdest episode of all) on a fat, utterly unsporting boy years ahead of them at school. A teammate who could not bowl but fielded excellently would in 'Spartanworld' skittle teams with his spinners and then let the ball through his legs at a finely balanced moment in a match. Preston Hale, the Old Owens' legendarily economical Underwood-style bowler who took wickets galore, is carted for stacks of runs and never takes a wicket in a season, while Les, a purveyor in life of costly leggies, takes hatfuls for the Spartans.

The Old Owens dressing-room would share the laugh at the prank's latest phase. Some players would press to be named in a write-up. One player who barely scored a run was highly insistent, and Les got him into the paper as scoring a century for the Spartans. When, however, the man took to showing people the cutting as if the ton was real, Les had it reported that he managed only five runs in his other eight innings. *Norseman* of the *Press* regarded this as a typically harsh twist of cricket fortune. Later, Les drew on an Old Owens' post-war tour to Norfolk. (On it a cash-strapped young Les, sponsored by an older player at the rate of a pint for every 10 runs or so, scored 120 in his first knock.) Les turned it into the Spartans' 1951 tour to Flintshire, north Wales. The report in the *Press* has them losing a two-day match and three others, rained off against The Optimists (of all people) and another team, and 50 without loss on the way to a win in the last when food poisoning lays low seven of the tourists. 'Defeat, Rain, and Sickness on Spartans' Tour' was the headline.

Typical of the on-going joke is 'Hooley Sets An Example' from August 3.

> Hooley, St. Pancras Spartans' stylish opening bat, celebrated his marriage on Saturday morning by turning out for his team against Finchley Electric in the afternoon. Opening with veteran Charley Baker, Hooley showed little of his cricketing skill but set a fine example to all married men in his reluctance to be parted from his wife. He was back in the pavilion after only three balls had been bowled.

If he was not to have real clubs calling the sports editor to say they had never heard of the Spartans, Les of course had to invent all the opposition teams too or at least situate them a long, long way away. Thus, for example, in June the Spartans play the Done Our Bit Club (Primrose Hill Branch). Keeper Baker takes five victims standing up to the pace of Attrill and Les's medium-paced leg-breaks and googlies, and Hooley, at No. 11 for some reason, seals a last-wicket win with a six

The real Spartans? Old Owens CC in the '80s, skippered by Les, seated centre
INSET: When the North London Press ran histories of local clubs, Les rose to the challenge and supplied this photo from his actual club, Old Owens CC

over long-on. In August they thrash Mr R St J. Day's XI, despite their opponents having no less than four capped Club Cricket Conference batsmen in their line-up and opening bowlers who used the new ball "with an ingenuity rarely encountered in club cricket." R. St J. Day is respectfully referred to as Mr Day throughout the report, as befits a man with a name such as Saint John in a time of Gentlemen and Players. Then, on August 17, across the page from an advertisement for *Alice in Wonderland* playing at the Islington Gaumont, a report celebrates that man Hooley again.

HOOLEY THE HUMORIST WAS A HERO
Against Southampton Police on Sunday, St Pancras Spartans groaned when they lost the toss. Police opened on an easy-paced wicket and went into lunch confident in the knowledge that 62 runs were on the board without the loss of a wicket.
Then rain fell. When play was resumed, Stephens and L. Williamson found the pitch suited their spinners and from a commanding position the local side were skittled out for 83.
Spartans decided that aggression was the only policy on such a wicket and reversed the batting order so that Hooley found himself batting in the unaccustomed position of number eleven. The plan only partly paid dividends for when he did go to

> the wicket to face the last ball of the day, five runs were still wanted for victory. Hooley was humoured by the situation. He carefully took guard, batted down a suspect piece of turf, glanced round and settled down. The last ball was hurled down – and Hooley calmly hit it out of the ground for six!

In fairness to local newspapers and their sports editors, it is worth recalling the challenges faced by the grizzled veteran in charge of the sports pages on the large-circulation London suburban weekly on which I began in journalism in the 1960s, not so long after Les was fooling the *Press.* I can still picture him vividly. The ash on his fag never less than an inch long, he would stab away two-fingered at his upright typewriter behind the sliding glass screen of his editorial booth. On a summer Monday reports from 30 or so cricket clubs on weekend matches would arrive by post for the Thursday edition. The paper, part of a national group which probably used the same method across the country, gave out to clubs standard forms to fill in as match reports, just indeed as the *North London Press* did in the 1950s. The veteran (another Les, as it happens) would get along to a ground or two in the summer, and even attend some club dinners, and would be familiar with regular players' names, but he would have had to take much on trust. He would, I like to think, have eventually rumbled a sustained sham, but then again Veteran Les never took on Les of the Spartans. What I am more sure of is that, if he had ever heard of the Williamson hoax, he would, between puffs and coughs, have had a good chuckle.

The sports editor of the *Press,* if he ever learned how he was taken in, may well have reached for the nearest typewriter ribbon and sturdiest office beam to hang himself. It should, though, be some comfort to know that he is not the only person in such a position to be hoaxed. Whereas these days fans who throw sickies to enjoy a midweek day at a Test need disguises, or at least low-pulled hats, to avoid being spotted on television by their bosses, club players going sick to help out their clubs in a midweek cup round or Cricket Week fixture would often in the past simply change their names for the press report, so that their employer would not read of their exploits in the local paper and catch them out. There were then also weekday matches for shop staff on half-day closing, and far from everyone playing in them was a retailer. At my club in the 1970s, one player would appear in our local gazette under the give-away pseudonym of Donald Jokes. Another named Roy became Reg. Once started, embellishment crept further, as whoever the captain picked on Sunday evening for the duty of doing the weekend's match reports for the newspaper sought relief in some creative indulgence. Thus a pugnacious, immobile wicketkeeper with the sand-blasted Aussie-style name of Russ would routinely be in the paper as 'fleet-footed Rupert,' and an Indian player by the name of Bhattachargee went in as 'Harry Bhatterycharger.' Hard-fought draws would be like Dunkirk, captains' pep-talks match-winningly Churchillian, all cover drives Gower-like, and trundlers raised to Holding-esque velocity. The fun was to see, when it came out a few days later, what of the florid phrasing made the paper. Much of it did.

At another Middlesex club, in the 1980s, when a future MEP took charge of reports, modest club matches were written up like grand international sporting events and, in particular, batting line-ups were tweaked. When the opponents were the Met Police, Nos. 5, 6, and 7 in their batting order in the newspaper were Dixon, Dock, and Green and, at Nos. 8, 9, and 10, A Lo, L Lo, and E Lo. A neighbouring club used to arrange batsmen's initials to send the sports editor messages of a strong Anglo-Saxon flavour. After one or two got through, they opened the paper to see the initials now read 'NICE TRY LADS.' In a north London club, the matter of what to call ringers making up the team was resolved by giving them all one set name. Thus Hunt, Isaac regularly figured in the local weekly's sports pages. For nearly 20 years the club's captain wrote triumphally one-sided accounts of his men's feats, all printed nearly word for word. In the 1960s, a leading Surrey club, when phoning in scores for the Saturday edition of the then *Evening Standard*, would use an alias for a high-scoring batsman who went on to be a chairman of the England and Wales Cricket Board. The tycoon who founded the company for which he worked liked to think that his rising executives spent weekends visiting branches. It would be no surprise at all if other instances of fiction getting into print abounded in club cricket but have remained private jokes.

Even *The Cricketer* has been a victim, though in a case not about club cricket. In his first ever piece for the magazine, David Rayvern Allen, later a cricket writer and anthologist of renown, got published in 1977 an article 'Cricket in Tibet' featuring a match between Gyantse County (78 all out) and Tsona County (79-3). In the next issue the editor had to admit it was a wholly false spoof for April Fools' Day. In another sport, a north London old boys' rugby side, I am told, included in match reports an invented Italian centre called Sebastian Broccoli. In the week he scored a wonderful – but utterly fictitious – try, the local gazette graced it with the headline 'Broccoli Spears Through.'

In 1951, as the Spartans' fabulous season went on, Hale still failed to capture a wicket. Les took many. Hooley stayed married, despite several times lasting at the crease for more than a few balls. When cricket overlapped with soccer again, Les provided *Norseman* with material to sympathise with the hard-pressed lot of groundsmen. In *Norseman Looks Around* on September 14 the columnist rose to the occasion:

> To get down to personalities in this short tribute to groundsmen, I should like particularly to wish Mr A Heath a successful retirement. Better known as 'Pop' to members of the St. Pancras Spartans Cricket Club, Mr Heath served the club for 35 years.
>
> **Silver Lawn Mower**
>
> At the Finchley ground, on Saturday, Spartans' president, Mr Harry Susser, presented 'Pop' with a miniature silver lawn-mower and roller.
>
> The happy ceremony took place after the Spartans had defeated the Metropolitans by seven wickets to conclude what must be their most successful season, even in Mr Heath's long memory.

Les's proudest moment in the whole two-year pretence was probably the headline given this piece by the sports editor: 'Groundsman gets a mower he need not push.' A twist yet more surreal, though, would be the finale. The figure of 'Pop' Heath was inspired by 'Pop' Coleman, groundsman at The Old Owens' ground not in Finchley but then in another part of north London, Barnet. Mr Coleman did retire, to be succeeded by his son, but I doubt that he received any miniature mementos.

Inspiration more generally came to Les from the whole post-war cricket scene in inner north London. The very columns carrying the fake Spartan reports in the *North London Press* teem with dozens of teams (real ones!) and list results for several leagues, such as the Gospel Oak and Hampstead League, the Regent's Park League, and the Finsbury Park League. Representative matches were held between park leagues, with selected teams announced in the paper. Sea cadets and scouts and boys' clubs played cricket. Teams were reported as angry that London County Council park pitches were dangerously poor and that captains could safely put on only slow bowlers. The return of local cricket after the war and the leagues of the 1950s and 1960s are recalled by Les in another article for *Cricket Lore*, 'Cricket in the Parks.'

> Park cricket catered for the ordinary man's love of sport... For me the centre of this cricket revival was Regent's Park, where on the central field by the zoo, fifty games would be played each Saturday and Sunday. Finsbury Park could stage a mere eight or so. Parliament Hill Fields had two pitches in splendid isolation and, on the field sloping down to the lido, eight in parallel with thirty yards between each.
>
> Roads, factories, churches, offices, social clubs, and just groups of friends spawned teams...

This was a scale, and social spread, of participation which the ECB would these days die for. Les himself played some matches for a Camden Town park team, Lyonton, and was picked for the Gospel Oak and Hampstead League rep side. With his local knowledge, Les had ideas at the ready when, to his delight, the sports editor of the *Press* invited clubs to submit stories of their origins for a new series, 'How They Started.' Seizing the chance for further fakery, Les told the paper that in 1902 St Pancras Sea Cadets, commanded by an old 'sea salt,' Petty Officer Hooley, played a street team from Camden Town, and the two teams went on to form the Spartans. A photo of the Spartans appeared in the *Press* with their history, according to Les's *Cricket Lore* article, which reproduced the photo. Les wrote that it was an old one from the Old Owens, but nobody I have spoken to from the club recognises it. The surviving perpetrator told me that it is of an occasional company team from a Mayfair property agency and was supplied to Les by an Old Owens member connected to the firm. It would be good to settle the mystery of who passed into history as the St Pancras Spartans.

After the summer of 1951, the Spartans went quiet for a while. Les went up to Cambridge; friends were away at college. Also, he recounts, his mother ran what he calls a 'guerrilla war' against the prank, fearful that her son would go to prison for fooling the press. Les and his pals were tiring of the joke but did not want the Spartans simply to disappear, disappointing the readers of north London. In 1952, towards the end of the summer, after holidays had brought the friends together again, Les hit on a way out with some of his wackiest detail. On August 8 the *Press* ran 'Spartans Hold Their Jubilee.'

> This season should have been a 'success season' for St Pancras Spartans cricket team, but Dame Fortune, who has blessed the club with a smile for most of its 50 years' history seems to have deserted one of the borough's keenest cricket teams.
>
> **On Edge**
> For 30 of those 50 years the Spartans have played at their own ground at Finchley. Last year's remarkable season in which they won 25 games and drew the other two, did not solve the club's financial problems and they were forced to sell their ground. The result: only one fixture for this season. But when skipper PJ Williamson tossed up against B. Russell on Saturday of last week the event was watched with more than usual interest. For one witness was 75-year-old Harry Susser, now president of the club, who as skipper and founder, tossed the first coin in the interests of Spartan cricket 50 years ago.
> Harry recalls that on that historic occasion the coin came down on its edge and had to be re-tossed.

Then came more of Les's phantom history for the Spartans.

> Opponents in 1902 were St Pancras's strongest side – the local sea cadets. In answer to a challenge by the commander, Petty Officer Hooley, Harry got together a team of Canal View, Camden Town, residents, met the cadets at Hackney and beat them by three wickets. This might well have been the end of Spartan cricket, for, although none were keener than Harry Susser and his neighbours, shortage of kit presented an insurmountable problem.
> Later in the year, however, the sea cadets disbanded, the rival clubs pooled their resources and the combined team went from strength to strength. A link with the past was provided on Saturday of last week when Mick Hooley, a son of the 'old salt,' opened the innings for the Spartans.
> It is sad that in their jubilee this old St Pancras side should have had such a lean season, but next year they hope to resume as a nomad side.

A dinner for the Jubilee was to be the Spartans' sign-off. Les and cricket friends did stage a dinner, in a large room in the Williamson family's extensive brewery house. Club relics, like the petty officer's cap worn by Mr Hooley in the Spartans' early fixtures, were on display for the occasion. Les actually invited the sports editor, and the friends would pretend to be the Spartans. Worried that they could not pull it off, he told the editor that they were no longer having guests because the president,

Harry Susser, had just died. Instead, someone his sister knew came along, posing as the sports editor. Les did not tell the friends or the fake editor about each other. Ever a lover of a sketch, Les and a few in the know enjoyed the spectacle of pretend Spartans mingling with pretend editor, neither realising about the other. At the dinner a place was laid for the late president. Courses were served, and removed, at the place. After food, a tape recording was played. My surviving insider says that one friend, an accountant with famous entertainers as clients, persuaded one of them, Michael Bentine of the Goons, to record a message pretending to be Harry Susser's mourning brother, and that that is what they all listened to. He says he can still hear Bentine's voice intoning crazy reminiscences such as 'I last saw my brother at the Siege of Sebastopol.' Whatever did happen, and whatever Les went on to tell the *North London Press*, on September 26, 1952, in its last ever item about the Spartans, the newspaper on page nine carried the gloriously more surreal report that the Spartans' dead president spoke to them from beyond the grave.

> **RECORDED HIS LAST SPEECH**
> Members of St Pancras Spartans CC heard the voice of their late President, Mr Harry Susser, at their annual dinner at St Pancras Way, on Friday. Some days before, he died on Monday of last week. Mr Susser recorded a short speech to be played at the dinner. He was one of the men who founded the Spartans in 1902, and was 72 [sic!] when he died.
> Over 30 members were present at the dinner, including a founder member, Mr J Hooley.
> Spartans, a wandering side, need fixtures for next season. Clubs able to offer them a game should contact Mr. J. Williamson, No 9, St Pancras Way, N.W.1.

There was prescience in Les's farewell notion of the Spartans as nomads. These days the big house at No. 9 is a St Mungo's hostel for the homeless.

• •

Times shape people. Les Williamson is a figure of his era of club cricket, a man who spent 50 years at one club, skippering teams or holding office or just helping out when needed. He could have played at the club game's most competitive levels but shared the view of his outstanding teammate, Preston Hale, who, when asked why he did not turn out for a 'top club,' would say, "Your mates, Leslie, you have to play with your mates." Les's mates also became the Spartans. It was a time when players would make a life in a club, generate their own affordable fun together, and make long-standing friends in other clubs. They'd stay late in the bar, sing round pianos, and do comic turns. Les had a wide repertoire of songs and would look fit to burst as he threw himself into them, rattling off lyrics like "Poor old coalman was a short-sighted fella, when he saw Jim's mouth he thought it was the cellar." Cricket dinners at Old Owens at one time attracted modest numbers. When, thanks to the member with the celebrity accountancy clients, speakers regularly included entertainers such as Tommy Cooper,

Sid James, and Peter Cook and Dudley Moore, they became for a while events at Lord's attended by hundreds. Les spoke at them and, a friend says, was never outclassed.

There was a subversive edge to Les as an after-dinner speaker and also to his prank about the Spartans, with its jibes about over-vaunted capped players from the Club Cricket Conference or about a posh captain. Mischief has its appeal. (Years back, when young, some cricket friends and I formed a team called The Ballbaggians, taking laddish glee at seeing the name in the fixture cards of clubs in whose cricket weeks we played. We even had a tie made: plain but for a horizontal B, the loops of the letter drooping.) Behind the mischief in Les's case, however, was a person of principle. He stood as a Labour candidate for his local council but never won, though he did achieve a wish attested by club-mates to be buried in the same cemetery as Karl Marx. He was critical of club cricket's then 'pecking order', as he called it:

> Starting at the bottom, it went something like this: park sides, works sides, business sides, wandering sides, old boys sides, club sides, posh business sides (posh park sides and posh works sides are contradictions in terms), posh wandering sides, posh old boys sides, posh club sides each desperately trying to maintain status or grab extra status for itself by gaining fixtures or dropping fixtures...

When Les died, the editor of *Cricket Lore*, Richard Hill, a teammate at Old Owens, described him as, after his father, the best cricket companion he ever had:

> I have never quite bought the idea that cricket builds character, but I have always believed that it gives ample opportunity for the best and worst of a man's character to be displayed. Cricket displayed Les's character to the full. He knew he was a fine player, but only in the same way he knew his phone number. There was no arrogance about him or his play, but no feigning mock modesty either. He was as ready to acknowledge that the bowler had beaten him as he was to accept the half-volley. League game or friendly, Les always played cricket *with* people, never against them. Yet he seemed never to be put out by the worst of petty displays of temper, unless from a player in his team. And after the match, he sought out the day's disappointed as readily as the successful and, as on the field, laughter was never far away.

Many years ago, Les had fun with a club that never was, one with a parade of characters and incident created from friends and the post-war cricket which he so affectionately and perceptively observed. The St Pancras Spartans have disappeared, but so have many clubs which were there and are no longer. Hounslow Cricket Club in Middlesex, for example, was once a thriving place with two pitches, where in the evening the pavilion would throng for hours with cricketers from four teams, a score or more bowls players just off the green, families, children, friends, social members, and guests. Now it stands empty, untended, awaiting decisions as to what will be built on the abandoned field. What is the chance it will be for sport? Others will know lost fields near them: spaces once for friendships and social bonding and unpaid toil by members and a ribald legacy all their own of jokes and nicknames and comic invention to match the Spartans. In the 1960s, after the so-called Beeching cuts had reduced the national rail network by a third, the singing duo of Flanders and Swann wrote a song *Slow Train*, hauntingly weaving together some of the names of the hundreds of axed stations and halts where trains would never stop again. The same might be done with names on a list at the ECB of folded cricket clubs where cricket will be no more. 'At Hounslow, Dover and Oatlands Park nevermore; at Hersham, Blackburn Northern, and Manningham Mills nevermore; at Islington, Tudor, and Crockham Hill, no play today or evermore.' As many clubs have ceased and society changed, more monetised modes of leisure have taken over. Fine fiction though they were, the Spartans are not a loss to compare in the slightest to the real clubs that live no longer, and the loss entailed by thousands of people and their communities. Of course we must be alert to the Fallacy of the Golden Past. Yet a strong case can be made, supported if challenged by rigorous analysis, that there was an optimal period, one covering the heyday of Les Williamson and his like, when factors – economic and social – combined to enable cricket clubs to flourish more fully and more roundedly than they do now. Clubs that have kept up that past spirit are to be admired, but they face growing challenges. Some changes responsible are to the good, such as the shift in the relation of the sexes and women's rightful resistance to being grass widows. Whatever the causes, space has gone from the social dynamic for clubs as they were to function and survive. It is not overall a compliment to how we are today. Gone, too, moreover, doomed by huge shifts in the media industry, are hundreds of local newspapers which once provided that little field of fame for the club game as well as that chance for clubs' in-jokes and humorous traditions to spill into print.

Returning to the Spartans – to conclude this true tale about untruths – some vital questions remain; questions that you might say the sports editor should have pursued. How was a club that had just sold an acre or so of prime Finchley in north London in financial trouble, even at 1952 prices? Why was so illustrious a club as the Spartans never known to the newspaper for 48 of its 50 years? How did Hooley Jnr of the Spartans keep hitting those last-ball sixes? Is he still married? How does a tossed coin land on its edge? What happened to that treasured relic, the petty officer's cap? What was Harry Susser's secret for losing three years of age? Why don't the sea cadets produce cricketers like they did? Where would England stand now if the Spartans were still playing? How would Kevin Pietersen get along with them? In saying that the Spartans had a ground, Les Williamson took a particular risk of being rumbled. Staff from the paper just might have sought to visit it. Then again, the mission had been to see how far they could go. The answer was: all the way. Even Les, though, believed that the sports editor, if he had attended the truly bizarre finale of the bogus jubilee dinner, would have suspected something. It seems that Les wrote out his fictions, most likely on the 'cricket forms' supplied by the paper, and posted them in, but apparently he did telephone the Press at least once. It is delicious to imagine Les, in his deadpan way, whispering his nonsense directly into the sports editor's ear. Did he stumble at all, or even once have to suppress a giggle? I think not.

• • •

VII

CLUB INSTITUTIONS
Sevenoaks Vine CC
by Will Macpherson

Sevenoaks Vine can boast a history as rich as any cricket club in the south of England. Their stunning ground on the Vine, just a stone's throw – literally – from the high street of picturesque Sevenoaks has had cricket played on it for 281 years and, unlike many of the earliest ovals, has an exact date of cricketing conception: a match played for 1,000 guineas between the Gentleman of Kent and Sussex on September 6, 1734, as recorded in the *Evening Post.* These days, a list of the club's alumni is full of impressive, respected names from Kent's recent past, such as Chris Tavaré, Mark Benson, Paul Downton (and his father George, a stalwart of the Club Cricket Conference who also played 10 first-class games), David Fulton and Ed Smith.

Their development has taken place before a backdrop as stunning as any in the country – and this remains very much part of the club's allure. Gavan Burden, chair of the club's management committee, jokes that much of the ground's undoubted beauty stems from its "utter impracticality." He says: "If you were building a cricket club in the 21st century this would be quite literally the last place you'd do it. It's 50 yards from the high street and has busy main roads running immediately either side. It's completely open and would just never be built today.

"It's in an incredible spot, the Vine has history going back to Roman times. It's where they used to grow their grapes and some still say it's a much better place to make wine than to put cricket pitches! Equally, we've got a Grade Two listed facade on our pavilion: it's stunning but a bit impractical – it can be very cold! Overall though, it's an amazing place to play and watch cricket and people love to come here, which is fantastic." As well as being the Romans' favoured wine-making spot, the site has acted as the vineyard of various Archbishops of Canterbury.

Cricket at the Vine is not all about that pretty ground, though. The club boasts three senior league sides, 150 junior players, an over-40s side that plays on Friday evenings and a T20 team on Sundays. The first team are Kent's 2014 champions and, just as important according to Burden, received the Brian Luckhurst Spirit of Cricket Award from the league's umpires for the way they went about their business. "That was a very gratifying award to receive," says Burden. "We're very keen to play the game in the right way and pass on that ethos to our juniors. We don't pay anyone to play the game, we're very clear about that. We may have professionals on our books, but we won't pay them, and sometimes they'll leave to go elsewhere as a result."

Clubs with history this deep often have their quirks and Sevenoaks Vine is no different. While the club funds the upkeep of the Vine without support from the council, despite it being a public space – and that doesn't come cheap – their rent for the playing surface is a little less taxing: a peppercorn. Every Wednesday of their immensely

Still going: Sevenoaks Vine's unusual 'Peppercorn Ceremony'

popular annual cricket week sees Burden present the Sevenoaks Mayor with the rent in what is known as "the Peppercorn Ceremony". Quirky indeed.

The club's social life is centred around major events such as cricket week, which also takes in a beer festival, various sponsors' lunches and plenty more frivolity. The event-centred social life is down to the number of members who are based in London and the standard cycle of membership: child joins as a junior, before heading off to university and, eventually, work in London, where they'll remain a member and get down as often as possible. More than half of the current first and second teams are London-based.

"Old Oaks" Friday evening cricket – which was pioneered by Burden when his kids were out of the juniors system and he reached his 40s – is aimed at commuters and now has a full programme of 22 fixtures a year, having started off with half a dozen. "We say that it gives us an eight-day week," says Burden. "We have loads of members who spend their whole week glued to their desk in London, starting early and leaving late, but they'll all make a huge effort to get out of the office for 4.30 on Friday so they're down to the Vine for 5.30-6, and we'll then play for as long as we can. It's great because you play a bit of sport and have some fun on a Friday night and still have the whole weekend to enjoy and relax."

Ancient and quirky they may be, but Sevenoaks are adapting to the times to keep cricket on the Vine growing and ripening by the year.

• • •

VII

CLUB INSTITUTIONS
Wanstead and Snaresbrook CC
by Will Macpherson

From the depth of its history to its sheer scale today – and its efforts in its local community – Wanstead and Snaresbrook CC is a genuine club cricket institution. In an age when the traditional community, family cricket club is under threat, Wanstead represents much that club cricket should. It marries the different facets of the recreational game, continually producing top-class results while remaining community-driven and working to nurture tomorrow's cricketers. This is no mean feat, and has not happened by accident.

Wanstead CC was founded in 1866 and moved to its current home in Overton Drive in 1880, by which point it had produced the first of its 12 international players, CA Absolom, who toured Australia with England in 1878/79. Shortly after the turn of the century they had three teams and continued to receive accolades for the high standard of cricket they produced and the sheer numbers representing them throughout the 20th century, in spite of the debilitating effects of the two world wars. In the days before league cricket arrived in the south, Wanstead regularly topped the *Evening Standard*'s Club Cricket Merit Table.

In 2006, Wanstead merged with neighbours Snaresbrook CC and today, the club is nothing short of a powerhouse. Looking at cold, hard figures, they boast as many as 1,000 members, six men's teams, a thriving women's side (women make up around 11 per cent of the membership) and a vast junior section of 350 kids. In the last decade, membership is up 42 per cent and there are three times as many girls involved as in 2002. In the same period, junior membership has climbed by 24 per cent and senior membership has more than doubled. Expansion has been the order of the decade.

But so has on-field success, at all levels. The first team – around 75 per cent of which are products of the club's youth set-up – have finished in the top two of the Essex Premier League nine times in the last decade and achieved various other accolades, including reaching the National Cup final. The other five league sides have all won titles in that period, while the women's side have twice won and three times been runners-up in five years in the North London League. The junior section plays a remarkable 350 matches every summer for all abilities and ages, with balls hard and soft. At both local and national level, the junior sides add to the club's trophy haul just as frequently as the seniors.

Club members commit around 18,000 hours of work – or £200,000's worth on the London living wage – every year to ensure the operation runs smoothly, according to coach and ultimate clubman Len Enoch.

"These days, we're a club with a team for everybody," Enoch says. He has been involved at the club for a quarter of a century and, now in his Seventies, his enthusiasm never flickers. "Fifteen years ago, we'd fallen a bit off the pace of some of the

other clubs around here. The first team never dropped out of the top flight but we needed reinvigorating a little bit, so we decided to focus on youth and the club from the bottom up. We wanted to make cricket a family affair and foster a love of the game among youngsters and to try to coach them well.

"I believe that a cricket club can be an immensely important place for a youngster growing up, second only to school, and that's what we aim to be. We're based in an area that sits the eleven plus exams and you see examples of kids taking a year out from their cricket because their schoolwork is that important. But it's just as important that they have other interests and get outside. Cricket is wonderful in that sense. Parents are prepared to travel a bit further to get their kids to a good club and people do come from a bit further afield to get their kids to play for us, which is wonderful and also says a bit about what we're doing here."

The sheer scale of youth involvement – and success – suggests that what they're doing is working. The stated aim is for whole families to be taking part: mums and dads playing as kids learn the ropes, too.

"What's really important to us is that the players in the club's top teams are involved in the development at grassroots level too, coaching the youngsters and trying to keep the ball rolling. It's great for the kids and strengthens the sense of community too. We also believe it's important to get kids when they're young so they grow up immersed in and enjoying the game. We're that kind of club, we have a team for everyone and haven't held a trial for years, that's just not our style."

• • •

GIANT KILLERS

THE DAY THE CLUBBIES BEAT THE AUSSIES

by Ed Kemp

"Lunch was delayed and possibly the Aussies had a good one"

VII

The Australian visit to England in 1961 was an old-fashioned sort of a tour. No quickfire fly in-fly out set of international fixtures as is now commonplace for national sides, this was a five-month marathon that saw Richie Benaud's men play 34 matches (mainly three-day affairs against county XIs) between their arrival in early May and their departure in late-September. They boarded their ship home having won many friends for their carefree approach both on and off the field: their amiability in towns across the country and the late, great Richie's commitment to playing positive cricket led *Wisden* to afford special praise to the tourists' particular "cheerfulness and boldness" and noted "the friendly atmosphere created by Richie Benaud and his team". The party – which included Bill Lawry, Neil Harvey, Barry Jarman, Brian Booth (who recalled years later: "I have no bad memories of the tour - it was terrific. There was a wonderful team spirit and everyone would go out together"), Wally Grout, Garth McKenzie and many other notables – had also retained the Ashes, having won the five-match series against Peter May's England 2-1.

That '1' for England – in the third Test at Headingley – was the tourists' first defeat of the tour. In all their encounters that summer, they would lose on just one other occasion.

The Club Cricket Conference had been playing representative matches since 1922, and by '61 a place on the international touring side's summer schedule had been secured. This, alongside the traditional MCC match, was the marquee fixture in the Conference XI's calendar that year. Maybe they caught the Aussies at a good time – just after their Test defeat in Leeds – or maybe the Aussies were unaccustomed to rain during such a fine summer, but whatever, at Blackheath CC on July 13 – at the picturesque Rectory Field ground in south-east London – something special happened. The Conference's club cricketers won the game by eight wickets.

• •

Genuine quick John Price – aka 'Sport' – would go on to play 15 times for England and in a total of 279 first-class games. While he had made a Middlesex debut that summer of '61, he had taken leave from work to do so: Price, about to turn 24, was still a keen amateur. But the fact of his imminent professional career made this his second and last match for the Conference side.

"I was playing club cricket at Wembley," Price says, "and probably happened to be bowling a bit quicker than most so got invited to play that one." The Conference would take this match seriously: nine of the 11 had played or would go onto play first-class cricket – meaning many wouldn't have qualified for the CCC representative side of today – although only Price, opening bat Philip Whitcombe (formerly of Worcestershire as well as Brentwood CC) and off-spinner Alan Hurd (an Essex CCC amateur and cricket master at Sevenoaks School) played more than a handful of times at that level.

Richie Benaud on the drive to a ball from Alan Hurd

The scorecard – and the first-hand accounts of people like Price – suggest that the Aussies' approach wasn't quite so serious. Overnight rain saw Rectory Field too damp to start play at the appointed hour, and instead the players took an early lunch. In Price's words: "possibly the Aussies had a good one."

Whatever the extent of their indulgences, the Australians seemed to have little answer to James Melville of Blackheath CC – yet to play first-class cricket – with the new ball. He saw off Lawry, Jarman, Norm O'Neill, Booth, Peter Burge and McKenzie to claim 6-46 as the Australians were bowled out for 149 in 39.2 overs. Benaud top-scored with 32.

This was a single-innings one-day match but pre-dated the days where limited-overs games were commonplace, so play would finish – no matter what – at 6pm. The Conference had 100 minutes to get the runs.

They were aided in their chase by a few things – not least the fact that neither keeper – Grout nor Jarman – actually kept wicket (those duties were handed to Burge) and both bowled – they were two of a full nine bowlers used by Benaud in total. Whitcombe (71) and opening partner Alan Day (38) took full advantage, taking the Conference close to the target. Their departures left John Swann of Brentham CC (38*), a veteran of four first-class matches for Middlesex and Cyril Gibbons (5*), a Wimbledon CC and minor counties man, at the crease in a race against time to finish things off.

Wally Grout bowled by Neville Griffin for 18

At 5:59pm and with the pavilion clock looming heavy over Blackheath, a nervous, excitable George Downton (of Sevenoaks Vine and 10 first-class matches for Kent and MCC), Conference skipper for the day, could celebrate. His men had beaten Benaud's Australians with a minute to spare, having hit 152-2 from 36 overs.

"George was a lovely bloke," says Price. "The fact that they used nine bowlers didn't stop him from being a very proud man."

Celebrations were heartfelt, and the ever-affable Australian party stuck around. But Price claims memory loss on the exact details of the evening. "Celebrations? Probably! And the old drink-driving wasn't quite so strict in those days… But I was driving back from Blackheath back to Harrow, so I probably didn't have too many…"

As far as the result goes, the memories have remained long and reliable. "I'm sure I'm not the only player in that Conference side that has just happened to mention now and again that they played in a side that beat Australia," Price says. "And down the years, when I've bumped into the lads who played, it's a topic of conversation that normally comes up... Sadly, I think this was the only time in my career [including England appearances] that I did finish on the winning side against them.

"What was nice was that when I occasionally met Richie Benaud in later years he remembered the day and the fact that I'd played in it, which was fairly flattering.

"Yes, the Australians played it in a fairly light-hearted way, but the lads were chuffed. We won it by eight wickets. We beat the Australians."

Among the countless wonderful gifts the great Richie Benaud gave cricket-lovers around the world, that day in July – a day for the club cricketer – is still one to be treasured.

• • •

CLUB CRICKET CONFERENCE V AUSTRALIANS

Australia in British Isles 1961

Venue: The Rectory Field, Blackheath on 13th July 1961 (1-day single innings match)

Balls per over: 6 **Toss:** Club Cricket Conference won the toss and decided to field

Result: Club Cricket Conference won by 8 wickets **Umpires:** FG Gaskell, GE Skinner **Scorer:** RE Driskell

AUSTRALIANS INNINGS		**RUNS**
WM Lawry	b Melville	13
BN Jarman	c Downton b Melville	3
NCL O'Neill	b Melville	32
BC Booth	c Griffin b Melville	22
*R Benaud	c Melville b Hurd	32
+PJP Burge	c and b Melville	1
ATW Grout	b Griffin	18
IW Quick	c Straw b Griffin	7
GD McKenzie	c Straw b Melville	4
FM Misson	c Griffin b Hurd	4
LF Kline	not out	0
Extras	*(11 b, 2 nb)*	*13*
Total	**(all out, 39.2 overs)**	**149**

Fall of wickets: 1-11, 2-22, 3-77, 4-77, 5-78, 6-106, 7-138, 8-143, 9-145, 10-149 (39.2 ov)

CCC bowling	**Overs**	**Mdns**	**Runs**	**Wkts**
Price	9	0	34	0
Melville	11	2	46	6
Griffin	10	3	18	2
Hurd	9.2	3	38	2

CLUB CRICKET CONFERENCE INNINGS		**RUNS**
PJ Whitcombe	c Kline b Benaud	71
AR Day	c McKenzie b O'Neill	37
JL Swann	not out	38
CBT Gibbons	not out	5

did not bat: JPF Misso, DS Straw, +GC Downton, NF Griffin, JSE Price, A Hurd, JE Melville

Extras	*(1 lb)*	*1*
Total	**(2 wickets, 36 overs)**	**152**

Fall of wickets: 1-82, 2-138

Australians bowling	**Overs**	**Mdns**	**Runs**	**Wkts**
McKenzie	4	1	5	0
Booth	3	0	8	0
Lawry	2	0	9	0
Quick	5	1	26	0
Jarman	5	0	21	0
O'Neill	4	2	5	1
Benaud	8	0	42	1
Kline	3	0	22	0
Grout	2	0	13	0

CLUB LEGENDS
Mervyn Mansell and Ted Jackson
by Stephen Chalke

Mervyn Mansell and Ted Jackson, two stalwarts of north London cricket, died a few days apart in 2009. Stephen Chalke wrote their obituaries.

Mervyn Mansell grew up in Rhodesia, for whom he played as an 18-year-old in 1936. His younger brother Percy, making his debut in the same match, went on to represent South Africa in 13 Tests, but Mervyn emigrated to England. He trained as a pharmacist and volunteered for wartime service in the Royal Navy, during which he won a Distinguished Service Cross for 'bravery, daring and skill' in combating German e-boats.

He joined the Ealing club in 1952. Playing in glasses like his brother, he was a classical batsman whose strength was on the off-side. Ealing was a top team at that time, but Mansell was among those who saw problems ahead. "Cricket in schools was declining," he recalled, years later, "so we had to start producing our own youngsters."

In 1955 a Colts side was formed, and Mansell became its driving force. He had a young family and a pharmacy business but, with his wife June's support, he always found time for youth cricket, extending his influence when he helped to found the Middlesex Colts Cricket Association in the 1960s.

The population of Ealing steadily changed, and many of his youngsters went away to university. But he stayed at the heart of the Ealing club, running the colts with quiet dedication for more than 50 years. He took an especial pride that three of his 1955 side were still playing for the club in the summer of 2009. Even as he lay dying in hospital, he wanted to know that week's results.

• •

Ted Jackson learned his cricket at Charterhouse and Cambridge University, playing as a fast bowler in the 1943 wartime fixture against Oxford. By the time he was captain of Brondesbury, however, he had turned himself into a top-order batsman and medium-paced leg-spinner.

A man of great intellectual energy, he worked as a barrister for the Inland Revenue, loved literature and music and threw himself with passion into cricket coaching. When the 11-year-old Mike Gatting arrived at Brondesbury, Jackson quickly recognised his potential. With evangelical zeal he nurtured the youngster, championing his cause so relentlessly that Gatting was playing in the Middlesex 2nd XI before his 15th birthday.

Jackson became a leading light in the developing world of coach education, describing his week at Lilleshall on the Advanced Course as "the happiest of my life – and I've had three honeymoons."

He held strong views on the skills of cricket, despatching long, densely written letters to all and sundry. One I received denounced the ECB's latest publication on Mental Skills: "They have the chutzpah to mention WT Gallwey in their bibliography but advocate rubbish like 'Positive Thinking' and 'Self-slaps on the Wrist'." Another began: "I'm in utter despair over ECB's obstinate stupidity over (1) the STANCE and (2) TRIGGER MOVEMENTS." Diagrams and quotations were enclosed, in various coloured pens, and a scribbled note on the bottom about a game he played in India in 1944.

He was a visionary, full of life, a passionate man who cared deeply about the game, and he left his mark on many – as did Mervyn Mansell, who was awarded an MBE for services to youth cricket in Middlesex. Ted Jackson's CBE was for services to the law – though it could just as easily have been for his coaching work. Without such men, always giving generously of their time, the game would not pass so well to future generations.

• • •

VII

CLUB LEGENDS

Ivor Chaplin: Storytelling scorebox dweller

by Stephen Chalke

It was a 2nd XI fixture that did it – back in 1963, nine years before league cricket came to Middlesex. The 25-year-old accounts clerk Ivor Chaplin was scoring for Turnham Green at Brentham, when his colleague in the box said he would be playing the following summer. "I looked out across the ground to the trees on the other side," Chaplin recalls, "and something seemed to gel inside me. I've been here ever since."

At the start of 1968 he was promoted to 1st XI scorer, and he hasn't missed a game in 47 summers: completing 700 league matches in 2014 as well as over 1,000 Sunday and mid-week fixtures, including – he tells with pride – a Wednesday afternoon in 1992 when he had to hurry back from his mother's funeral in Brighton. "The funeral was at 11, and I was on the train at 12. I only missed two overs."

The big wheels of numbers, with the ladder for putting up the 100s, have given way to an electronic system, and fellow scorers no longer smoke: "Thank God for that!" With his Jewish background, he used to be the odd one out, negotiating an alternative to pork at lunch, but now he looks after the dietary needs of all the Muslim players. "Have you tried halal chicken? It's much better than Tesco's, I'll tell you."

You argue with his scoring at your peril. "All the people starving in the world," he'll say, "and you're worried about one run."

"He's eccentric," says young club member James Overy, "but he's a great guy to have around. A dying breed, especially on Sundays when he's often alone in the box. He's got so many wonderful stories."

"You've got to talk," Chaplin says. "You're in the box for six or seven hours."

He is a man with many interests – theatre, gardening, square dancing, philately, scrabble – "but cricket comes first," he says. "The rest has to fit in. You're in the fresh air, with all the wild life, and it keeps your brain active, keeps you in contact with the young. I'll do it as long as I can."

• • •

Chaplin collected the Lifetime Achievement Award at the Middlesex OSCAs in 2014. Photo courtesy of Matt Bright Photography

VII

CLUB INSTITUTIONS
Ealing CC
by Will Macpherson

Cricket is a team game played by individuals and, perhaps more than any other 'team' game, lends itself to selfishness. But running a cricket club is a team game more suited to self*less*ness; to giving up time and to pulling together. First and foremost, cricket clubs are about groups of people working as a community.

This, according to Ealing's long-serving president John Poore, is the primary reason his club has enjoyed such success and longevity. From the dozens of volunteer coaches putting on clinics and courses for the club's 400 colts, to mums and dads providing transport, this is a collective effort. Poore cites the outstanding contribution and influence of certain individuals – Mervyn Mansell and Peter Hughes (father of Simon Hughes, who came through the colts system), for instance, who have been involved with the club's thriving youth section for 55 and 45 years respectively – but believes the club's strength is built on the sheer weight of numbers of those keen to give their time and energy to ensuring cricket at Ealing does not merely survive, but thrives.

The club's results speak for themselves, not just in terms of sheer longevity – it's approaching a 150th anniversary – but in recent on-field success too. The club won seven consecutive Middlesex Championships until 2012, while a national T20 triumph in 2011 was achieved by a side containing nine players who had graduated from the youth system that so many work so tirelessly to sustain.

According to Poore, there is a sense of duty about all of this. "It is our duty to ensure we leave a strong, viable club for the next generations, because more than a century ago, our forebears borrowed a vast amount of money to secure our ground, which has been the base of our success over all these years. It's held us in good stead for a century-and-a-half as clubs that don't own their own ground often find themselves being ripped off."

There's a sense of social responsibility about Ealing's success, again derived from the enjoyment that a generation – now the club's senior citizens – and many more besides, have had playing down at the Corfton Road ground and revelling in its handsome, century-old pavilion, of which the members are so proud.

"Coming out of school you latch on to something," says Poore, who has since fulfilled just about every role at the club, culminating in 19 years as president. "And cricket and Ealing really was my life. We would live and breathe it, winter and summer, living just down the road and always popping down. Certainly up until I was maybe 35 when family and four kids came along, it was an enormous part of my life. These days I still try to get down as much as I possibly can."

He's not alone in his unwavering commitment to the club. John Lindley, Bob Fisher and Alan Price played together in the club's very first colts fixture in 1955,

against Finchley, and were still playing together nearly six decades on. All were fine players, with Fisher and Price capped by Middlesex 2nd XI, with the former now playing, at the age of 73, for the England Over 70s side. But all three played many roles beyond the boundary at the club. Lindley, for instance, ran the club's fixture list for 48 years.

In 2013 the club merged with the struggling Hanwell CC, who were reportedly on the verge of closing down after the rent on their ground was ramped up. The club's entrenched ownership of its ground puts it in an enviable position, one that enables them to bring in income by hosting large-scale events such as the Bonfire Night party and firework display, a community-wide event that can bring in as much as £30,000 per year. That money is poured straight back into the club.

"We're not trying to make big money, just keep the place going," says Poore. "Our job is to provide cricket within our community and we've always taken that seriously. It's as much about us putting on courses and stuff for kids as having success with the first team. We have 12 weeks a year where we have kids at the club during the summer and Easter holidays. We hope out of it some of them will take up cricket for good and that is so important to our club and the future of the game in the area."

Those individuals and that teamwork – the stuff that makes any cricket club tick – has paid off handsomely at Ealing, and as their 150th anniversary approaches, there's no reason to believe it will slow any time soon.

• • •

AFTER THE WINDRUSH

THE RISE AND FALL OF CARIBBEAN CLUB CRICKET

by Peter Mason

"Caribbean clubs were the cohesive force that pulled the strands of Britain's West Indian population together"

VII

Before the arrival of the Empire Windrush ship at Tilbury in 1948 presaged the beginning of mass Caribbean immigration, the presence of anyone of West Indian origin in club cricket in the south of England was a rarity indeed.

While the northern professional leagues, especially in Lancashire, had played host to a number of West Indians during the inter-war years – including the great Trinidadian all-rounder Learie Constantine – the amateur game down south offered no opportunity for top Caribbean players to make a living. Thousands of people had emigrated from the West Indies to Britain before 1948 – mainly as seamen, soldiers or students – but the numbers were still relatively small, and the impact on southern cricket was minimal.

The Windrush changed all that. Although it had only 492 people on board, around 125,000 Caribbean migrants travelled to Britain on other vessels in the following decade, often to take up jobs in the transport sector or in the National Health Service. A further 113,000 arrived before the 1962 Commonwealth Immigration Act began to reduce the flow, and by the 1966 census an estimated 454,100 people of West Indian origin were resident in Britain.

Not all, of course, were Afro-Caribbean: a substantial minority were descendants of Indian or Chinese indentured labourers who had travelled to the West Indies (especially Trinidad and British Guiana) after the abolition of slavery. Others were of mixed race. But a great many nurtured a passion for cricket, and as the number of Caribbean immigrants grew, so their impact on the game in England began to make itself felt.

The broadcaster and writer Mike Phillips, who arrived in Britain in 1956 from what was then British Guiana, has argued that cricket "was the only thing that wasn't strange or alien to us and I suspect the one thing that was not strange and alien to the English [about us]". However, although there were plenty of cricket teams the new arrivals could theoretically have joined, in reality they found themselves treated as unwelcome outsiders at many clubs, little understood by the white majority and often treated with suspicion. Given this sometimes hostile reception – as well as the natural propensity for immigrants to stick together in an unfamiliar new society – dozens of West Indian cricket clubs sprung up across the south in cities and towns wherever there was a Caribbean presence. Many of these were in London, where the main body of immigrants had settled. But they also appeared in places such as High Wycombe, Hitchin, Luton, Oxford, Slough, and St Albans.

• •

Early beginnings

Although the first West Indian club side in England – Caribbean CC in Leeds – was formed in the north in 1948, the south was the epicentre of West Indian club activity. The lack of historical records makes it difficult to estimate how many Caribbean teams have existed in the area of the Club Cricket Conference since the Windrush docked, but it would appear safe to suggest that there may have been in excess of 60, perhaps up to 100. Among the earliest clubs founded in the south were St Albans West Indian CC in Hertfordshire, created in 1958, Sabina in south London (1964), Old Castletonians and Deckers in Streatham (1963) and West Indies United in Catford (1966), all of which are still around. But there were others that have few historical records and for whom foundation dates do not appear to exist: Starlight, Paragon, Cowley West Indians, New Calypsonians, Wilkinson Way, Milton Keynes Afro-Caribbean CC, Willesden Unity, Island Taverners, BWIA Cavaliers, Leyton County, Simba, and Boca, to name but a few.

A good number of the sides were created in the '50s, '60s and '70s as offshoots of West Indian social or church clubs, but others were founded by groups of friends or families, often from the same Caribbean island. A team might originally have had some affinity to a particular territory: the early Casuals CC in Oxford, for instance, was the creation of two Barbadian families, and Antigua Cavaliers in east London, as the name suggests, was set up by Antiguans. But it was rare for clubs to remain insular for long, and most soon became a mix of Trinidadians, Guyanese, Jamaicans, Barbadians and others from the 'small islands' such as St Kitts, Grenada, Anguilla and Dominica. While internal relations were not always 100 per cent harmonious, Caribbean clubs became a melting pot for West Indians who had often not encountered others from British West Indian territories before they arrived in England. Journalist Tom James has gone so far as to say that they were "the cohesive force that pulled the strands of Britain's West Indian population together".

Caribbean teams would typically field just a single side, although some grew in size over the years to the point where they could put out two or even three sides. In the early days they mostly played friendlies, but as the number of Caribbean sides increased across the country they found themselves able to set up and play in their own leagues and cup competitions (including the national Caribbean Challenge cup). These fixtures they would supplement with matches against 'English' sides, typically on a Sunday.

So big was the growth spurt in Caribbean clubs after Windrush that club cricketer Ollie Williams, in an account of his playing days on the London Fields cricket ground in Hackney, reports that in the 1960s "nearly all" the teams in the Clapton and District Amateur Cricket Association league were West Indian, with evocative names such as Rockets, Hurricane, and Sir Frank's XI "which communicated the vibrancy, aggression and confidence of the West Indian grassroots cricket community of the time".

Caribbean clubs boasted some excellent players, but they had few resources, and mostly were confined to playing on municipal grounds or to an existence as wandering clubs. Those that tried to venture outside the Caribbean competitions would usually find themselves playing in the lower leagues, excluded from a higher standard of cricket because their grounds were deemed substandard.

Cricket, however, was not the be-all and end-all. Caribbean clubs were a social centre, a community hub, and a support network. *Guardian* journalist Gary Younge, born in Hertfordshire to Barbadian parents, recalls that he spent much of his spare time as a youth at Stevenage West Indians Sports and Social Club, where his eldest brother and father used to play cricket and he would do the scoring. "The black community's life revolved around the cricket team," he remembers.

St Kitts-born Harwood Williams, who played for Caribbean CC in its early days and eventually became its chairman, says the club was often "a home away from home and a place where you could share knowledge of where the jobs were and how to get accommodation in the area". More than that, Caribbean sides were a refuge from the harsh world outside. Playing for one, as the author Colin Babb says, was "a badge of identity [that] expressed a sense of togetherness in often hostile surroundings", while one member of a West Indian club told the academic Ben Carrington (in Carrington's *Journal of Sport and Social Issues* essay entitled 'Sport, Masculinity and Black Cultural Resistance'): "It wasn't just a sports club, it was a focal point for those people who were black and in a vast minority."

Racial tensions

One of the main reasons to seek such refuge was prejudice, which took varied forms. Over the years many Caribbean clubs reported regular vandalism of their clubhouses, grounds or facilities, while others found it strangely difficult to arrange fixtures against mainstream clubs. In the early days, at least, racist comments were commonplace; umpires were occasionally hostile or biased, and when racism was challenged, administrators and leagues would typically do their best to brush the issue under the carpet. There was also a feeling that the quality of home grounds was used as an excuse, rather than a real reason, to deny such teams promotion – or even to exclude them altogether.

Even if prejudice was not expressed in a tangible way, it was noticeable behind the scenes. "It may not always be right there in front of you but you know it's just lurking around the corner; you can tell by some people's attitudes," one player told the *Crossing the Boundary* study into racism in league cricket. "There's not many people that come up and say they don't like you because of your colour or whatever. But you'll hear it going on behind your back."

More often that not, tensions stemmed from ignorance or fear. 'White' sides thrown into battle against a West Indian team might be nervous and unsure of what to expect, especially if they were from an area that had experienced little immigration. Such tensions were well captured in the gently humorous 1987 film *Playing Away*, written by St Kitts-born Caryl Phillips and directed by the Trinidadian Horace Ové, which drew on almost 40 years of experiences among Caribbean cricket clubs in England. Focusing on a fictional meeting between a south of England village side and the Caribbean Brixton Conquistadors in a charity match (with scenes filmed at Botany Bay CC in Enfield), the film exposed the stereotypes entertained by both sides, with the villagers worrying that the Conquistadors would be liable to bring drugs and bad behaviour to their quiet home and the Conquistadors lost and confused when they arrive in 'alien territory'.

Crucially, however, the film also shows many of the protagonists building new relationships and understandings. For all the real-life difficulties that were exposed when Caribbean teams came to town, there's no doubt that the presence of West Indian sides in English club cricket was a powerful force in promoting racial harmony. Cricket may have exposed divisions, but it also helped to reduce them.

Into the mainstream

In the beginning there was little cross-pollination between the newly-arrived Caribbean cricketers and those who played the game in mainstream clubs across the south. West Indian sides played against 'white' teams on an occasional basis, most often in friendlies, or might appear sporadically for works teams. But it was exceptional for a West Indian to fetch up at one of the more established clubs as a player, and rarer still to be welcomed with open arms. Immediately after the Second World War, Learie Constantine played regularly for Chalfont St Peter in Buckinghamshire, and the West Indies batsman, Allan

Rae, from Jamaica, joined Winchmore Hill in north London while studying for his law degree. But at the time these were exceptions to the rule, and the elevated cricketing status of both players gave them a relatively easy entrée into such clubs. For the mass of West Indian immigrants, playing in a Caribbean side was the only comfortable option.

This was especially so in the early post-Windrush days. But by the mid-1960s, many newly arrived West Indians were of school age, and in addition a host of 'second generation' children were being born to Caribbean parents in Britain. By the late 1960s many players of West Indian origin would typically play for their school team and then hook up with a local Caribbean club once they started work. But others would also be brought into the mainstream club circuit by 'English' schoolfriends. This might happen either straight from school, or perhaps at a later date when they were seeking to move away from the Caribbean circuit to play on better pitches or seek some kind of recognition. The progression was hit and miss, but significant numbers did begin to make the transition, and to stick with it.

Playing for mainstream clubs was rarely easy, especially for the pioneers. They might find they were the only player of Caribbean origin at a club, and that the welcome was not all they had hoped for. There was often a suspicion that they were being batted in the wrong position, or bowled infrequently; that they were being singled out for some kind of particular attention – critical or otherwise – or, on the opposite end of the spectrum, being paid very little attention at all. There was also greater exposure to the individual perils of racism. As one player who was exposed to racist sledging while playing for a 'white' club told Ben Carrington: "If I were playing for [my Caribbean side] he wouldn't have dared say it because he'd really be saying it to the whole team". There was safety in numbers at a West Indian club, less so in the mainstream.

For the most part, however, the early players soldiered on. Sometimes it became a question of trying one club, finding it inhospitable, and moving on to another. But eventually, by the mid- to late- '70s and early '80s, some large mainstream clubs had become well known for possessing a significant contingent of Caribbean players who had settled for the long-term, and were being supplemented by second and third generation recruits. In the Middlesex League, for instance, there was Shepherds Bush, and in the Surrey Championship there was the Wandsworth-based side, Spencer. Other clubs, too, found homes for players of Caribbean origin, though in lesser numbers.

That club cricket benefitted is beyond doubt, though difficult to assess precisely. Shepherds Bush and Spencer both went through some of their strongest periods when such players were to the fore, while other teams such as Wycombe House in Osterley used their Caribbean input to punch well above their weight. Less tangibly, 'Caribbean' players over the various generations, but particularly the first, may well have brought some of the proud West Indian traditions of flamboyant, aggressive batting and bowling to the more conservative mien of amateur cricket in southern England. Off the field, too, cultural marks were laid down. Some teams still order jugs of Barbadian Cockspur rum to celebrate an especially fine victory; many a club still has a highly popular Caribbean evening in their social calendar, even if their number of Caribbean players has now diminished.

The great West Indian Learie Constantine played regularly for Chalfont St Peter in Buckinghamshire after the Second World War

Decline

West Indian teams have always come and gone. Some have merged with each other, others have thrown their lot in with a mainstream club. But something different happened at the beginning of the 1990s. Many Caribbean clubs began to take a nose-dive, and the number of teams diminished rapidly.

The picture in Luton was fairly typical. For many years the town had a healthy West Indian club scene, yet in the winter of 1993, with Luton Caribbean Cavaliers and Luton United having already fallen by the wayside, the two remaining clubs, Chevette and Luton International, came together to discuss the possibility of a merger. Chevette reported that for three years they had been unable to attract any new players to the club, while International said they had been having much the same problem. In 1994, lamenting that "all the black cricket clubs from the past 50 years are now down to one", the two decided to amalgamate as Luton Caribbean Cricket Club in a bid "to secure the long standing future of West Indian cricket in Luton".

At other clubs a similar story was unfolding. According to Jack Williams, in 1990 the London-based Clive Lloyd Red Stripe league for West Indian teams could boast 10 clubs, but by the end of the decade it was existing only as a knockout cup competition, and the only other Caribbean league in London was also on its last legs.

Partly this was a reflection of a wider trend that began to show itself in the 1990s: while Williams found that between 1990 and 1999 the number of CCC-affiliated Caribbean clubs in Middlesex fell from 11 to nine, for example, over the same period the total number of affiliated clubs in the county fell from 403 to 334 – roughly the same proportional drop. However, as the base numbers of Caribbean clubs were small to start with, any losses were more keenly felt. Often the demise of clubs left entire areas more or less bereft of any Caribbean cricketing presence – as with the disappearance of Hitchin West Indians and Stevenage West Indians in north Hertfordshire.

Since those dramatic years in the 1990s, the rate of decline has slowed. But nothing has happened to reverse the overall downward trend, and few people – least of all those in the clubs themselves – are optimistic that it can be stopped.

Why should such a collapse have come about? One reason can be found in the fact that by the beginning of the 1990s many players and administrators who had been the backbone of West Indian clubs had reached 60 years of age and beyond. When these individuals departed or reduced their role, holes were left that others failed to fill. Partly, too, there was also a diminution of the importance of Caribbean clubs in the eyes of younger cricketers of West Indian origin. As the sports consultant Russell Holden has pointed out, as people of Caribbean descent have become more integrated into national life, West Indian clubs "struggle to play a key socio-political role" which meant their significance was lessened and their appeal to those from younger age groups was reduced.

As new generations have become more 'British' in outlook, so their attachment to cricket, ironically, has waned. "The connection… used to be contemporary – now we have a third and fourth generation, and each one is disconnecting a little more from the game," says the former Gloucestershire cricketer Mark Alleyne. Or as *ESPNcricinfo* UK editor and former *Guardian* cricket writer David Hopps has put it: "Cricket has become something their grandad used to talk about."

Add to this the rapid decline of the West Indies regional team as an inspirational international cricketing force from the 1990s onwards, and throw in the growth of football as an all-engulfing counter-attraction in the UK, and it is perhaps not surprising that new generations prefer to look elsewhere for their pleasure – especially if one takes into account the fact that state schools have all-but withdrawn from playing cricket in many areas. "Away from the social reasons, in simple terms, life has moved on," says Rodney Hinds, sports editor of the black newspaper *The Voice*. Former England cricketer Alex Tudor, now a coach at Spencer CC, told *The Voice* in 2013: "It's those of us who are aged 35 and over who will talk about cricket. The youths are interested in playing bigger and more glamorous sports."

Former England man Tudor now plays and coaches at Spencer CC in Surrey

An uncertain future

The cricketing authorities, and their allies, are hoping they may be able to change this sad position. While not all specifically targeted at people of West Indian origin, myriad initiatives, including Cage Cricket, Chance to Shine, the Grass Roots Cricket Academy, the Wisden City Cup and the Taverners Cup, certainly have them in their sights. The African Caribbean Cricket Association has also been established to identify the reasons for the lack of interest and participation in cricket, and is working with various cricketing bodies to find ways of attracting and retaining cricketing interest at youth and grassroots level among young people of West Indian origin.

But once the Caribbean clubs have gone, it is unlikely they will ever come back. Even the most optimistic of commentators find it hard to see a turnaround on the horizon. Historian Colin Babb believes that a resurgent West Indies team, with the ability to beat England convincingly during a series in England, "could command an increase in interest and optimism", but even he feels there is "limited evidence" that the once intimate connection between cricket and the Caribbean diaspora in Britain will be restored in the foreseeable future. The game, he argues, "is no longer a premier site of expression and identity" for people of Caribbean descent.

Many would like to see him proved wrong, but it is difficult to escape the conclusion that he is probably not.

CLUB INSTITUTIONS
Sabina CC: 50 years old and still going strong

So many West Indian clubs have fallen by the wayside in recent years that it's heartening to find one that's not only surviving, but appears to be retaining its strength.

Sabina CC celebrated its 50th anniversary in 2014, and still holds its own on the London cricketing scene, where it has been a regular winner of the South London Sunday League.

The club was founded by a group of eight Caribbean immigrants in Peckham in July 1964. Originally called the All Star Cricket Club, it changed its name to Sabina in 1966 when one of its founders, Joseph Bryan, tried to register the club with the CCC and was advised that it might be mistaken for a showbiz team. Being a proud Jamaican, he looked no further than the legendary Sabina Park cricket ground in Kingston for inspiration, and the dye was cast.

Initially the club had 16 players, with Bryant taking on the roles of secretary, treasurer and fixture secretary – not to mention general bag carrier and kit man. He was, by all accounts, 'very strict on discipline' and determinedly intolerant of bad behaviour. But his iron fist was concealed beneath the velvet glove of the club's first captain, Lance McKenley, who was so easy-going that after managing to secure the services of a star player, Norbert Mattis, he called a team meeting and handed over the captaincy to him.

Sabina played initially in the rather rough and ready surrounds of Dulwich Park, and had nets on Peckham Rye. But from the outset they were able to build up an impressive fixture list across the south of England.

One well-remembered early encounter, however, neatly encapsulated the tensions experienced by many West Indian clubs in those fledgling days. When Sabina approached Horsmonden CC in Kent for a game, they were told that most of the village players 'had only seen black people on TV' and were nervous about setting up a fixture. Eventually the day was won through the intervention of a Horsmonden grandee, who informed his committee that he had once been to Trinidad and could vouch for the fact that 'black people are nice'. The match went ahead, and such a good time was had by all that Sabina were invited back the next year, with a request that they bring a steelband with them. The fixture continued for many years afterwards, and warm friendships were built up between players and supporters on both sides.

As with so many other West Indian teams, Sabina has since spent many years trying to secure a clubhouse and ground, and in the days since Dulwich Park, has flirted with at least nine different venues in the local area without finding a long-term home.

Nonetheless, the club is in a relatively stable financial state, has a healthy membership, and has even managed to attract some sponsors over the years. The finances are helped by a good roster of social events and day trips, as well as a netball section that was originally formed by girlfriends and wives of the cricketers and has been running now for more than 30 years.

There was no steak and kidney pie at Sabina's 50th anniversary dinner and dance – or roast beef for that matter. Supporters tucked into curry goat, jerk chicken, rice and peas and fried plantain, among many other Caribbean delicacies on the menu.

At the heart of the celebrations was a modern-day stalwart in the mould of Joseph Bryan – Sabina's secretary, Marlene Wander, who has been in post for more than 30 years. Sadly Mr Bryan himself didn't live to see the club celebrate its 50th year – he died in 2013, aged 87, having returned to Jamaica. But like other departed members who created such strong foundations for the club, he is fondly remembered as part of the Sabina family.

•••

CLUB LEGENDS

Alf Langley: How I left Jamaica and found a home at Shepherds Bush

Alf Langley was a much-admired opening bat and regular CCC representative who captained Shepherds Bush for many years in the Middlesex League. The Aussie Test seamer Carl Rackemann once wrote that he was the hardest-hitting batsman he had ever bowled against. Alf is now chairman of the CCC.

My uncle Ronsford Hamilton was a keen cricketer who played at senior level in Jamaica. He emigrated to Britain in the early 1960s, so when I came over from Jamaica myself in August 1968 the first games I played here were with him, as a 15-year-old for a London Transport garage in Peckham. There were six or seven West Indians in the team and that's where I first met Barbadians, Trinidadians and people from other islands. Up to that point I'd only really known Jamaicans. I learned more about the West Indies from playing in those games than I did living in the West Indies.

Cricket was such a big thing at home in Jamaica that it was a massive culture shock to come to England and find so many people weren't really interested in the game. I couldn't even find anyone to play with in the local park. Back home if I'd have walked out into the street with a bat and a ball there would have been 30 or 40 kids playing within a few minutes. I went to Aylestone High School in Willesden, where the cricket pitch was just a horrible thing in the middle of a field, and the PE teacher wasn't interested. But in the sixth form our music teacher organised us into a side, and some of us started playing for Middlesex Schools Cricket Association.

Lambert and Butler Trophy winners 1981
J. Grimmer, T. Howard, B. Partridge, C. Menzie, B. Howard, R. Walker, J. Walker
S. McInnes, A. Langley (capt.), S. Doughty, A. Bhattarcharjee, B. Kelly

Shepherds Bush CC's 1981 Lambert and Butler Trophy winners, captained by Alf - front row, second from the left

My brother Mikey had come over to England six months before me, and he went to a different school, Wealdstone Grammar. He played club cricket for their old boys team, Old Uffingtonians, so I used to turn out on the weekends for them, around 1969/70 – I enjoyed that.

Then I started to play for a West Indian side called Holmwood, who were based in Sudbury. At the time there were quite a number of other Caribbean teams in our area – including Starlight and Willesden Unity. We used to play them in a West Indian league, and then there was a knockout competition, which eventually became the Clive Lloyd cup; that was really popular. You'd get lots of people coming to watch those cup games, even though we used to play in some pretty horrible places. On Sundays we'd play friendlies away from home, often against some pretty good sides. I remember we played Lordswood in Kent once, and Ford CC in Essex.

Sometimes we'd go on a long coach trip to play cricket on a Sunday – maybe Margate or Herne Bay, or out in the country – and they were great multicultural experiences. We'd bring lots of our own food and a bit of rum. We'd have tea with the local people and there'd be a disco in the evening. I remember those occasions as an unbelievable pleasure for everyone – a real exchange of cultures.

At home and against other West Indian sides we played on some horrendous wickets. You'd walk out and you wouldn't be able to tell the strip from the rest of the field. But there were lots of excellent players in those teams. I remember we played Slough West Indians with Cardigan Connor (Hampshire) opening the bowling, and Norbert Phillip (Essex and West Indies) played against us for some Caribbean side in Essex. We even had the current prime minster of Nevis in our side – Vance Amory (Leeward Islands) – he was a bloody good player.

People were reluctant to leave their West Indian teams because they were concerned about the reception they'd get elsewhere. But if you wanted to play at a higher level and on decent pitches then you really had to look outside of the Caribbean clubs. Eventually I went to South Hampstead. I have to admit that I went there reluctantly, because I was really enjoying it at Holmwood; I was comfortable with that group of guys. But I made the move anyway.

I found it really difficult. I remember the first game I played, in the second XI. We batted second and I went in at No7, got 56 not out and we drew the game eight or nine down. I came off thinking I'd done quite well, but the captain gave me an enormous bollocking. I was opening the batting for Middlesex U19s and Middlesex Young Cricketers, but at South Hampstead they kept sticking me in the second X1 and batting me at seven or eight. I didn't really settle at the club, and they just weren't encouraging enough.

I think it was partly just being at a new club, but I also believe that if I'd emerged from a different set of circumstances then they would have given me better opportunities – I remember thinking that quite clearly at the time. There was a group of West Indians there – including myself, my brother, Carl Menzie, and Steve Doughty – who all lived locally, and I don't think it was a coincidence that we all left in the end. For a time I went back to Holmwood.

Then I moved to Shepherds Bush CC in 1974. There was only one other person of colour at the Bush when I arrived, but from day one I was made to feel wanted. It was just a completely different vibe and I was very comfortable in persuading other West Indians to come along. There was no question that we were young and different, and that we did things our own way. But the contrast in reception that we got at Shepherds Bush was so clear. I couldn't believe it. When I first began to play for them, I only had a cheap pair of plimsoles to run around in, and one day Steve Wright, our captain, quietly asked me what size feet I had. The next week there were two brand new pairs of cricket boots waiting for me – no-one even mentioned it - they were just there for me. There were so many kindnesses, and that's why I'm so passionate about the Bush as a club.

Because of the reception we got at the Bush, by the late 1970s there were lots of fine Caribbean players at the club – including people like Martin Jean-Jacques (Derbyshire, Hampshire) and Algie Corbin (Glamorgan) – and through the 80s and 90s the Bush became known as a club with a large Caribbean presence, right through to the second and third generations.

Even when I was at the Bush, especially in the early days, I'd still play for Holmwood sometimes - in cup matches on a Sunday, maybe. But the Bush is where I found my home.

• • •

WE DIDN'T JUST MAKE THE TEAS

THE STORY OF WOMEN'S CLUB CRICKET

by Raf Nicholson

"We discussed how cricket could become real for us – no longer to be an illusive thing... one played half afraid of ridicule"

VII

Early women's club cricket

Women's cricket has been around for centuries. The first ever recorded match took place in 1745 at Godsden Common near Guildford, between "eleven maids of Bramley and eleven maids of Hambledon, all dressed in white". It was reported in the *Reading Mercury* that the Bramley maids wore blue ribbons in their hair and the Hambledon team red ribbons, and that Hambledon won by eight "notches" (runs). Over the next 100 years, reports of other women's matches regularly appeared in local newspapers. Cricket was introduced into some women's public schools, such as Roedean in Sussex (which opened in 1885). It was also played by women at garden parties.

But the first women's cricket club was not formed until 1887. This was the White Heather Club, founded in Yorkshire by eight upper-class ladies who had played the game in their schooldays. The most famous of its members was Lucy Ridsdale, who in 1892 became Lucy Baldwin when she married future British prime minister Stanley Baldwin. In 1930, aged 61 and retired from the game, she wrote that: "The crack of the bat against the ball amid the humming and buzzing of summer sounds is still to me a note of pure joy".

During the 1890s a small number of other women's clubs appeared. This included a club called the "Derbyshire Butterflies", and another based in Bristol, the Clifton Ladies. WG Grace is reported to have said that: "Cricket is not a game for women, and although the fair sex occasionally join in a picnic game, they are not constitutionally adapted for the sport". Even so, his daughter Bessie regularly played for Clifton Ladies. It is unknown whether she eventually changed WG's mind about cricket's suitability as a game for women!

Additionally, of the one million British women who worked in munitions factories during the First World War, many participated in factory cricket teams. A photo in the *Daily Mirror* from May 1918 contains the caption: "Women war workers, having done brilliantly at football, open their cricket season. The wicket-keeper arms for the fray in a match between Woolland's and Harrod's." And long-standing clubs including Redoubtables WCC (formed in 1921, now part of Purley CC) and Gunnersbury WCC (formed in 1925, now part of Finchley CC) also came into existence. But there remained only a handful of women's cricket clubs by the 1920s. What was really needed was the support of a national governing body, to facilitate the formation of clubs.

• •

The Women's Cricket Association and the growth of women's club cricket

This happened in 1926, when the Women's Cricket Association (WCA) was formed. The organisation was the brainchild of a group of female hockey players, who in October 1926 travelled to Colwall for several days of cricket on the Malvern College Ground. Among them was Marjorie Pollard, who recalled:

> After play was over we sat in the Park Hotel at Colwall... and discussed how cricket could become real for us – no longer to be an illusive thing, that one played half afraid of ridicule. We pondered, mused, talked.

Out of this came the decision to form an association. At the first meeting of the WCA 19 women met, elected a chairman and formed a committee to arrange fixtures around the country. One of the initial aims was "to encourage the foundation of cricket clubs throughout the country".

It was a bold step, but it paid off almost immediately. For the 1927 season the WCA arranged a fixture list and 49 matches were played; by 1929 37 clubs and 39 schools were affiliated members, and the first public women's cricket match was played on Beckenham Cricket Ground, between London District and the Rest of England. Public matches continued throughout the 1930s, with some played on Test grounds including the Oval. In 1933, county associations were formed in Middlesex, Lancashire, Kent, Nottinghamshire and Surrey. And there was a massive expansion in women's club cricket: by 1938, the WCA reported that 105 women's clubs had been formed.

A wide variety of different types of club were formed during the 1930s, including Women's Institute clubs, hospital nurses clubs, a Ministry of Labour club, and workplace clubs based at companies including the Mansfield Shoe Company, the John Bull Rubber Company, Symingtons Ltd, Rolls Royce, Lever Brothers, and the Lyons Corner Houses. Even the BBC had its own women's cricket team.

An official WCA magazine, *Women's Cricket*, was set up in 1930 and edited by Marjorie Pollard. Much information about how these WCA-affiliated clubs functioned can be gleaned from the "club pages" of this magazine. The main problem was how to secure access to pitches, which was often an issue given that many men shared WG Grace's views about cricket for women. The founder of the Rainham Ladies Cricket Club, for example, spent time "wrestling at Town Hall meetings, against all the local men's clubs, for allocation of home pitches". She and her husband eventually set up a practice wicket in their own back garden!

Women's clubs often had to make do with poor facilities. Netta Rheinberg, an early member of Gunnersbury, recalled that one of their early grounds "sloped not only towards one side, but downwards as well, and your off-breaks became leg-breaks at one end". The Harlow Club, formed in 1934, found a pitch at a farm near High Wycombe – the only problem being that their cricket field was shared with a herd of cows. One club in Baxenden in Lancashire reported that they used the same pitch as two men's teams, and therefore had to play all their matches in the evenings: "Very often our matches end in a draw because of the bad light". As for Baxenden's cricket teas: "the poor visitors often wonder, we are sure, what on earth are in the sandwiches but have no way of telling until they have tasted"!

Groundsmen for women's pitches were practically unheard of. The captain of Hastings Ladies, Marjorie Bull, would take her own garden lawn mower to and from their cricket pitch the day before matches to ensure that it was fit for purpose. It also had to be swept before the other team arrived, in order to get rid of the sheep droppings!

It could also be difficult for women's clubs to raise enough money to function effectively. One article in *Women's Cricket* suggested that the typical club might possess just seven pads ("some completely strapless"), one bat, four stumps and one bail. Much of the off-season was taken up with fund-raising activities, including whist drives, jumble sales and bazaars. Clubs like Dukesmead WCC, founded in 1927, were lucky: their members were all civil servants, which meant that they had access to the Civil Service Ground at Chiswick and received generous grants from the Civil Service Sports Council.

There was undoubtedly still a great deal of opposition to women's cricket at this time. Pollard quoted a male-penned letter which she had received after *Women's Cricket* magazine was launched in 1930:

> Women seriously betaking themselves to the greatest of all British games? Why it is a sacrilege! It is tempting the gods themselves to rise in their wrath...a direct insult is thus hurled at the heads of those who call themselves men. If this attack is not 'nipped' in the proverbial bud, we predict a rapid decline in the noble art of cricket, a decline which will be merited if this movement is allowed to proceed. Now, once for all, a 'truce to this foolery.' Men will not invade the work-basket and the feminine domain of the kitchen, but, we beseech you – let us have this one sport to ourselves... we may conclude with an earnest prayer that women will never gain admittance to the pavilion at Lord's.

This is less hilarious when it is recalled that women did not in fact gain admittance to the pavilion at Lord's until 1999!

However, many clubs also described increasing support from men's teams during the 1930s, once they realised that women were serious about their cricket. For example, one village in the Weald wrote in 1939 that the local Women's Institute had challenged the men of the village to a cricket match:

> The men had to play left handed with broom sticks and field one handed. When this was first started, the men always won... but the girls became very keen to defeat them and by practising their bowling and fielding hard, defeated the men easily the following year. This was so encouraging that it was decided to form a proper club.

The women's club were allowed use of the men's ground on Tuesday and Wednesday evenings, and the men's club lent them bats and balls and provided coaching and umpiring.

Local newspaper editors could also provide useful support: many women's clubs attracted members by advertising their activities in the local press, and some clubs were directly supported by their local newspapers. In the North, in 1931, a *Yorkshire Evening Post* women's cricket team was launched, with the newspaper helping fund its activities. And in 1935, two members of the St George's Club in Reading scored centuries during the season, and received *Berkshire Chronicle* cricket bats as a reward.

The WCA certainly felt that it was important to demonstrate that women were playing cricket seriously. Many photographs which appeared during the 1920s showed women playing cricket in bathing costumes, or short frilly frocks, both of which were clearly unsuitable for cricket and promoted an image with which the WCA did not want to be associated. It was for this reason that strict rules regarding dress were laid down from the beginning, dictating that "WCA teams must play in white and wear long stockings. Dresses, divided skirts or tunics must not be shorter than 4 inches from the ground when kneeling. Coloured jerseys and sleeveless dresses are not allowed."

In the late 19th century women had played cricket in long skirts and blouses, but most club players had switched to white shirts and knee-length divided skirts (culottes) by the 1930s. Nonetheless, Pollard complained that many did not bother with stockings (which presumably could be quite uncomfortable on a hot day). Clubs like St George's in Reading even reported that cricket was being played in coloured frocks and high heels!

Pollard was concerned that "the sight of bare legs (and often our legs are not too attractive to other people) may have repercussions... Women cricket players are entirely dependent upon the goodwill of the owners of cricket grounds". This was of course true, given that women cricket players did not (and still do not) own a single cricket ground. But skirts could cause problems of their own. In 1939 it was reported that a Miss Oliver of the Cuckoos Club had "recently been 'No-balled' twice when bowling, because her skirt brushed off the bail at the bowler's end". The MCC's Laws of Cricket never quite got round to grappling with this particular problem!

Clubs that were not affiliated to the WCA also ignored their rules regarding dress. A number of independent women's cricket leagues were established in the north of England during the 1930s, and many of these women played in trousers. In 1933 the *Lancashire Daily Post* announced that the secretary of the Preston and District men's league was interested in forming a women's league and invited local workplaces to form teams. The following year, the Preston and District Women's League was established with teams including Ensign Lamps, Preston Steam Laundry and Penwortham Mills. The league ran until the 1960s, and the *Daily Post* awarded a bat and ball annually to the players who topped the batting and bowling averages. Similar leagues were also formed in Leeds and Manchester.

Relations were not overtly hostile between the WCA and the northern leagues. But the WCA, much like the MCC, was a southern-dominated organisation which disapproved heavily of 'competitive' league cricket. All early WCA club matches were friendlies, and until 1966 there was a section in the WCA constitution which forbade the awarding of trophies. In 1949 it was agreed that clubs belonging to leagues would be permitted to join the Association, and that those playing for trophies would be allowed to continue doing so – but the WCA stated that they "would view with disfavour any affiliated bodies starting to play for new trophies". Yet women's matches in Yorkshire were probably the best attended women's club matches anywhere in the country. A women's 'Test match' at Headingley in 1931 between Bradford and Leeds attracted nearly 7,000 spectators (Leeds won with 11 balls to spare).

Some of the growth in women's club cricket was arrested by the Second World War. Wartime meant upheaval for both the men's and the women's games; official matches were cancelled immediately war broke out in 1939, pitches were dug up, and most clubs ceased to function. However, the war also provided new opportunities for women's cricket to develop. One member of the Berkshire and Oxfordshire WCA reported that her first experience of cricket had been playing the sport with a baseball in a Japanese internment camp during the conflict. And there was also cricket on offer for the 445,000 British women who served in the women's branches of the armed forces during the Second World War – the Auxiliary Territorial Service (ATS), the Women's Royal Naval Service (WRNS) and the Women's Auxiliary Air Force (WAAF). In the first edition of *Women's Cricket* after the war, one cricketer who served in the ATS described her experiences as the Commander of a Platoon and the Sports Officer for 13 companies at Aldershot. She organised matches every weekend, and nets most evenings, with the ATS providing the grounds and equipment. By 1943 ATS districts and commands played regular matches, and there were inter-service matches with the WRNS and the WAAF. These matches continued, even after the war ended.

Rationing during and after the war could cause problems for women's cricket clubs. Beaconsfield WCC reported in 1948 that members had struggled to secure petrol coupons for the mower for their pitch, and that finding ways to procure cricket clothing had proved problematic. Eventually they bought white overalls and made them up into cricket shorts, although one member also "clothed herself in the best parts of a discarded sheet"!

Even so, the existence of the WCA seems to have been enough once again to facilitate growth. By 1955 the WCA reported its highest ever number of affiliated clubs: 170. Women's cricket would not reach such heights again until the boom of the late 1990s.

The postwar years, and the decline of women's cricket

Men continued to be heavily involved with women's club cricket in the postwar years. Local men's teams often provided opposition for women's sides: Gunnersbury, for example, played an annual fixture against a men's London Transport team who they had met during a net practice session at Chiswick – the men having hired the next net along. The *Daily Mail* reported in 1966 that the Exeter WCC had entered the Devon Club Cricket Association's knockout competition, of which the other 71 teams were all-male. How they fared went unreported, aside from the fact that they defeated five of the men's teams in a quiz on umpiring before the start of the season.

Men also often helped with umpiring – though this did not always go smoothly. In 1954 the *Dereham and Fakenham Times* reported the following incident:

> Men umpires who offer unnecessary advice when officiating at matches in the Fakenham and District Women's Cricket League were criticised by Miss MD Ellicott, the secretary, when the annual meeting of the league took place at Fakenham Secondary Modern School on Monday.
>
> Miss Ellicott gave instances of advice given by male umpires to women bowlers and said that umpires were not supposed to speak to any members of the team. It was a little bit awkward sometimes and made 12 players in a side instead of 11.
>
> She added: "I think every umpire in the league has been guilty of it; it isn't cricket really, and we must see to it that they don't do it. If it were men

Women's cricket club institution Redoubtables CC in 1967

> playing they wouldn't do it, and if it were women umpires umpiring for men they wouldn't do it."
>
> Miss Ellicott said she appreciated that the men umpires were trying to help, but there had been some feeling about it which she rather deplored, because it had spoilt the league for some of the women players.

Some men evidently still felt that women did not fully understand how to play cricket!

Women's club cricket, however, could also turn traditional gender roles on their head. In 1989, *Cricket World* magazine were forced to change their "Tea Lady of the Month" competition to "Tea Person of the Month", when Pat Siderfin of the Thames Valley women's club wrote into the magazine in praise of her husband Steve. "The Thames Valley Women Cricketers have played 50 and 55 over matches this season and the Lunches have been prepared by Mr Steve Siderfin, my husband," she wrote. "The other members of the squad were delighted at Steve's effort at quiches and sausage rolls and he has always made an excellent cup of tea... In his first session, he was taken from washing the lettuce to check a slow puncture and change a tyre, fortunately another man stepped in to help with the lunch preparation."

Some famous male cricketers had little-known cricketing wives: Basil D'Oliveria's wife Naomi played for Malvern WCC for a number of years – though was apparently more talented at baking chocolate cake for cricket teas than at emulating her husband's achievements with the bat. But forget cricket widows – there have always been many "cricket widowers" out there. One poem entitled *The Married Woman's Apology* to her husband was published in *Women's Cricket* in 1951:

Tell me not John, I am so strange
That from the scullery
Of our good home and quiet life
To bowl and bat I fly.
True, a new venture now I chase,
The Aussies must be beat;
And with a firmer grip I brace
My bat, my nerves, my feet.
Yet this desertion from my hearth
Which you, I know, deplore -
I could not love thee, dear, so much,
Loved I not cricket more.

Netta Rheinberg reported in *The Cricketer* in 1970 that she had recently overheard a conversation during the tea break of a women's match at which the players had concluded that they generally advised their husbands to "carry on with the chores at home" while they were out playing cricket of a weekend. As for when children arrived, one Cambridge cricketer wrote to *Women's Cricket* in 1963 advising women to "take your husband along [to matches] to babysit"!

There were problems ahead for club cricket, though. From 1956 onwards there was a slow decline in the number of women's clubs. In fact, neither men's nor women's cricket went unaffected by Britain's 'swinging Sixties': the rise of home-based leisure activities such as television, as well as the increase in many newer sports such as badminton and squash, saw a decline in those participating in cricket during the 1960s and 1970s. For the women's game, this meant that by 1970 club numbers had sunk to 68, and by 1980 there were only 55 women's cricket clubs operating in the whole of Britain.

One problem was that tensions seem to have emerged at this time between the WCA and its member clubs over how club cricket should function. The most extreme example was in 1954, when the Hertfordshire Association actually threatened to sue the WCA for defamation. In autumn of that year a club called the Vagabonds had written to the WCA complaining of the "inefficient organisation of the Hertfordshire County Association, coupled with its apparent disregard both of the spirit and letter of its Constitution". It is unclear exactly what their grievance was, but the WCA attempted to resolve the dispute by chairing a meeting of the county and appointing their own replacement association committee. The original Hertfordshire committee were clearly angered by this. In July 1955, the WCA executive received a letter from a solicitor acting on behalf of two of the county officials:

> Threatening an application to the High Court for an injunction should any attempt be made to put the resolution into force, and further suggesting that the WCA or your Executive were liable to an action for defamation.

Huge amounts of paperwork followed. On the advice of their own solicitor, and subject to heated debate, at the 1955 AGM of the WCA the executive introduced a ruling whereby in future they would have the power to suspend any affiliated body or member if their conduct was "prejudicial to the interests of the Association or of the Game". The Hertfordshire association never carried out their threat – but relations continued to be tense.

There also continued to be disagreements about uniform, as well as general behaviour at club matches. One England player, Betty Birch, complained of club cricketers turning up in clothing that was too revealing, arguing that: "Nothing looks more ridiculous than short shorts, showing an expanse of thigh above pads". An article in *Women's Cricket* in 1960 criticised players for having short hairstyles, wearing trousers, and chewing gum while en route to matches.

Emphasis on correct "etiquette" in women's club cricket in fact remained strong at least until the 1980s. One letter sent by the captain of Redoubtables to club members in 1985 listed "do's and don'ts" on match days. The "don'ts" list read as follows:

> Ignore the opposition
> Show dissent when batting or fielding
> Grab your tea and slouch off
> Field with your socks down
> Wear short socks
> WASTE TIME
> WEAR COLOURED SHIRTS, SOCKS ETC.

Sledging was also frowned upon. And in 1993, one of the bowlers in the women's Varsity match was actually banned from bowling for grunting while she released the ball, as this was seen as "unladylike behaviour"!

Another area of tension stemmed from the fact that many women's cricket clubs disagreed with the WCA's rulings regarding Sunday cricket and competitive cricket. WCA rules dictated that Sunday matches should not be played: the executive committee of the WCA when they discussed the issue in 1957 felt that "Sunday matches should not be made official... some players did not wish to play on Sundays on religious grounds, and... it was unfair to penalise them for not doing so." However, Sunday matches were actually a fairly common occurrence at club level, because it was far more difficult to secure good pitches on Saturdays, as this tended to be when men's league and club games were played. Additionally, more and more clubs felt that a good way to inject life into club cricket, given the year-by-year decline in affiliations, would be to introduce some kind of challenge cup – but the WCA continued to resist this.

The WCA executive did slowly begin to appreciate that they needed to take action to attempt to stem the decline of women's club cricket. In 1965, it circulated a questionnaire to all clubs entitled "The Future of the Association". Questions included:

> Would you support some form of inter-club competition cricket?
> Do you favour the award of trophies for competitive cricket?

In the wake of this, a working party was set up to consider the "Future of the WCA" in order to take into account feedback from grassroots clubs. Several key changes took places as a result. Firstly, given the success of men's Sunday League cricket (the John Player Sunday League was introduced in 1969), the WCA decided to "fall into line with the present day trend towards more Sunday sport" and introduced a rule change which permitted official matches on Sundays – as long as these matches commenced after 2pm.

Secondly, during the 1965 season a national knockout women's cricket tournament was instituted. Twelve teams entered, and the final, which took place at Bedford Physical Training College, featured Wallington LCC (based in Surrey) and Brighton and Hove WCC. Wallington were the eventual champions. Two years later, Vagabonds WCC ran the first ever women's single wicket competition. At the 1966 AGM, it was agreed to delete the section of the WCA constitution which forbade the awarding of trophies. Competitive cricket gradually spread through women's club cricket during the 1970s and 1980s, with more women's leagues being introduced.

However, this did not solve the main issue for women's cricket in the postwar years, which was a financial one. Many other activities, such as athletics and swimming, were much more affordable than cricket. In a 1956 editorial of *Women's Cricket*, Netta Rheinberg wrote that one player had written to her complaining that she had spent £56 on cricket in the last season (approximately £1,282 in today's money). "Here is a real problem," she concluded, "which is not easy to solve".

It was not just the travelling to matches, which required at least some players to possess their own cars, and the payment of club fees, which were often expensive, but the purchase of uniform. The WCA dictated that divided skirts for representative cricket could only be bought from official suppliers Lillywhites and (from 1970) Len Smith's. Enid Bakewell, England's star allrounder of the 1960s and 1970s and the daughter of a miner, recalls that as a young club player: "Mother nearly had a heart attack when I had to have some proper cricket shorts. They were seven guineas! Eventually Hazel Sanders (a fellow England player) gave me a pair of her old ones, so that kept my mother from having a heart attack!"

The economic climate of the 1970s and 1980s only made matters worse, as clubs struggled to survive during periods of depression and high unemployment. Leicester WCC, for example, was established in 1984, and reported in 1987 that it had an active membership of over 20, with most members having never played cricket before they joined the club. In an article for the WCA newsletter in 1987, their founder Ann Woods wrote that one of the main problems for any new club was finance: "Women's cricket can become prohibitively expensive for some". An effort had been made by Leicester to keep costs low, with special club subs for juniors and the unwaged, but their survival had still been a struggle, even with a grant of £120 from Leicester City Council.

Many other new clubs simply could not afford to survive for long. West Essex was a new Middlesex club, established in 1980, who complained in 1984 that the club was "struggling to meet the financial commitments involved – its own running expenses and affiliation fees and levies to the County and National bodies". It dissolved the following year, surviving only five years in total. In fact, the examples of Redoubtables, Riverside, Gunnersbury and Dukesmead stand out because they are the *only* women's clubs which have managed to survive for the whole of the postwar period right up until the present day.

The shortage of clubs meant that often, for those women who wanted to play cricket, even club matches could involve travelling long distances. Invicta LCC, based in Kent, had one member who regularly made 375-mile round trips from her home in Cardiff to play in "home" games! In fact, one of the distinctive things about women's club cricket is that it has always involved lengthy travel: some years, members of Gunnersbury (based in Ealing, south-west London) actually travelled 460 miles to and from a weekend cup fixture in Catterick, North Yorkshire.

Clubs did attempt to secure sponsorship in order to alleviate financial problems. In the north, Lancashire and Cheshire reported that during the 1990 season, their clubs were provided with support by McVities. Apparently "the free biscuits came in extremely useful"! But sponsorship was not, as it was for struggling men's clubs, the solution to all financial problems. One letter in the November 1986 edition of *The Cricketer* described the formation of a club in Halifax by two sisters who had:

> Wanted to play for a long time. After writing to all of the clubs in the area, they at last received a reply from the Halifax Cricket and Athletic Club, who invited them to join the club.
>
> The team was duly formed but all the expense, advertising for players and buying the equipment, had to be met by the girls themselves. They have written to several businesses seeking sponsorship, but most did not bother to reply.

This experience was far from atypical. Women's club cricket was often not an attractive financial prospect for potential sponsors.

It also continued to be difficult for women to gain access to pitches. One woman wrote to *Women's Cricket* in 1960 complaining that her village team had secured use of the village ground "at great cost from the ever-jealous men who watch anxiously and clutch their brows in despair whenever our newest recruit dispatches the turf to the boundary instead of the ball". Where men's clubs were not co-operative, the alternative could be to hire a local authority-owned pitch, but during the 1980s, when the Thatcher governments made the decision to sell off numerous school and municipal cricket pitches, it often spelled the end for those women's clubs who relied on school pitches for practices and sometimes even for home games.

And the quality of local authority pitches was often poor. Shirley Hodges, who kept wicket for England between 1968 and 1982, recalls that at club matches in Sussex,

Old Actonians Ladies. Photo courtesy of Carlene Bender

"we had to mark out our own pitch, put the whitener out, put all the boundary flags out... The pitch was awful... It was hilarious, because you never knew what was going to happen!" This is borne out when looking at some club scorecards. On one occasion Beaconsfield were bowled out for just four runs by Wallington. Wallington's opening bowler took 10-0 (Hedley Verity eat your heart out!). The four runs were byes.

There continued to be a tremendous shortage of women's cricket clubs, right up until the 1990s. This meant that the best women players often came through boys and men's cricket, instead of through the women's club system. Of the 14 players who participated in the 1997 Women's World Cup in India, for example, seven had a background in which they had played the vast majority of their cricket with boys. One famous example is Clare Connor (England captain 2000-2005 and now ECB head of women's cricket), who played for the age-group sections of her local men's club, Preston Nomads, from under 9s all the way through her teenage years, and later made headlines when she became one of the first ever girls to play 1st XI public school boys cricket, for Brighton College. She recalls: "I wasn't really even aware that other women played cricket, or that there was this thing called 'women's cricket'". Clearly the women's game could not survive much longer like this. Radical change was needed.

The revival of women's club cricket

Radical change was to occur during the 1990s and 2000s: more radical than the women's game had ever seen. Just look at the statistics. In 1993 there were reportedly only 39 women's cricket clubs in the whole of Britain. By 2000 there were 204 – more than at any time in the history of the sport. And by 2010 there were 309. What changed in such a short space of time?

Kwik Cricket was a major factor. Launched by the Cricket Council in January 1988 to "bring the game to new generations of boys and girls and ensure cricket is a mass appeal sport well into the 21st century", Kwik Cricket was aimed at both boys and girls from the very beginning: the funding made available for the project was on the basis that both boys and girls would participate in coaching sessions held in schools.

By 1998, 374,000 primary school girls and 83,000 secondary school girls were participating in Kwik Cricket. It brought many girls into the club system who might otherwise never have played cricket. Future England captain Charlotte Edwards was actually "discovered" by a scout for Huntingdonshire Boys while playing in her regional Kwik Cricket final.

But Kwik Cricket also helped those involved in men's cricket see that they should be involving women and girls in other development initiatives, too. Surrey WCA, for example, reported in 1995 that they had "established a good working relationship with various members of the Surrey Cricket Council and the Surrey Cricket Association at the Oval and now the Oval staff are carrying out development work on our behalf within the county." A number of development plans created by men's county associations in the early 1990s formally incorporated women's cricket for the first time. By 1997, cricket development officers with special responsibility for women's and/or girls cricket had been appointed in Surrey, Yorkshire, Lancashire and Kent.

During the 1990s, too, many local authority sports development officers (SDOs) reported that they were running women's cricket initiatives in their areas. In one typical case in 1993, the SDO for Tameside, after being approached by the mother of one of the boys who attended colts sessions at a Tameside club and asked why there was no local women's team, rounded up several interested women, and organised an indoor coaching course. This was attended by 33 women, and resulted in the establishment of two new women's cricket clubs in the area.

Some men's clubs began to start "women's sections", and club-level "mergers" by established women's clubs with men's clubs also began to take place. There were many potential benefits to this type of relationship – not least that it helped solve the problem of access to pitches. Shepperton Cricket Club in Surrey was an early example. Having begun separately in 1980, the Shepperton Ladies team was officially incorporated into the club constitution five years later, when the men's club management committee voted to incorporate a "Ladies Charter". One member of the club wrote in 1985:

> There is no doubt in the minds of Shepperton members that a joint venture benefits men and women alike, with the men providing undying support, encouragement and technical expertise to help the women, and the women and their visiting opposition sides contributing fully to the social side of the club, fundraising and of course the bar profits!

Funding by the Sports Council for clubhouse improvements began to be dependent on the provision of "equal opportunities" for women at clubs. This provided an incentive for men's clubs to open their resources up to female cricketers. And regular access to good-quality facilities helped make those women's clubs which did form more sustainable.

Another big change which took place during the 1990s was more visible: the introduction of trousers. Even by the 1990s, most women's clubs still played all their cricket in the divided skirt or culottes which had been the official uniform of English women's cricket since the 1930s. But for a new generation of England players, many of whom had spent much of their early years in cricket playing with boys in trousers, skirts were seen as a throwback to the 1950s, and totally unsuitable for the increased athleticism at all levels of the game. In the words of Charlotte Edwards: "People said we looked nice, but we were there to play cricket! If we played in skirts we'd have no skin left on our knees now."

At national level, trousers were introduced for the first time in August 1997 during England's series against South Africa. At club level, though, it was decided to introduced a compromise whereby clubs could vote themselves on whether they wished to introduce trousers. For a few years matches took place in which sides would play in skirts or trousers according to preference. But as a younger generation of players came through and began to dominate domestic cricket in the early 2000s, trousers gradually became the norm. The hope was that this would make the women's game more accessible: trousers were cheaper and easier to obtain, and many girls and women felt much less exposed in them. Many clubs believed, as Dukesmead expressed at their 1998 AGM, that "we would rather have people playing the game than just looking the part".

The biggest change of all, though, came in 1998. On March 29 that year, at an Extraordinary General Meeting of the Women's Cricket Association, members voted to merge with the newly formed England and Wales Cricket Board. After 71 years as an autonomous organisation, 97 out of 128 delegates who attended the meeting voted in favour of dissolving the WCA: women's cricket would now be administered by those who ran the men's game.

What did this mean for women's club cricket? Firstly, since the ECB took over, their plans for cricket development have fully incorporated women's cricket at all levels – including club. Initially, this meant that in 2000, four women's club development officers (WCDOs) were appointed, to revitalise women's cricket in the Home Counties, the north, the east Midlands and the south-west. Their role was to form new clubs, establish more local women's leagues, and to facilitate the formation of age-group under 13 and under 15 sides. Within a year, these WCDOs had increased the number of clubs in the 14 counties they covered from 46 to 77 adult clubs and from 16 to 54 junior girls' sections.

Secondly, it became ECB policy to support and promote the kind of club-level mergers which had already been taking place during the early 1990s. Before this, taking on a women's team had sometimes been mere lip service for men's teams and genuine equality could be difficult to secure. The Bury Ladies team, for instance, joined with Bury Sports Club in 1989. The club promptly gained £18,000 from the Sports Council for the improvement of club facilities, specifically to help women's sport, but by 1994 the women's cricket team were complaining that:

> Men's friendly games... take precedence over women's league games in use of the square... We were graciously offered the use of the artificial pitch in another corner of the ground, a seemingly generous offer until the slippery surface and rutted, pot-holed outfield are taken into account... We are thinking of renaming ourselves the Bury Wanderers.

Under the ECB such mergers became commonplace – but more importantly, they have generally taken place in a way which supports the interests of the women's side. Take Somerset Wanderers LCC as an example. The club had been formed in 1969 by Nicola Tranter, a teacher at the Bath Convent School, but as their name suggests, they had often had difficulty securing access to decent pitches. In 2001, it was agreed that they would form a partnership with Bath Cricket Club, and by 2003, this led to a full merger. The merger was negotiated by Jan Godman (who played for England between 1991 and 1996, and is now a fully-qualified ECB coach). She recalls: "Bath couldn't have been more helpful. They wanted to become an all-inclusive cricket club, which is what they are now. They just promote cricket."

The women's team have become the "Bath Wanderers" – but they are no longer a wandering club. They now have access to Bath's beautiful centrally located ground on Sundays throughout the season. There are three women's XIs, and 50 girls train each Friday evening at Bath. Jan also coaches a mum's team. And this has all been done with the encouragement of the ECB: Bath is now a designated "focus club", meaning it receives additional financial support.

Jan describes Bath's ethos as "treating everybody the same, giving everybody an opportunity to play. The girls have every opportunity to play cricket at whatever level they want to, and not be treated any differently to the blokes." If any further evidence were needed of the positive environment which Bath has created for the development of women's cricket, you need look no further than one of the stars of England's 2009 World Cup victory and recent double Ashes-winning squad, Anya Shrubsole. She was 10 when Somerset Wanderers went to Bath; she has grown up playing cricket there. The club has brought to maturity one of the best women's bowlers in the world.

Other club mergers have been equally successful. The fates of the oldest women's clubs still in existence are telling. Riverside WCC, who for many years relied on poor-quality council pitches, made the decision to merge with Twickenham CC in 2000, becoming Twickenham Riverside. They now have access to the clubhouse, and play on the club's main square on Twickenham Green. Gunnersbury have become Finchley Gunns – the women's section of Finchley Cricket Club – having moved to Finchley in 2010; Dukesmead merged with Old Actonians CC in 2011. Both women's sides now have access to their clubs' first team pitches on Sundays throughout the season.

Most recently, in 2012, Berkshire-based club Ridgeway, which had been in existence since the 1980s and is now the home club of both Charlotte Edwards and England vice-captain Heather Knight, has moved to play at Wokingham Cricket

Club. Why? Not only do they have access to the club's excellent facilities – but the women's side, who were national champions in 2006, now have priority over their male counterparts when pitches are allocated. Those at Wokingham see the move as an advancement of the club's status – and treat the women's side accordingly.

Perhaps most importantly, these type of mergers have meant that women's clubs have a constant stream of juniors coming through into their ranks. Previously, while girls sometimes played age-group cricket with boys at men's clubs, they had nowhere to progress to once they hit their teenage years. That has now changed. Clubs like Old Actonians, who used to simply have girls attending their largely male colts training sessions, now run under 11, under 13 and under 15 girls sides; many of these girls eventually progress to the Old Actonians senior women's side.

Beth Morgan, former England batsman, has been a member of Gunnersbury since 1995, aged 14, and has witnessed this transformation: "I look back to when I started and they had this one open day, and I think four girls turned up. That's not enough to keep building the club. At Finchley we have a constant feed of players through from the juniors. It's a more professional structure now in place. And the facilities and the quality of grounds that we get to play on now has hugely improved the standard."

In short, since the merger with the ECB, there has been a revolution in women's club cricket. The perennial problem of access to facilities has finally been solved. And female cricketers have at last been recognised as the asset that they are.

Women's club cricket today

In March 2015 I attended a meeting at Lord's, led by the current women's cricket development officer at the Middlesex Cricket Board, detailing all the activities available for girls and women in Middlesex. It was quite incredible. The MCB has now had a full-time WCDO since 2000. In that time, women's and girls cricket in Middlesex has grown exponentially. There are now 18 girls sections at clubs within the county, with leagues at under 11, under 13 and under 15 levels. Middlesex girls are some of the 14,000 annually who take part in the age-group soft and hard-ball competitions organised by the Lady Taverners. Eight under 13 girls from the Bushy Park Girls Cricket Club recently played in the final of the London Youth Games competition, held at Lord's. And clubs around the county are welcoming girls like never before. North Middlesex CC even held a special weekend during the 2013 season to celebrate girls cricket – deliberately designed to coincide with the 100 year anniversary of their pavilion being burned down by a group of militant suffragettes!

At senior level, there are now 14 women's clubs in Middlesex. Most run at least two XIs, as well as age-group girls sections. All have access to regular coaching and excellent facilities. Several of the Middlesex clubs play in the Women's Cricket Southern League, an independent league established in 2004, which has recently begun to receive financial support from the ECB. Some also play in the North London

Women's Cricket League, which was established in the 2006 season as a friendly league for teams in and around the north London area, as a response to demands by newly formed clubs who wanted to participate in league matches, but at a standard more suitable for beginners.

Pauline Osborn, whose team, Wanstead Heronettes, was one of the league's early members, is full of praise for the initiative. "It started as a development league playing 20-over games whenever pitches could be made available, either on Sunday or during the week in the evening. Other leagues were more formal and rigid, playing 40 overs on a Sunday afternoon, and many of the clubs involved were several hours' drive away. Most of the ladies in our club were new to cricket, and we have young mums in our team who would not play if matches plus travel took up the whole day.

"That is why our league is so good. It is competitive but friendly; it is flexible; we play 30 overs on a Sunday, morning or afternoon to suit the needs of the club; and we are finished in time for ladies and girls who are playing to get home at an acceptable hour."

The North London Women's Cricket League began with eight teams; there are now two divisions and a total of 15 teams. The league, which is run outside of the auspices of the ECB, is just one example of recent local initiatives which have helped provide more competitive opportunities for women new to cricket to progress within the sport.

Overall, women's and girls cricket in Middlesex is simply unrecognisable from where it was 20 years ago. And that experience is being replicated around the country. Since 1998, the number of cricket clubs offering women and/or girls cricket has increased by 507 per cent, from 93 to more than 600. There are now 30 women's leagues operating in England and Wales. And the ECB's recent National Playing Survey revealed that more than 63,000 women and girls over the age of 14 played cricket in 2013.

While women's club cricket still relies on local initiatives by volunteers, like the North London League, the influence of the ECB has achieved something important – something less tangible than the opening of access to facilities. Even in the 1990s, many men (and women) still saw cricket as a man's game. Members of the Bury Ladies team complained that even when England Women won the World Cup in 1993, it was still looked down on as: "only women amateurs (in skirts!) taking an afternoon off the housework... there is still a hard core attitude, at least up here in the North, that these things are best left to men". One letter published in *The Cricketer* in 1993, by a P Holland of Lincolnshire, complained about the magazine's coverage of that World Cup:

> I find it deeply disturbing that with such a wide range of quality cricket being played throughout the world you should decide to dedicate in September issue's coverage of the Women's World Cup two full pages to a form of cricket which is little more than village green standard.
>
> At present I am introducing my young grandson to the vagaries of cricket, and I feel that scenes on programmes such as *Grandstand* showing such a consistently poor standard of cricket can only be confusing to a boy of tender age. I feel that members of MCC are fully justified in their decision to allow male only membership...

> I am sure your readers will agree with my sentiments, as does my cricket loving wife whose cricketing ambitions extend no further than making teas, which role she has dutifully fulfilled for the past 35 years.

Contrast this with the coverage which England players now regularly receive in the national media: every ball of the 2015 women's Ashes series broadcast live on Sky. The ECB's support and financial investment has made this possible. The ECB are also running projects to raise the number of female umpires and coaches; and through the Chance to Shine scheme, run in partnership with the ECB, a million girls have accessed the sport in schools across the UK. The best female players in the country – including England skipper Charlotte Edwards – now regularly go into schools to carry out coaching sessions. You couldn't ask for better role models for the girls who will be the cricketers of the future.

The ECB's backing has therefore done something crucial for the future of women's club cricket: it has helped demonstrate that cricket is a sport for everybody, boy or girl, man or woman.

Middlesex are still looking to the future. Their own Middlesex Women's Cricket League, and a "Club20 Competition", are both due to be launched in the 2015 season. The Club20 competition will be six-a-side, with weekly 20-over matches leading up to a finals day – a more informal, less time-consuming type of competition, specifically designed to draw in more girls and women to clubs. Given that still only seven per cent of cricketers within the UK are female, there is evidently room for growth, both in Middlesex and nationwide.

In fact, it is pretty clear that for women's club cricket, the only way is up.

• • •

CLUB LEGENDS
Netta Rheinberg: Administrator extraordinaire

Netta Rheinberg (1911-2006) was one of the pioneering administrators of women's cricket. Born in Middlesex, the daughter of a Jewish export merchant, she learned cricket at South Hampstead High School for Girls. She joined Gunnersbury WCC in 1932; the club had formed in May 1925 and by that time was running three XIs. Rheinberg later recalled that she was placed in the 3rd XI as punishment for failing to bring the correct attire – namely white stockings – to the club trials. However, she went on to captain the 1st XI, and helped to ensure that Gunnersbury was one of only a handful of women's clubs which continued to function during the Second World War.

Rheinberg had attended secretarial college, and later became the company secretary in her father's textile business in the City. Her organisational skills served the cricket community well: she was secretary of the WCA between 1948 and 1958, as well as later becoming membership secretary and vice-chairman of the Cricket Society. She was also manager of the England teams which sailed to Australia and New Zealand in 1948/49 and 1957/58. Due to injuries, she was selected to play in the Adelaide Test of January 1949, but she made a pair, and never got another opportunity at England level.

She was secretary of Gunnersbury at a difficult time for the club, as women's cricket sought to rebuild itself after the disasters of the war. Gunnersbury were ousted from their home ground at Bedford College in 1947 as the pitch was to be let to a men's club which had recently reformed, and Rheinberg reported that she spent hours finding alternatives, labelling cricket grounds "a secretary's nightmare". Thanks to Rheinberg's hard work, the club has continued to function to this day (its members now play at Finchley CC).

She was editor of the WCA's magazine, *Women's Cricket*, between 1950 and 1967, and ensured the magazine continued to regularly report on club activities and print end-of-season club averages. Her editorials reflected her traditionalist attitude towards club cricket: she complained about club players turning up to matches "in the briefest of flimsy tennis shorts... However slim, young and beautiful she may be, this is not cricket." She argued that it detracted from the skill of the sport.

She remained involved in club affairs throughout her life, and in 1999 she was rightly honoured as one of the first 10 female members of the MCC. She died, still living in Middlesex, in 2006.

•••

VII

CLUB LEGENDS
Marion Collin: Stats queen

Marion Collin is a legend in women's cricket across the world, and it is all thanks to her work with statistics. She took early retirement from her job in local government in 1993, and became the first-ever official International Women's Cricket Council statistician the following year. The job involved entering records of all international women's matches (the first of which took place in 1934) into a computer database. She has kept records of all matches since then, and is now the ICC's honorary statistician for women's cricket.

Marion's involvement in women's club cricket has been long-standing. She began playing cricket at Sutton High School in Surrey, over 50 years ago. On leaving school, she joined Redoubtables WCC, and played for them for 35 years, until illness caused her to retire in 1997. She also represented Surrey. She served on the Redoubtables committee for many years, later becoming club chairman. A qualified umpire and scorer, she has officiated in countless club games, as well as in four Tests and several ODIs.

Yet perhaps her main contribution to women's club cricket has been as the keeper of records. When Marion joined Redoubtables, the then-Women's Cricket Association statistician, Margaret Dickens, belonged to the club; Marion began to help her compile records and averages, for club cricket as well as for county and England matches. She took over the role herself after the 1973 World Cup. This work was all done manually, painstakingly, for many years – and without it, we would probably have no record at all of domestic women's cricket.

More recently, Marion's efforts have ensured that some club scorecards, including for Redoubtables, have appeared online at cricketarchive.com. A trawl through them shows that Marion herself once took 6-37 for Redoubtables with her trundling medium-pacers, against Dukesmead, back in 1975.

She can be found at all Berkshire and England matches, scoring, making sure all records are up to date – she currently collects all scoresheets and compiles the points for the ECB's women's County Championship – and keeping journalists on their toes with her incredible recall of statistical records in the women's game.

• • •

CLUB LEGENDS
Pauline Osborn: Contemporary Hero

Pauline Osborn's involvement with women's cricket began at Wanstead Cricket Club back in 2002. Her sons were members of the club's colts section at a time when several girls, whose brothers were club members, decided that they wanted to play themselves. "We agreed that there was no reason why girls should be excluded," Pauline recalls. "Wanstead always strives to do things properly and with girls playing it was decided that there should be female coaches to support them – which is how I quickly found myself on an ECB Level 1 coaching course!"

Once it became known that girls were welcome, numbers swelled. A women's section was soon formed, too, initially made up of the mums and aunties of the girls who were playing, as well as Pauline herself. In 2007, after a few seasons of struggling to find local clubs to play "friendlies" against, Pauline was instrumental in the Wanstead Heronettes (as they named themselves) applying to join the recently formed North London Women's Cricket League. Since then, coached by Pauline, the Heronettes have won the league on several occasions – doing so in 2011 and 2012 without losing a game.

Pauline is now head of women's and girls cricket at Wanstead CC, manager of the women's team, and chairman of the North London League, as well as a level 2 ECB coach and a qualified scorer and umpire. When asked about her personal highlights since becoming involved in women's club cricket, she cites leading Wanstead under 13 girls to the national Lady Taverners final, and twice winning the London Youth Games as manager of the Redbridge borough team.

Thanks to Pauline's hard work, Wanstead now have over 50 girls and women participating in cricket, ranging in age from five to 60. Pauline is currently making arrangements for a women's team to travel to Barbados in November to take part in the club's centenary celebrations.

•••

VII

CLUB INSTITUTIONS
Redoubtables WCC

Redoubtables WCC, based in Surrey, lays claim to being the oldest women's cricket club in the UK still in existence, having been formed in 1921. Its members now play at Purley Cricket Club as Purley Redoubtables.

In February 1921, eight women of St Matthew's Church in Brixton met and agreed to form the St Matthew's Ladies Cricket Club. The club was the initiative of the wives and daughters of the men's church cricket club, and in the first year, all of St Matthews' matches were played against the men's team. Edith Child, the club's first captain, regularly bowled at her father, who was the treasurer of the men's team. This doesn't seem to have caused too much familial tension – probably because initially all bowling was underarm! Coaching was given by the men in exchange for an agreement that "the ladies of the club should get the refreshments ready for the men's cricket club".

It appears that the club was formed largely for social purposes. Councillor Child, Edith's father, had to arrange for a chart showing standard fielding positions to be given to each member during the first season after the acting captain had to ask for assistance in placing the field during a match, as she was not "sufficiently acquainted with the positions"! However, their cricket steadily improved and in 1926, it was decided to award medals each season to the women with the best batting and bowling performances. By the 1930s, club fixtures included matches against Battersea Polytechnic, Unilever, the London School of Economics, Lyons, and the Civil Service.

In 1935 it was agreed to change the club name to Redoubtables Women's Cricket Club as by that stage only one member lived in Brixton and certain members apparently disliked the label of "Ladies"!

Some of the club's early fixtures were played on a pitch in Regent's Park which became known as "Dead Man's Corner", which gives some idea of the quality. However, from 1935 the Wallington Hockey Club invited the club to share their "beautiful" ground at Beddington Park in Surrey. Unusually for a women's club, they also secured access to a groundsman. They continued to play at Beddington Park until the 1980s. At one stage Alec and Eric Bedser even became joint club presidents, and assisted with coaching.

Redoubtables have always been one of the strongest women's clubs. Many England players have passed through their ranks, including England captain 1982-85 Jan Southgate, and Enid Bakewell – who aged 74 still plays club cricket for Redoubtables!

• • •

CLUB INSTITUTIONS
Riverside WCC

Riverside WCC, based in south-west London, was formed in 1946 by Aline Brown, the sister of England captain Freddie Brown. Their mother also played cricket and both she and Freddie attended some of Riverside's early matches. The first club meeting was held at the Methodist Church Hall in Barnes and the first match was against the "Southern Railway", which Riverside won by 16 runs. Umpiring was provided by the husband of one of the members, Mrs Coysh, who herself topped the batting averages in the 1947 season with 136 (it is unclear whether her husband was influential in this!).

There were initially many problems with finding a home ground. Aline wrote that she "cycled many miles, wore out many pairs of pants, but the answer was always no, no, no. 'The men need the pitch every weekend'..." The headmistress of St Paul's Girls' School allowed them to use the school nets free of charge and eventually a permanent home ground was found at the Barnes Council Sports Ground. There was no clubhouse, though, and for many years the team changed in a tent hired from the council!

The club were very active at organising tours, going to Holland in 1957 and 1961 to play the Dutch women's association. In 1977 they visited New Zealand at the invitation of a former club member, Prue Hyman, and played at the Test ground Lancaster Park in Christchurch. The match was umpired by a Test-level umpire and local radio stations featured coverage of the game.

Riverside won the national club competition in 1978 and have continued to experience success. In 1999 they moved to play at Twickenham Cricket Club as Twickenham Riverside in order to improve their membership and to secure access to Twickenham's excellent playing facilities. They can currently be found playing on Twickenham Green throughout the season.

• • •

THE PASSION AND THE GLORY

THE GROWTH AND POTENTIAL OF ASIAN CLUB CRICKET

by Sahil Dutta

"British Asians in mainstream clubs, the recognised parks leagues and unseen streets hold the future of cricket as a popular national sport in their hands"

It felt like the first day of every English cricket season, cold. Gun-metal grey, gusting winds and under their coloured cricket jerseys, players wore two, sometimes three layers. Also, it was clearly still football season, in a football country.

The Ford Social and Sports Club in Ilford, Essex, was established in the 1950s when Ford's Dagenham factory fed the area's economy. It was now drab, transfixed in a style from a generation past. On a mid-April Sunday morning it played host to an endless expanse of football matches. It was also supposed to host the National Cricket League's season opener: a charity T10 tournament.

Eight teams had arrived for the big day, and eight more were already in action at the Walker Ground in Southgate. At Ilford many of the cricketers milled about on the outfield, rubbing hands together, wincing at catches, and 'warming up' with stiff-looking bowling actions. Others, like much of the 'Oceans XI' team, thawed out at the bar. Just tea and cola, of course, since many of Ocean XI's players didn't drink alcohol.

Their cricket outfits were bright green (all the teams were in technicolour) and had nicknames emblazoned on the back: 'Mr Khan'; 'RAZZY D'. The fronts and arms were plastered with sponsors' labels, a local fried chicken and pizza shop.

Around the ground some young men had spiked, dyed hair, others reversed baseball caps, and others still the traditional Muslim taqiyah. Almost everyone who could wore some kind of beard. It was a sweep of Greater London's south Asian community. Dads and uncles with their boys; wives, mothers, daughters and aunties elsewhere, apparently. It was already past 11am, the tournament was supposed to have started more than an hour ago. But still everyone waited.

"There's been a bit of a problem," Sajid Patel, secretary of the NCL who was organising the day, told me. "The groundskeeper has said we can't play here today. It's a real shame, all the guys were so excited for it. I'm trying to make some calls to see what we can do."

Sajid is a huge guy, six-foot-five he says. His downward-sloping eyebrows and toothy smile give him a gentle manner, but he was clearly annoyed. Whether a misunderstanding or something more pointed, the ground's facilities manager had decreed "round robin" events prohibited. It felt arbitrary. The ground had been hired for the day, the teams had arrived and "round robin" or not, there would only ever be one match happening at a time.

Despite Sajid's protestations it wasn't to be. The tournament was postponed and almost 90 players drifted back to their normal Sunday lives. The Ford ground remained football only for another week, and cricket took another, quiet blow. As I was leaving Sajid smiled and explained: "We're used to these kinds of challenges."

The 2015 edition of the *Wisden Almanack* warned that English cricket was becoming distant from the British population. The ECB's own figures, though hardly scientific, showed participation flagging and spoke of a sport struggling for popular relevance. Over the course of a year the equivalent of 5,818 playing XIs had been lost, and of the thousands of people that were still playing cricket, many did not do so regularly.

All of which makes British Asian cricket something to celebrate, because the south Asian game is thriving in England. Officially, they play over a third of all recreational cricket, but that ignores the fevered matches that take place in carparks, street corners and council-owned pitches around the country. This off-grid cricket lies outside ECB oversight and is unregulated and impossible to catalogue. Between them, British Asians in mainstream clubs, the recognised parks leagues and unseen streets hold the future of cricket as a popular national sport in their hands.

Yet when so many British Asians play for fun and so few (about six per cent) professionally, something is awry. For the last two generations the mainstream English game and the British Asian game have stood apart, though things may finally be changing. The ECB has recently attempted to bridge the gap and in 2014 announced a 'national south Asian engagement programme' to try and 'connect' with 10,000 south Asians. Counties received funding for diversity training, the ECB brought England players to community cricket festivals, and goodwill was extended all round. No panacea, but after decades of mutual neglect, an important step.

Changing attitude though, does nothing to shift deeper infrastructural problems. Simply, there aren't enough cricket grounds left in urban Britain. Twenty thousand playing fields have been lost since 1990 and in London, where luxury housing developments are more lucrative to cash-strapped councils than cricket grounds, there has been a 40 per cent fall in the number of pitches over the last 20 years. The ECB is experimenting with new forms of the game, adapted for tightly enclosed urban settings and in years from now this might prove fruitful, but they are no replacement for what has been lost.

It is why places like Victoria Park in east London are so sacred. Among the fashionistas revelling there in summer you also find an authentically retro scene: inner-city cricket. Teams play cup games on weekday evenings and all day on weekends as part of the Victoria Park Community League. The league was founded in the early 1990s and at the time was almost the only organised cricket in Tower Hamlets and Newham, two of London's most-populated and ethnically diverse boroughs. The community league is successful and recruits players that well represent the multicultural population, but the cricket is gentle. More akin to the village game than anything more flinty. Instead, it's a couple of miles up the road from Victoria Park – at the Leyton County Ground – where south Asian cricket really gets serious.

• •

Saturday afternoon players in Victoria Park, east London

It is in Leyton where you'll often find Sajid Patel and the best matches from the NCL. Like so many, Sajid owed his love of the game to his family. His dad, Dilwar, had come to England in 1968 from the Bharuch district in Gujarat, north India. Dilwar was a keen cricketer and he and fellow migrants from the same community immediately came together to play cricket. They founded the Leytonstone Cricket Club two years later which played park games mainly, but also entered an XI in the Middlesex League and the Colour Assembly League in Essex in the 1970s. Of course, they didn't have a ground, and were sub-letters to the mainstream English clubs, playing their 'home' games at Leyton, Hackney Marshes and Lea Valley Park.

Seventies London was not always accommodating to these still fairly recent migrants. Many of Dilwar's friends and relatives preferred to play among themselves than deal with the hostile attitude of other teams. With his family steeped in the game Sajid was always going to play cricket, and he wanted to play it properly. For a while he was at Wanstead CC but couldn't get a fair outing. Eventually his dad's frustration turned to innovation as Dilwar helped found the Gujarati Metropolitan Cricket League in 1993. The league still runs today with two divisions and a cup tournament and, affiliated to the Essex county, is 'open to anyone'. When it started, though, it was a haven for London's Gujarati Muslim community. "It was a similar concept to the IPL in a way," explained Sajid. "Seven players from each team had to be Gujarati Muslim and four players could be from any background." Though Sunday cricket, the GMCL was a high standard.

What Dilwar couldn't have known when he helped start Leytonstone CC in 1970 is the legacy the venture would have. The GMCL continues today and its spin-off, the NCL, is now a behemoth of south Asian cricket in London and Essex. On first sighting 'National Cricket League' is a misleading name. The league comprises 39 clubs, none of which hail many miles out from Leyton. But with players from Britain's Bengali, Pakistani, Sri Lankan and Indian communities, it is more representative of 'the nation' than much of the English game. They play across four divisions, with a T20 tournament, Pro40 cup, and a four-stump 10-over knockout event for charity. A lot of cricket. The club names give an insight to their role models: Leytonstone Cricket Club are now called the Leytonstone Lions, and their opponents include the Cornered Tigers CC, Smashers CC and the Mumbai Indians.

The league entered its fifth season in 2015. Each year it has expanded: more clubs, more teams, more people playing the game that is supposed to be on the wane. Playing stocks are never a worry, the only real limit on growth is the lack of facilities. Leytonstone Lions still have no permanent home, and neither do most of the teams in the league. It is only a recent partnership with Essex to use the Leyton County Ground that has allowed the league to grow.

"We're trying to get away from the parks cricket label and see ourselves as potentially mainstream cricketers," said Sajid. "Essex have managed to help us get meetings with different groundsmen and Leyton County Ground is our hub. We got that two years ago and it's crucial."

Unlike the GMCL, which mostly plays traditional-style games, the NCL concentrates on short-form cricket. "A lot of people are actually coming over from Saturday league cricket to come and play Twenty20 with us. With work or family commitments people have moved away from the traditional English-style clubs to play three hours of cricket instead."

There might be a lesson here. With world cricket's professional game skewed ever further towards the shortest form, is traditional club cricket not out of step with its half-speed, all-day format? Certainly another successful south Asian cricket adventure in London takes its cue more from the IPL than the Ashes.

The Telugu Premier League, made up of the South Indian community that live in and around north-west London, is a 16-team, franchise-owned, 20-over tournament that started three years ago. Having found it hard breaking in and committing to regular league cricket in Middlesex, Sanjay Bhiraju, the TPL's founder, and his friends were playing tennis-ball cricket in parks. Inspiration struck when they saw the IPL.

"We are a community who come from India and we were impressed by their tournament," Bhiraju told *All Out Cricket* in 2014. "We immediately called a few people and decided that the business owners would be the franchise owners." It grew from there and the tournament raised an estimated £35,000 in sponsorship. In keeping with the IPL ideal a touch of glamour was allied to commercial acumen, with Tollywood actor Manchu Vishnu attending the tournament's opening ceremony last year. Though the TPL was recently recognised by the ECB, it was built by the community itself.

• •

"He was unknown but very skilful, a wonderful bowler back then. Before he went down the drain." Salim Yasin, chairman of the Elliott Davis London Cricket League, is speaking about Mohammad Asif, Pakistan's once magical seam bowler who was banned for spot fixing in 2011. "You know, he was very open, very helpful, used to talk to anyone about the skill of bowling."

Asif was actually very well known when he played for Marshes CC in 2009, and was one of a number of Pakistani internationals to have played in the EDLCL. Abdul Razzaq, Zulqarnain Haider, and even umpire Aleem Dar have all featured recently. Salim's personal links with Pakistan Cricket Board insiders keep a conveyor-belt of first-class Pakistan cricketers coming to ply their skills on unremarkable and unreliable park pitches around London. The league has been running for 26 years and though now dominated by the Pakistani community, included eight African-Caribbean sides and two traditional British teams when it started.

Salim is an enthusiast. He speaks eagerly and warmly of everyone who's been involved in the league at any point, and is clearly an enterprising force himself. He started the Hackney Marshes cricket club with school friends in 1968 and Marshes CC, as it has become, is now the London institution for Pakistani cricket. The premier division is very strong and Salim isn't shy to talk it up. "We could compete against anyone, any-one," he said. "Some of the traditional clubs, their Saturday cricket is like tour games. The way our league is structured with the bonus points and all that, we play very fast and furious! Attacking cricket!"

There are now 15 teams spread across two divisions but despite its history and international stardust, the league cannot overcome the familiar obstacle of insufficient facilities. More than anything else the EDLCL needs pitches. "Our teams cannot enter the top Essex leagues because we don't have any home grounds," Salim explains. He is now more optimistic but describes how in the past bids for grounds have been rejected for spurious reasons. Though on-field prejudice was limited, these off-field barriers were deeply damaging. "Despite having the best bid, the most players, sponsors and all that, we were passed over, again and again." he says. "And we still don't have home grounds."

This inhibits the development of the communitarian culture that is such an important feature of mainstream club cricket in England. There is no pavilion bar to run, no square to cut, and most significantly, no colts to coach. Both Salim and Sajid Patel of the NCL see youth development as their first priority, but both are limited by the lack of facilities.

• •

It's clear that where there are south Asian communities, there will be cricket. Look widely enough and you'll find British Asian cricket played all over southern England. Why something so everyday feels so marginal is the riddle waiting to be solved. One issue is that because there are no home grounds or colts system, parks cricket is still played independently, or within specific diasporas. Rarely are these disparate pieces knitted together. Unlike the traditional club scene, there are few development pathways or umbrella organisations under which the many players, teams, clubs and leagues can belong. The ECB hopes to fix this by increasing the board's own 'visibility' in these areas, but perhaps more significantly the British Asian community itself is trying to find a collective voice.

Gulfraz Riaz, development officer at the Club Cricket Conference, has spent the past few years pushing for greater recognition for south Asian cricketers in England. Starting in London and the sout-east, Gulfraz took to his car to personally seek out and speak to teams and league secretaries that were previously unseen by the English game.

His aim was expanding the network of teams affiliated to the Club Cricket Conference, but the more he visited the more he felt they needed fuller representation. "It wasn't a case of picking up the phone and telling them they now belong to us," he said last year. "It was a case of going there, talking to them, and understanding their achievements and needs." There are now 13 leagues affiliated to the CCC, totalling over 300 teams and 5,000 players and plans are in place to establish an organisation dedicated to representing British Asian cricket. "For the first time [these clubs] have a chance to share ideas and concerns with each other," he tells me. "It's given them a voice."

It was through Gulfraz that Essex built a partnership with the NCL that is now so important. "At first we thought 'oh here we go it's another Asian talk-shop guy'," says Sajid Patel. "But we found they really care about this stuff and could deliver. Through Gulfraz we are now working in partnership with Essex."

The links forged have given British Asian cricket a toe-hold on the professional game for the first time. In May 2014 a select south Asian Cricket Leagues XI, featuring the best players from the various parks leagues, played Essex Second XI in a bank holiday Twenty20 game. Though a festival match for the county and good all-round fun, it is spoken of very seriously by those involved in south Asian cricket in Essex. It catapulted Pakistani-born Tanvir Sikander into the Essex County Championship team in 2014 and many of the British Asian players I spoke to now feel they too have chance, however slight.

That is a huge change. It has been almost 50 years since people like Dilwar Patel, Salim Yasin and Gulfraz Riaz came to Britain and established a cricket welcome to migrant players. After decades of mutual suspicion with the mainstream English game, it is proof of how attitudes are beginning to thaw. A flood of cricketing love and talent is poised to burst through, but the question is whether resources can be unlocked and shared in the other direction too.

Whatever happens at the elite level, though, it is worth celebrating the weekend heroes, who in the scrappy parks and built-up cities around England, have helped keep cricket thriving.

• • •

In action: the National Cricket League

CLUB LEGENDS
Joe Hussain and the School of Hard Knocks
by Phil Walker

The Hussain family. Monuments to cricket. Father Joe, hauling his family from Madras to Ilford in search of 'English morals', taking over the running of a legendary cricket school in Gants Hill; the gifted oldest brother Mel, who could have turned pro, and the boy Nasser, the failed leggie with the yips who went on to captain England. Phil Walker, a kid cricketer himself when he first set foot in 'Joe's place', sits down with Nasser to hear the story of a singular cricketing family.

I was 13 when I became properly aware of Nasser Hussain. It was 1993. He was about to become a regular Test player. I was a schoolboy whiling away the hours just up the road from Chelmsford's County Ground. When there was a match on, I'd sneak in for the last session, perching myself on the wall, my wall, just behind the lifers in the Tom Pearce Stand.

I always thought of Nasser then (as I still do now) as slightly removed from the other homegrowners. He was young, swaggering, furious: one of our own and yet so exotically different. Perhaps it was the name; more likely the strut. Or maybe it was because he always appeared, in my head at least, to be in cahoots with the overseas star of the day, perpetually in partnership with any one of Mark Waugh, Stuart Law or Salim Malik. I guess even then he was sizing them up, studying the form, taking notes; in a sense we both were. I've been drawn to his story ever since.

• •

Salty tales shook the pavilions of Essex cricket long before the world cared to take note. In style and background there was no other county cricketer quite like him, at least not in Essex, and this fact, coupled with his precocity, made him an early star. But it went deeper than that; in this case, there was no other family quite like the Hussains.

Everyone knew old father Joe. He was a famous figure to many of us growing up in Essex. Here was a man who moved his young family from Madras to Ilford in 1975 in search of experience and 'English morals', and who took over the running of a shabby old cricket school in Gants Hill which, under his watch, solidified its reputation as the most fertile breeding ground for young cricketers across the whole Essex/East London region. Founded by the great Ilford stalwart Harold Faragher in 1957 and originally the place where Trevor Bailey's old Essex teams trained, by the Eighties the Ilford Cricket School had become 'Joe's place'. It was here that young Nasser, middle brother Abbas, and older brother Mel would cut their teeth. And a few thousand others, for that matter.

I would have loved our first meeting to be at Joe's place – I used to go there myself as a kid. Instead we meet at a posh pub near his house in the Essex countryside.

Nasser and his dad with yet another keen youngster

Nasser has agreed to meet for lunch. Truth is, I'm a little apprehensive. Reverence can have that effect.

In the event it's easy. It turns out I've been having a one-way conversation with him for 20 years and more. Recollections of the school come easily too. For a way into Nasser's story, you have to walk through those doors.

• •

I wanted to take you back right to the start. Because your cricketing education began at the school itself, I thought we should start right there, at that mythic old shed behind the pub...

It's funny, as you grow older you get used to certain things in life. But when you're young and desperate to play cricket, you're not so worried about it being freezing cold and smelling that typical Ilford Cricket School smell, with the gear all over the place. I wasn't worried about any of the peripheral things, as long as it was open, as long as there was someone there to put the nets up.

What did it mean to have that place there, with your dad in charge of it?

As kids we were very fortunate to have it. It's been well proven since those days that in cricket, you need to get a kid bowling balls and facing balls – don't worry about the coaching and the technique and all that. It's just purely on the amount of balls you face, hit, bowl or catch: that is the way to get better. So, you know, just to have that facility there that your dad runs – or before that a bloke called Bill Morris ran – and to be able to just ring up, "Is the cricket school open today?" "Yeah, come down. Bung us a few quid if you want, if you don't, don't worry about it." To us kids, that was everything.

And what of the place now?

It's still going strong. I have to be honest, since my dad passed away I've not been… My association with the place was through my dad in the latter years. He used to ring me up every year and say, you know, "Prize-giving evening for the indoor league, will you come down?" And I used to love going down there. He'd still have all the old photos of me up and it was good fun seeing the young lads and seeing the British-Asian community down there. It's changed over the years from when I first started. There used to be a big West Indian community, British-West Indian community. And there was a lot of banter, especially Sunday morning nets. There used to be a West Indian net, an Indian net, or a Pakistani net, you know. And an English net, if you want to call it that. That's just how it was. It was a great development.

• •

When Jawad 'Joe' Hussain died in 2008, aged 68, cricket lost a true loyalist. With a devotion to the game first fomented at the Chepauk Stadium in Madras – where he played a single first-class game in 1964 – he found its truest expression in East London during that period in the Eighties and Nineties when the English game was straining to find its place in a faster, coarser, more fragmented world. His style, they say, both as coach and man, was blunt, brusque and to the point. In a touching tribute to the school, former England and Essex stalwart Doug Insole described Joe as a "genially explosive" character tightly laced to the advancement of cricket, who was at the heart of "helping to redress the imbalance" caused by the falling off of cricket played in our state schools. It was here, Insole asserted, "that the Ilford School made its most telling contribution to cricket."

His commitment to the game, the school and his boys was legendary. "My dad brought me up," Nasser says, "with that Indian mentality of, 'This is important, cricket is important and if you're going to do it, you do it properly.'" It helped that his boys had enough talent to make it feel worthwhile. If it wasn't Nasser being put through his paces, it would be Abbas, who would go on to play for Essex Second XI, or Mel, the tall, charismatic strokemaker who chose the City over a cricket career.

Is the rumour true, I ask the younger brother, that Mel was the best? "He was more talented, yeah. But how do you define better? Who's better, Pietersen or Cook? Pietersen seems more talented. Who would you want batting for your life? Cook." Although Mel was snapped up early by Essex he was also coveted by Hampshire, who offered him a better contract. He took it, but it didn't work out.

"Unfortunately there is more to being a professional cricketer than just raw talent. Mel was always an outsider in Hampshire. Back then they were a difficult side to break into with all their star names, and Mel probably didn't do the right things. You go and ask around league cricket in Essex, you will be able to wind up a few people."

I may have heard that.

"You may have heard that. You would have heard that. He breaks records, he'd play innings, and he still does. He plays with his lad now and they run each other out and they have arguments about it! And he'll go back and play the next day. He's got cricket in his blood more than me."

Mel Hussain in action for his club

Mel is one of those regional guns who embody the class-less nature of Essex club life. With its borders overlapping with the ethnically diverse boroughs of east London and its history of urban overspill out towards the coast, Essex, both as county and cricketing culture, has long been infused with multiculturalism. For south Asian immigrants in particular – first, second, third generation – the county delivers a style of unvarnished cricket played in the raw where individual and collective identity can be given full expression.

It's certainly a much pricklier world than the one evoked by the old, generally misleading clichés of cucumber sarnies and Sta-Prest creams, and it's into this scene, where fair play are dirty words and dirty words are fair play, that certain bruisers emerge, vast in scale, hauling their numbers wherever they roam, embellishing their myths with every new scrap, century and set-to. As a legendary presence at three of Essex's grandest clubs, Ilford, Fives & Heronians and Gidea Park & Romford, Mel was one of those totems of club life, Essex-style.

Mel may, at a push, have been the more naturally talented sibling, but Nasser was still a precociously brilliant leg-spinner. An England Schools Under 11s player at eight, here was a rough diamond being lovingly polished day after day by his relentlessly driven father. I remind him of a story about the time when, as a schoolboy playing for Forest School, he hit a hundred and took the first six wickets against the Westminster School lads over the other side of town, only for Joe to demand to know why he hadn't taken all 10.

Was Joe ever satisfied?
That story... I was upset, but I wasn't that bothered because I'd ended up getting runs and wickets. But it sort of defined me at the time, because it was about always trying to be as good as you can be. If you've got nine wickets, why didn't you get all 10? It was my dad's way. My dad never coached me. My dad never, ever said to me, "Well, your head's falling over. You're playing across your front pad. Oh, you've got half a bat face open." His attitude was, "Right, do you want to be on that Gameboy this morning? No you're not, you're going down to Ilford Cricket School." And on days I didn't want to go, "No, you are going." It meant that you would always strive to be as good as you possibly could be.

What was he like as a coach?
I see two types of coaches. You get someone who is very technical, very driven by technique and bowling machines and, "Let's have a look at where your head is". And I see other coaches, where it's just, "I love the game of cricket. And if any boy or girl wants to know anything about the game of cricket, I'll be there. They can talk to me." And in his case, it was a few beers and a brandy, and he would feed the bowling machine or chuck balls for hours on end, because he loved the game of cricket and he wanted them to love the game of cricket and to be good at cricket. And my dad was in the latter. I can't remember any real coaching tips he gave me.

Who did 'coach' you then? Were you self-taught?
I was a little bit. I think coaching is overrated, to be honest.

During those early years, you weren't far off being as good as you could possibly be. But then at the age of 15, you lost your leg-break. How harrowing a time was that?
That year was traumatic for me because, you know, I was a leg-spinner, up until England Schools Under 15s, myself and Mike Atherton used to bowl leg-spin, though he was a batter as well. But I used to go in at No. 8 or something. And, you know, I was much revered at the Ilford Cricket School because Graham Gooch would come for a net, and I'd spin one past him and bowl these loopy leg-spinners and get everyone out, and all this sort of stuff. And then, one year, I shot up in height by half a foot, and I couldn't hit the cut strip. It was basically the yips, and it was very traumatic.

And this put a strain on yours and Joe's relationship?
My dad couldn't work it out. Because he wasn't a technical coach, he went from seeing his boy getting everyone out, to a lad who couldn't land it. So, it wasn't a case of, "Oh, bless, you've shot up in height a little bit. We're going to have to work this out." It was: "For f***'s sake, what is going on here? Why aren't you landing? Are you taking the piss or something?" You know, the default setting was: "Right, we'll work even harder on this." And the harder I worked, the worse it got. The trajectory changed, I couldn't spin it. I just got the yips. So the only other thing I had to do was to work on my batting. That was a difficult time, that year.

It's both extraordinary and entirely consistent that within seven years of the sky falling in, Nasser was taking guard as a Test match batsman, the leg-breaks discarded, his game flipped on its head, against Marshall, Patterson and Walsh.

• •

I get off at Gants Hill station and walk up the A12, past the pebbledashed roadside terraced houses, past the Burger King and the Self Storage block, and on past Chas & Phil's Jewellers. It's been so long since I've been here that I have to pop into the pub on the corner to ask for directions. The European barmaid draws a blank, but the old Asian fellas huddled around their pints watching the IPL on the TV send me round the back. I'm transported back immediately. Nothing's changed. I meet up with Pal Shukla, who runs the joint from his tiny office out the back and has done for the best part of 30 years. He was here when, in his prime, Joe Hussain bestrode the place. So come on then, what was the old boy like to work with?

He suppresses a laugh. "If Joe saw talent he would really work hard with you," says Pal. "He wouldn't mince his words – if someone was doing anything wrong he would let you know about it! But on the other hand he was very generous, if someone did well he would show his appreciation."

Was he a tough man to please? "I let him do what he wanted! There was no middle ground. But they still all came here..."

Joe's place

I say I was speaking earlier to another coach out in the nets. He said that while he didn't always agree with Joe's methods, he always got the best out of his players in the end. "Yeah, absolutely," says Pal. "You have to judge him by the players that came through. The thing with Joe was that he was strict. When he lost his temper he was just… fearsome! But he was very careful to know when to do it and when not to do it – otherwise he would have driven everyone mad! But, yes, he would give everything for you."

Mel brings his boys down from time to time. He'll show up during the winter months and get his lads working in the nets. "Our surfaces are the best surfaces," says Pal. "The bounce it gives you, you will not find anywhere else. People really like batting here."

He shows me a list of 40 names. All are involved in county representative cricket, from Varun Chopra, doing classy things at Warwickshire, right down to the latest batches of talent coming up through the Essex Under 11s squad. "All from here. In the winter you'll be lucky if you get a slot here."

In these straitened times for cricket, and indeed most active sporting life in this country, I ask Pal what the purpose of the school is today.

"Previously we used to have just a few hours for private coaching and a lot of clubs used it. But now it's changed to concentrating on one-to-one coaching with youngsters. And we keep our charges to a minimum. The idea is to promote cricket, and we are cheaper than anywhere else you can think of. We hire our nets for £15 an hour. For our Saturday session for beginners aged nine to 11, it is £4 – I don't think it's changed in 20 years! The whole idea is to make it accessible to people. If we wanted to make money we could have demolished it and built something else but it's not about that. It's about promoting cricket."

Survival and renewal. At club level – at any level – this is cricket's story. The story of this school is cricket's own. On this chilly, spring Thursday evening, the place is packed. "We've never advertised," says Pal. "Everyone who knows about cricket knows where the cricket school is!"

• •

Just before I leave, Pal finds the cuttings file. I turn to one of the old testimonials written in honour of 'the shed behind the pub'.

> It is impossible to do justice to the Ilford Cricket School in a brief article such as this. I thought about doing it justice to the cricketers who without the school may never have gone onto have the careers that they have had. Gooch, Hussain, Lever, Rollins, Lilley and others have been a product of what seems to many as a large wooden shed behind the Beefeater pub. This shed, with its intoxicating mix of noises and smells and people from all walks of life creates an atmosphere that can never be duplicated in these new cricket schools that seem to be popping up all over the place. All of this however misses the point about Ilford Cricket School. It has provided a facility for young kids and schools to go and spend some time, and have some fun, and dream about becoming some of the names that I have already mentioned. Every Saturday morning I am sure there are hundreds of Graham Gooches and Nasser Hussains practising in the indoor school.

Nasser's words.

• • •

THE LIE OF THE LAND

WHAT NOW FOR CLUB CRICKET?

by Ed Kemp

"It is time to take stock and to think about just what our cricket is going to look like in 10 years' time. Because it could be very, very different from what it is at the moment"

VII

Much of this book about the history of club cricket has fostered a kind of nostalgic glee, as it celebrates the very best in participation, volunteerism and revelry. This has generally been set against what seems a comparatively troubled outlook for our sport. But I believe the history touched on in this volume gives us clear and significant cause for hope. In all the 100 years this book has covered, a sense of crisis has never been too far away. Indeed, the Club Cricket Conference, whose centenary year this volume marks, was formed specifically – as Duncan Stone has put it, "to keep club cricket in wartime London going, protect and preserve private grounds and provide cricketers, both civilian and military, with opportunities to play."

Clubs and recreational cricket in general have survived, and occasionally prospered, through countless obstacles in the last hundred years: the enormous drain on the stocks of young men, finances and available space brought about by the two world wars – which saw clubs fold, re-start, struggle on, rebuild – were followed by a significant expansion of rival leisure opportunities in the Sixties and Seventies, then the fragmenting impact on community-based living of the socio-political order of the Eighties, through to the bewilderingly granular world in which we find ourselves today. As Andrew Miller has written in his chapter on the impact of the Great War: "most of the problems that beset the club scene back then – a shortage of decent players, a surfeit of the reluctant and inept; an over-reliance on the goodwill of the few and a chronic lack of funds – were not so fundamentally removed from what most match managers encounter to this day."

Former Conference official Leo Bennett once wrote, in a piece entitled 'Whither the British Club?': "I fear the threat of apathy to our sport, and I see too much indifference to the reasonable discipline we must all observe if the game is to have any meaning. Club cricket, in the south, anyway, is beginning to suffer from lassitude; it needs a stiff dose of something. But what? And who is to administer it?" That was in 1951, in his book *The Weekend Cricketer*. Save for the odd sprinkle of 'establishment' phrasing, the passage could have been written yesterday. So just what is the scale and nature of today's 'crisis' in participation at the grassroots level?

• •

In the autumn of 2014, the ECB commissioned a long overdue landmark survey about recreational cricket in England and Wales. Over 37,000 people completed it, providing cricket's stakeholders with their clearest vision yet of the game's rugged landscape. "The survey has helped us identify where the challenges are, and where the opportunities are," says the ECB's chief operating officer Gordon Hollins. His colleague at the ECB, Mike Gatting, cricket partnerships ambassador, agrees with him: "You know what? I was concerned that [before the survey] we didn't have any figures that we could really rely on. Only now, at long last, have we got some real insights that we can work with."

Now we have figures. And the bottom line makes stark reading. Participation numbers dropped by 64,000 in a single year, down from 908,000 in 2013 to 844,000 in 2014. Just as alarmingly, five per cent of all organised fixtures were conceded in 2014 because at least one of the teams was unable to field 11 bodies, with the obvious knock-on effects of such cancellations breeding disillusionment among those who have given up their weekends for a cause they want, with profoundly good reason, to believe in. And there's more: less than a third of those 844,000 regard themselves as 'core' players – defined as people who would commit to at least 12 matches in a league season; reliable Saturday-to-Saturday members in other words – with the best part of the remaining 600,000 deemed 'occasional' or 'cameo' players.

Such patterns are not uncommon. Participation in sport is down generally, and Sport England figures show that this is not a problem unique to cricket. Fewer people are playing games. For administrators and the rest of us, the great struggle of the modern age has little to do with England's performances against the Aussies – though let's not for a minute discount the relevance of *that* – but how the overarching trend towards less participation is bucked.

"We recognise and accept," says Hollins, "that over time participation in cricket has dropped slightly in line with the trends of the vast majority of other sports, particularly team sports. We recognise there are challenges out there and we need to step up to the plate to address those challenges."

Many point to the lack of cricket on terrestrial TV – and who wouldn't, in an ideal world, like to see more of the game on free-to-air? – or to the limited facilities for cricket in state schools – albeit that the Chance to Shine charity is doing brilliant work in addressing that. But these points alone miss the crux of the matter. For this is not a problem unique to cricket, nor one that can be laid at the door of any administrator, but, principally, the result of long-term societal changes. People work long hours, into the weekend, conference calling, skyping, emailing beyond the nine to five, and when the working week does relent, they are rightly expected to play an active part in family life. Cricket's drawn-out charms are rarely conducive either to successful careers or thriving relationships. Even where free time is abundant, there are countless options for how to fill it, and why would you miss a night out on the town because you're still driving back halfway across the county after batting at seven and not getting a bowl? These days you cannot spend the evening putting money behind the bar when you have to drive home at the end of it. Cricket clubs depend on hours and hours of voluntary work, but young people are more mobile, they go away to university, travel the world; online they can find and communicate with people whose interests align closely with their own regardless of where they live. Their connection to their immediate communities is weaker and more short-term. They may have worked numerous hours unpaid just to get a foot on the career ladder; perhaps they are therefore less inclined than their parents were to give up time for free in the cause of running of a sports club. Perhaps individual sports are better suited to the modern sensibility than team games, which require greater organisation, regular appointments and an investment beyond the self. As *ESPNcricinfo* UK editor David Hopps has written: "How do you save a game that demands hours when many people only want to give minutes, that only reveals its secrets slowly when everybody wants instant gratification?"

So, armed with the data, which indicates a desire amongst many of today's "time-poor" participants to move away from the traditional formats of all-day cricket (often favoured by the generation occupying the administrative roles at clubs and leagues) towards a shorter, more streamlined version, the ECB is, it seems, prepared to act.

"We need an overarching strategy for recreational cricket. The game has to realise that if it's to maintain relevance it needs to change and adapt to society, and become more inclusive," says Hollins.

While the participant-demographic of club cricket's microcosmic society evolves at a bewildering rate, so the old models become outdated. Hollins recognises the scale of transformation, and with it, the task that confronts us. "In some ways," he says, "it's about us actually changing the conversation from 'England and Wales cricket' to 'cricket in England and Wales'. And it's a very significant change in our conversation, because we recognise that a lot of people in England and Wales aren't England cricket fans.

"In particular, we have our south Asian communities, who we're really focused on engaging. That's a massive growth opportunity for us. Unique to cricket. Most sports would give their right arms to have their game in the DNA of such a large section of our society. We've got to do more to engage people from that group."

As illustrated expertly by Sahil Dutta in his chapter on Asian club cricket, while participation totters in more 'traditional' areas, the reverse is the case among south Asian communities, whose recorded cricket accounts for over a third of participants throughout the country. It's a trend the ECB (or CEW?) with help from the county boards, Chance to Shine, the NCC and its newly formed National Asian Cricket Council, is keenly seeking to capitalise upon. As Sahil notes: "Between them, British Asians in mainstream clubs, the recognised parks leagues and unseen streets hold the future of cricket as a popular national sport in their hands."

• •

The Asian cricketers and organisers who are increasingly being brought within – and supported by – 'established' cricket have also set it an important example. That is, the most notable start-up leagues or tournaments cited in these pages have featured matches of 20 overs or less, often, but not always, modeled on the IPL. While 20-over cricket has been played in supplementary cups and evening leagues for decades, it is still tricky for those who have grown up playing traditional, longer-form cricket to adjust to the idea of playing shorter forms alone. For some, who treasure the complexities and intrigues – not to say, the greater likeli-

Have Asian park leagues shown mainstream cricket the way forward?

hood of getting a bat – offered by 45, 50, 55-over or even declaration cricket, such a change might be enough for *them* to pack up playing. Finding formats of the game that suit both the more casual player – yet to be attracted as regular participants, perhaps – and those whose commitment and enthusiasm maintain the established clubs that currently underpin the recreational game, is critically important.

Hollins says: "We know that 2.3m people a year pick up a cricket bat at some point, which is a sizeable number. The review told us there is a significant latent demand for cricket, and the vast majority of those who play it want to play more of it. It's about offering them cricket at the right times in the right format to allow them to play and to combine playing with their busy lifestyles.

"The important thing is to make it easier for people to play formal cricket as well as informal cricket, accepting that you have two different segments that we've got to cater for. We've got a responsibility to both segments." That's been the reason for the introduction of schemes like Last Man Stands – an eight-a-side, 20 (five-ball)-over format laid on in parks as well as established club grounds, and endorsed by the ECB in the last few years. It's also the reason for the ECB's new national under 19 T20 competition, which was trialled in 2014 and launched in full in 2015 – complete with coloured clothing and walk-on music – an attempt to retain cricketers at the post-age-group stage when they are routinely lost to the game. Similar projects – the 20-over, even 10-over formats and competitions outlined in Raf Nicholson's chapter – are in place to engage even more women and girls in the game, to make further increases on the progress already made in that regard over the last 15 years since the ECB took over the running of women's cricket.

These more casual participants – the ones cricket cannot take for granted – are more likely to respond to these shortened forms than play a 120-over declaration match every Saturday for 20 weeks a year.

• •

Even amongst club cricket's most devoted, high-level players, the length of travel and playing time is a real problem – enough to put an early end to many playing careers. Former England man Alex Tudor – who, interestingly, developed his cricket through the now-defunct London Schools system rather than the county academy pathway – has played for and coached his club Spencer CC in Surrey since retiring as a professional in 2009. "The 2015 season is my final year, " he says. "I can't do it anymore. I've got a little boy and my family's growing and I can't be gone all day Saturday. You can't get away with that for too long! If it was 50 overs, done and dusted, maybe – but I can't do the all-day stuff. I did that when I was playing, I don't want to do that at club level. I can't be leaving at eight o'clock and getting home at 11, especially when I've got my daughter jumping on my bed the next day because she wants me to take her swimming."

Tudor is one of many playing club cricket who would prefer to see an end to the all-day declaration format. "I moan about the timed games every time we have one. I can understand the reason why they try to play it but listen, 15 overs here or there isn't going to make the difference in telling whether someone's a good cricketer or not."

It's a point that is raised time and again in conversations about the club game, and frequently the discussion comes back to the landmark changes made to recreational cricket in 1999 following the formation of the ECB out of the old Test and County Cricket Board (TCCB). As we have heard from Benj Moorehead in these pages: "English cricket, back in the doldrums, was streamlining the amateur game in an attempt to fast-track the best cricketers in the country. The ECB – under the guidance of its first chairman, Lord MacLaurin – mapped out a new pyramid system for club cricket, with new premier leagues supported by 'feeder' divisions." The masterplan aimed to mirror the lean structure of Australian cricket, where talent was concentrated and the recreational game was efficiently geared towards funneling the best players through to first-class level.

As CCC secretary, NCC managing director and seasoned league cricketer and administrator Simon Prodger says: "That had a fairly fundamental effect on the demographic of people playing the game, where they were choosing to play, whether they continued to play 1st XI; people were making choices about the type of cricket they wanted to play, possibly for the first time."

Feeder leagues – which had previously been separate from each other – covered a larger geographical area when put together, meaning that matches in the premier league they fed into would be contested between sides sometimes substantial distances apart. At the same time, due to MacLaurin's desire to develop the club game as a means of accessing first-class cricket, premier leagues were incentivised to play a format in excess of 50-overs a side. Suddenly the best club players were being asked to start earlier, finish later and travel further.

"A lot of people, particularly those in their early thirties who had just started families, did not want to play all-day cricket, did not feel that they wanted to commit that kind of time," Prodger says.

"Increasingly clubs weren't taking a credible side to away games – you had to be up at 7.30, and weren't getting back until 10 or 11 o'clock at night."

Legendary league cricketer of north and south Alan Burridge tells us: "It's happening in the north-east as well, where a side from Northumberland would have to travel all the way to Middlesbrough. It's a major problem. I know of umpires who have decided to pack it in because of the long journeys. At Sunderland in the 1960s we mostly played against clubs who were nearby geographically. So there were local derbies and there was a great deal of competitive humour between the players and the crowd, because they knew each other."

According to Prodger, all of these factors meant that the aim of the reforms – to raise standards – was being undermined as many of the best players opted to play 2nd XI cricket – or even refuse their club's promotion to the premier league.

It's also true that leagues maintained a certain amount of autonomy; indeed, since the premier divisions were introduced there have been almost as many systems for matches and points as there have been leagues. Then there has been the issue of win-lose cricket. Despite the fact that 50-over limited-overs cricket has been the staple at professional level for decades, many leagues have persisted with formats in which teams can bat out for the draw. Indeed, the Middlesex league is the last to switch to having half a season of limited-overs matches, a change made for 2015 after years of debate. In Prodger's words: "One of the big reasons was player pressure. The players want shorter games and they want win-lose cricket."

Paul McMahon, the former England under 19 captain who played 21 first-class games for Nottinghamshire, has a more positive view of MacLaurin's reforms. Having grown up playing in the Nottinghamshire league for Wollaton CC, he now plays for Peterborough Town CC in the Northants premier league, as well as captaining Cambridgeshire in Minor Counties cricket.

"People don't always appreciate quite how much changed in a relatively short space of time in terms of league cricket," he says. "If you asked players in the Middlesex and Surrey premier leagues what league cricket looked like in the 1960s I think they would be absolutely staggered to find out that it didn't exist. To go from no league cricket to what we have now in two generations is remarkable.

"I personally benefitted enormously from the creation of the ECB premier leagues. My first season of first team league cricket was in the first year of the new premier league, which helped massively. By all accounts that was a much higher standard than the previous constituent leagues, and through the ongoing concentration of talent that it led to, that standard increased. It was a fantastic base for me at 15, 16, 17 to move on to the cricket I then played at 18, 19 – county 2nd XI level and beyond."

Good or bad, the changes were in many areas strongly resisted by those organising local leagues. That recent history helps to underline the magnitude of the task that lies ahead for the ECB and its local representatives in instituting another kind of reform. McMahon again: "A lot of people in cricket administration are probably small c conservative and there's a desire to see the time and effort and energy that local administrators put into the running of their leagues give them some kind of control over that. You get a tension between the more macro interests and the micro."

The task is in bringing everyone together – including the volunteer administrators who are so crucial to the successful running of clubs and leagues. Prodger, who is also chairman at Watford Town CC, acknowledges this. "The make-up of most committees is on the older side. The young element doesn't take up the opportunity of becoming officers. The club is probably being managed by ex-players who have a bit of time to give back, who are not playing the game any more. Even inside clubs you have this gap between what the players think and want and what the people running things think. And that just goes on into the league level and beyond."

All of which is fine providing that participants aren't put off the idea of playing the game altogether. The lack of ECB-enforced uniformity, and the consequent degree of flexibility allowed for local league organisers, can sometimes grate when decisions over league rules and promotion matters come up for discussion. While one club is routinely refused promotion due to some ground issue or other, another team down the road is given enviable leeway, with little explanation offered as to the reasons for the discrepancy. Such matters of petty politics are no joke, creating real anger and damage to the game in the localities involved – even leading some to question why they give up their time to the game at all. In amongst all the rules, regs, whys and why-nots, the grander cause of promoting cricket can sometimes be forgotten.

"Without doubt there is an arrogance within the recreational game that sometimes comes to the fore," Prodger admits. "On the grounds issue for example, Totteridge Millhillians were twice rejected promotion to the Home Counties league – having won the Hertfordshire league – because of their ground. It was very difficult to believe that there were not more Machiavellian reasons for that rejection other than on the premise of the grounds. They've got a pleasant ground, private, enclosed, they'd made good on providing dedicated umpire facilities and they had covers, which other clubs within the Home Counties set-up didn't have. The application criteria were very inconsistent. You had to feel that there were other issues influencing the decision. The arrogance of the management of a league to simply make those decisions and not feel that they need to be responsible for demonstrating consistency is shocking sometimes. That does come from way back. It comes from somewhere else in the history of the game.

"I guess I can understand why maintaining a certain level of quality is important and relevant, but you've still go to give clubs that are developing and progressing through the league structure the opportunity to play at that level; give them the opportunity of improving their facilities so they are fit for purpose at the highest level. There is still an element of old-school, but that is because the people who are organising it to a large extent *are* old-school!"

Such issues – the age disparity between administrators and players – has an impact when discussing formats of the future, Prodger says. "At the end of the day, who am I, at 55, to determine and define what the 20-30 year olds should be playing? The brutal fact is that cricket at this level, if it doesn't adjust, could die. Does that mean that different types of leagues will be created, some dedicated to 100-over cricket and some to 20-over cricket? Possibly. It is time to take stock and to think about just what our cricket is going to look like in 10 years' time. Because it could be very, very different from what it is at the moment."

• •

All of which brings us to the question of what club cricket is for in the first place. For McMahon, bringing club cricket closer to – indeed, feeding – the first-class game raises standards while also boosting support for the England team. "In Australia you see a stronger emotional connection with the national team at the apex of the pyramid from people playing a relatively low standard. I think in England the rigid demarcation of the amateur and professional game is unhelpful." But with the ECB's backing of county academies, the lean pyramid of Australian cricket was never really created anyway. Players are developed within counties from a young age rather than being brought in following success in the leagues. Access to the first-class game from club cricket is limited – restricted to the Minor Counties route and the CCC rep side – while the number of new professionals

to have played significant amounts of cricket for their local club is lower than ever. That perpetuates a feeling of distance between amateur and elite cricket.

Perhaps it was ever thus, and many people question the aims of MacLaurin's reforms more fundamentally. "I think the ECB now see the amateur game and the professional game as being two different things," says Prodger. "One is not necessarily a means to an end of the other. I think that's probably how we have always seen it as clubbies." In his foreword in this volume Angus Fraser, not only a former international but Middlesex's director of cricket and an England selector, has chimed with this view. "Should club cricket exist just to produce England cricketers? I do not think so. I believe club cricket in the UK exists to provide 22 people and their families with regular opportunities to play and be involved in this wonderful game." Rather than being there to provide a service, clubs must aim to provide a hub for the local community.

Club cricket brings generations together in a way that few other games or institutions can. From a young age I watched my dad and older brother every Saturday, I sat on the boundary with the rest of the team, listening, talking, and without fail went (with the rest of the club and my family) to the pub afterwards. From 13, I started to play in the senior teams myself, in teams not only alongside my peers but with men in their fifties. At a time when the only adults many of my schoolfriends had spoken to were their parents and teachers, I counted men and women between 18 and 60 as friends, learning social skills, cricket knowledge and plenty more besides along the way. Now the entire senior club is largely filled and run by former junior players who are also each other's best mates. If recreational cricket is in terminal decline then no one has told them.

Those fortunate enough to have such an introduction (Fraser describes Stanmore as having been like a "second home" to him and his brother during teenage years) will all have had the feeling of being a part of something larger, and learnt to enjoy doing something that, while giving personal satisfaction, is also of relevance to the local community. It is not something that goes away.

For my own part, though I am fortunate to work in a job that involves studying and writing about the game at the professional level, it is increasingly the heart and soul of the game: the weekend heroes, the mates and volunteers and human lives, that shine most brightly in the imagination. Amongst the glitz and media coverage and opinion about who tweeted what and whether X should be dropped from the England team, it is the community cricket club – down-to-earth by virtue of its being physically rooted in its own sweat and soil – that seems to carry the most meaning.

As Fraser's foreword shows, this is even true for the generation of England players who had the opportunity to learn their game in club cricket. I interviewed Graeme Swann just after his retirement in 2014, and though – despite the horror Ashes tour he'd just departed – he was in typically chatty spirits, it was when I began to ask about his early days playing for Northampton Saints (in the days before county academies) with his dad and brother, that he really lit up.

"If you look back at the cricket you enjoy the most, it's Saturday afternoon with your mates, playing for your club," he said.

"We were a very successful senior club, but they were just the greatest lads in the world. All the young ones would go out on a Saturday night, and they'd drag me along – I was 14, 15 getting dragged along into town with a fake driver's licence trying to get into a pub. Just experiencing life and growing up together, highs and lows and laugh until you cry and cry until you laugh kind of thing… I loved cricket so much playing there, it was just amazing.

"You'd play these games and there'd be a real, tough edge on the field. But it would be with your best mates, guys who'd live and die for you. And I still look back on my days there – especially my first forays into senior cricket with the Saints – as the most fun games of cricket I've ever played in my life." There are echoes here of the inspirational Les Williamson, David Perrin's wonderful Fifties 'Spartans' hoaxer, who learned early on: "You have to play with your mates!"

Cricket clubs – as has been highlighted – can be of immense significance to people's lives, and despite his many international successes it is through club cricket that Swann feels he has experienced the best of what our wonderful game has to offer. Likewise, Ealing president John Poore has explained the central role of the club in his life: "Coming out of school you latch on to something. And cricket and Ealing really was my life. We would live and breathe it, winter and summer, living just down the road and always popping down." Meanwhile Wanstead stalwart Len Enoch has highlighted the educational aspect. "I believe that a cricket club can be an immensely important place for a youngster growing up, second only to school, and that's what we aim to be."

The point of a cricket club, then, is to have a significance beyond the game itself, to mean something to its people.

• •

"If you look back at the cricket you enjoy the most, it's Saturday afternoon with your mates, playing for your club" – Graeme Swann

This is essential if club cricket is to thrive. We have heard how leagues have become increasingly competitive, with the recruitment of players having a draining influence not only on club finances (league rules notwithstanding) but on the overall cohesion of the clubs as institutions. Prodger explains this has intensified in the years since 1999, as players who might formerly – like Les Williamson – have unquestioningly played "with their mates" at their local club, sought instead to move around in order to play at the best and most lucrative level available to them.

"Suddenly you had a mass migration," Prodger says. "The changes meant that young, thrusting, ambitious players would move to premier league clubs, so if their team had a poor season and was relegated they'd disappear. Clubs got drawn into a cycle of paying players – irrespective of the rules of the league these things as we all know, are a reality – so it became messy, and I don't think it did any service to club cricket at all."

Brook CC in Surrey are a fascinating case study here. A traditional village club (Brook is in fact so small it's technically a hamlet) with a long history of providing 'cricket on the green', Brook developed to such a stage that by 2012 their first team was fifth in division one of the Surrey Championship – ostensibly the 15th best team in the whole county. But their success was not built on solid, sustainable foundations. Good side though they had, the majority of their players were from outside the area – old boys from Charterhouse School with little connection to the club long-term. They also felt they needed an overseas player – and all his attendant costs – each year, just to compete. As Alan Hardy – the club chairman who has been involved at Brook since playing his first match at the age of 11 in 1948 – admits: "There wasn't the infrastructure; we didn't have a junior section." Increasingly, they struggled to fill a 2nd XI, and after a couple of failures to fulfil second team fixtures (which put them in breach of Championship rules) they decided to pull both Saturday teams out of the leagues. The following year, in 2013, they re-entered a side in the very bottom division of Surrey's much less competitive I'Anson league. First team player and committee member Jonathan King explains the thinking: "What we really discovered is that within the small little hamlet that is Brook and its surrounding area, there were quite a few locals who wanted to play at their local club but knew the standard that we were playing at was far too high for them, so never bothered to make any contact with the club.

"Once news got out that we were going to start off again in division six of the I'Anson at a level where pretty much anyone with a basic knowledge and ability could play, word spread and locals came forward, signed up and now play regularly. Bringing the club back to the village and playing at a level where anyone could play has been a major part of the success. With the locals playing, their partners get involved (as the ground is nearby) and the children come down and play on the boundary. All away fixtures are just a maximum of 20 minutes away too, so there's no more traipsing around the South Circular for two hours as I did when I played at Cheam a few years back!" Brook have been promoted in both of the last two years.

At the same time, establishing a junior section helped to connect Brook more closely with the immediate community and build something sustainable. Starting small with under 7s and 8s, but offering professional coaching, the section has rapidly grown to 80-strong. Hosting social events after junior training on a Friday in the summer, or at one of the race nights Hardy organises, the club can expect 100-150 people – a mixture of kids and parents and senior players. The club, it seems, has made itself an attractive social centre for the surrounding area. "We've reaped the benefits of that," says Hardy, the architect of the club's revival. "One or two of the fathers who were quite good cricketers have now come along and are playing for the club as well." Next year, Alan hopes, the club will have its 2nd XI back, completing a full and virtuous circle.

"What we did was really to bring the club back within the village," says Hardy, who has played for Brook in eight different generations. If the club hadn't taken the action it did, the other option was to merge – as many clubs around the country have and will no doubt continue to do. Concentrating resources at larger playing centres rather than having two neighbours competing can often make good deal of sense, and a merger must always be preferable to a closure. But at the same time, where a club can be of significance to its community – can provide a service, unite people and improve their lives – there is something worth preserving.

"Whether or not merging would have been the right decision, who knows?" Hardy says. "But you have feelings. I just felt that it was a takeover rather than a merger, and in my view it wouldn't have been beneficial to the people within Brook.

"There was the selfish, emotional side, too, of course," says Hardy. "Being involved with the club for all those years, I couldn't bear to see it go."

• •

In an individualistic world, creating cultural spaces where people can come together – to work for a common cause and call it 'leisure' – is a challenge. But as this book helps to highlight, the enduringly enchanting power of cricket clubs is what they mean to the people who make them.

Clubs will merge. Clubs will come to arrangements with Asian park sides; share facilities, players, experiences. Clubs will set up new women's sides, and if they haven't got enough numbers themselves, do so in conjunction with their neighbours. Clubs will arrange games with local businesses, invite unconnected local residents down for a barbeque, set up links with other sports clubs, add crèches to their pavilions, join new 10-over leagues for casual players. They might one day look very different, but clubs will find ways to survive and thrive as meaningful communities in their space and time. They will keep the show going.

Because cricket clubs are, in the end, entirely about people. That the game is – as CMJ said – "certainly the best invented by man" is actually secondary: any institution – a football club, hockey club, dominoes club, mother-and-baby group, school, Women's Institute, church, mosque, am-dram society or book group – can bring people together within communities, creating relationships, experiences; giving purpose and meaning to people's lives. Society might be increasingly individualistic, even hedonistic, but we are social animals, and somewhere in this disconnecting world of glaring laptop screens, viral videos, 24-hour news, five-minute celebrities, email-on-the-go, 60-hour working weeks and social media fury, not far from the surface, people are desperate for something simpler and more meaningful to grab on to. Something they can touch, and feel. Ultimately, most of us just want to feel like we're a part of something. To be involved in club cricket is exactly that.

• • •

BIBLIOGRAPHY

Thanks to the many dozens of clubs and volunteers who have provided club histories, centenary booklets and photographs to help in the production of this book.

Chris Arnot, *Britain's Lost Cricket Grounds*

Colin Babb, *They Gave the Crowd Plenty Fun*

Colin Babb, A History of West Indies Cricket in England, *Blood Sweat & Fashion* website

Norman Baker, 'A More Even Playing Field? Sport During and After the War', in 'Millions Like Us?' *British Culture in the Second World War*, edited by Nick Hayes and Jeff Hill

Norman Baker, 'Whose Hegemony? The Origins of the Amateur Ethos in Nineteenth Century English Society', *Sport in History*

ACL Bennett, *The Weekend Cricketer*

Derek Birley, *A Social History of English Cricket*

Martin Bishop, *Bats, Balls and Biscuits: A Brief History of Cricket at Reading Biscuit Factory*

Rowland Bowen, *Cricket: A History of its Growth and Development Throughout the World*

Ben Carrington, Sport, Masculinity and Black Cultural Resistance, *Journal of Sport and Social Issues*

Tony Collins, 'The Ambiguities of Amateurism: English Rugby Union in the Edwardian Era', *Sport in History*

David Day, 'Walter Brickett – a Respectable Professor', *Recording Leisure Lives: Sports, Games and Pastimes in 20th Century Britain*, edited by Robert Snape and Helen Pussard

Peter Fryer, *Staying Power: the history of black people in Britain*

Jermaine Haughton, Black English Cricketers Are Extinct: Fact or Fiction?, *The Voice* website

Richard Hill, *Cricket Lore*

Russell Holden, A Crying Shame, *The Nightwatchman*

David Hopps, 'England lose the generation game as black Britons abandon tradition', *Guardian* website

David Hopps, 'A Crisis that Defines the Age', *ESPNcricinfo*

Andrew Horrall, *Popular Culture in London c. 1890–1918: the Transformation of Entertainment*

Tom James, 'Caribbean cricket in the UK entering a new era', *Pitchare.com*
John Kay, *Cricket in the Leagues*

BIBLIOGRAPHY

John Lowerson, *Sport and the English Middle Class, 1870–1914*

JA Mangan (ed), *The Cultural Bond: Sport, Empire, Society*

Tony Mason and Richard Holt, *Sport in Britain: 1945 to 2000*

G Mellor, 'English Cricket, Amateurism and National Identity: A Sociological and Historical Study', *unpublished MA dissertation, University of Leicester*

Martin Pugh, State and Society: *A Social and Political History of Britain since 1870*

Allen Steel and Robert Lyttelton, *Cricket*

Duncan Stone, 'Cricket's Regional Identities: the Development of Cricket and Identity in Yorkshire and Surrey', *Sport in Society*

Duncan Stone, 'Regional Cricket Identities: The Construction of Class Narratives and their Relationship to Contemporary Supporters', in *Recording Leisure Lives: Sports, Games and Pastimes in 20th Century Britain,* edited by Robert Snape and Helen Pussard

Duncan Stone, '"It's all friendly down there": the Club Cricket Conference, amateurism and the cultural meaning of cricket in the South of England', *Sport in Society*

EP Thompson, *The Making of the English Working Class*

Richard Trainor, 'Urban Elites in Victorian Britain', *Urban History*

Martin Wiener, *English Culture and the Decline of the Industrial Spirit 1850–1980*

Jack Williams, *Cricket and England: A Cultural History of the Inter-War Years*

Ollie Williams, *London Fields Cricket Club* website

Jack Williams, *Cricket and Race*

VII

CONFERENCE CLUBS

List of clubs affiliated to the Club Cricket Conference in May 2015, with year established.

Bedfordshire

Ampthill Town, 1834
Biddenham, 1986
Dunstable Town, 1891
Eversholt, 1900
Ickwell, 1885
Lewsey Farm, 2010
Luton Town & Indians, 2002

Berkshire

Boyne Hill, 1890
Bracknell, 1880
Braywood, 1920
Cold Ash, 2001
Cookham Dean, 1881
Cranbourne, 1931
Datchet, 1869
Englefield (Berks), 1896
Falkland, 1884
Finchampstead, 1857
Holyport, 1844
Hurley, 1959
Hurst, 1862
Ibis Mapledurham, 1999
Littlewick Green, 1810
Maidenhead & Bray, 1798
Newbury, 1945
North Maidenhead, 1918
Odney, 1929
Old Leightonians, 1977
Pinkneys Green, 1885
Purley-On-Thames, 1969
Reading, 1859
Reading Lawyers, 1936
Royal Ascot, 1883
Royal Household, 1903
Slough, 1849
Sonning, 1870
Thatcham Town, 1878
Theale & Tilehurst, 1829
Twyford & Ruscombe, 1791
Wargrave, 1860
Welford Park, 1900
White Waltham, 1879
Windsor, 1995
Windsor Great Park, 1861
Wokingham, 1825
Woodcote, 1880
Wraysbury, 1926

Buckinghamshire

Amersham, 1856
Beaconsfield, 1825
Bledlow Ridge, 1919
Bledlow Village, 1889
Burnham, 1828
Chalfont St Giles, 1874
Chalfont St Peter, 1850
Challoners, 1949
Chenies & Latimer, 1878
Chesham, 1848
Chesham Bois, 1880
Coleshill, 1921
Denham, 1892
Dinton, 1908
Farnham Royal, 1889
Fiddlers, 1948
Fulmer, 1895
Gerrards Cross, 1882
Great Kingshill, 1890
Great Missenden Pelicans, 1964
Hawridge & Cholesbury, 1885
High Wycombe, 1823
Hyde Heath, 1963
Ivinghoe & Pitstone United, 1840
Jordans Taverners, 1923
Knotty Green, 1904
Ley Hill, 1947
Little Marlow, 1960
Little Missenden Misfits, 1976
Marlow, 1829
Marlow Park, 1892
Open University (Milton Keynes), 1970

Penn & Tylers Green, 1909
Penn Street, 1906
Phoenix Rugby Football Club, 1963
Princes Risborough, 1837
Stoke Green, 1815
Stokenchurch, 1861
Taplow, 1850
The Lee, 1875
Wendover, 1865
West Wycombe, 1890
Winchmore Hill (Penn), 1918
Wolverton Town, 1894
Wooburn Narkovians, 1936

Essex

Abridge, 1838
Ace Cricket & Sports, 1970
Alderton, 2005
Anson St. George, 1951
Antigua Cavaliers, 1975
Ardleigh Green, 1940
Aztecs, 1986
Barking, 1901
Belhus, 1960
Benfleet, 1948
Billericay, 1875
Bow Green, 1976
Brentwood, 1881
Brookweald, 1949
Buckhurst Hill, 1864
Canewdon, 1981
Canvey Island, 1946
Capricorn, 1979
Chadwell Heath, 1903
Chelmsford, 1810
Chigwell, 1988
Chingford, 1884
Clacton-on-Sea, 1882
Cloghams, 1870
Club Cricket Academy, 2013
Colchester & East Essex, 1862
Coopersale, 1920
Cosmopolitan A&S, 1966
Craven, 1932
East Essex Stallions, 1996
East Hanningfield & Great Burstead, 1887
Eastons, 1972
Epping, 1865
Farnham Harlequins, 1974
Fives & Heronians, 1937
Forest Gate, 2005
Frenford, 1985
Galleywood, 1931
Gidea Park & Romford, 1863
Goodmayes & Blythswood, 1995
Goresbrook, 1981
Great & Little Warley, 1948
Great Baddow, 1850
Great Canfield, 1920
Hadleigh & Thundersley, 1946
Hainault & Clayhall, 1919
Hamilton Lions (formerly Ilford Lions), 2008
Harlow, 1774
Harlow Town, 1960
Harold Wood, 1896
Havering-Atte-Bower, 1860
Herongate & Ingrave, 2008
High Beach, 1948
Hornchurch, 1783
Hornchurch Athletic, 1936
Horndon-on-the-Hill, 1956
Ilford, 1879
Ilford Catholic, 1920
Island Taverners, 1994
Jaguar, 1979
K2, 1985
Kashmir, 1975
Kelvedon & Feering, 1868
Langley, 1884
Leigh-on-Sea, 1907
Leyton Orient Supporters, 1985
Little Baddow, 1904
London Fire Brigade, 1920
Loughton, 1879
Maldon, 1975
Marshes, 1965
Matching Green, 1925
Mathews, 1938
Maylands Green, 1942
Mountnessing, 1994
Navestock, 1768
Nazeing Common, 1883
Newham, 1987
Newport, 1953
North Weald, 1984
Oakfield Parkonians, 1906
Old Brentwoods, 1954
Old Chelmsfordians, 1937
Old Sectonians, 1951
Old Southendian & Southchurch, 1924
Old Victorians (Thursday), 1878
Orsett, 1900
Potter Street and Church Langley, 1865
Rainham, 1896
Rankins, 1881
Rayleigh, 1902

Rayleigh Fairview, 1953
Redbridge Parks, 1932
Roydon, 1939
Saffron Walden, 1859
Seven Kings, 2004
Sheering, 1947
Shenfield, 1921
South Loughton, 1938
South Weald, 1927
South Woodford, 1884
Spartan, 1925
St. Clements, 1895
Stanford-le-Hope, 1887
Stansted Hall & Elsenham, 1888
STM, 2008
Stock, 1769
Tennyson, 1918
Thaxted, 1878
Theydon Bois, 1868
Thurrock, 1991
Tillingham, 1750
Upminster, 1858
Waltham, 2000
Walthamstow, 1862
Wanstead, 1866
West Essex, 1921
West Ham, 1999
Westcliff-on-Sea, 1902
Wickford, 1887
Wickham St Pauls, 1920
Willow Herbs Blackmore, 1951
Witham, 1847
Woodford Wells, 1864
Writtle, 1850

Hampshire

Aldershot, 1947
Cove, 1935
Crondall, 1879
Eversley, 1787
Fleet, 1896
Hartley Wintney, 1770
Oakley, 1863
Odiham & Greywell, 1764
Vagabonds, 1980
Yateley, 1881

Hertfordshire

Abbots Langley, 1844
Aldbury Entertainers, 1960
Aldenham, 1972
Allenburys, 1912
Archway Ladder, 1983
Baldock Town, 1879
Bamville, 1932
Bayford & Hertford Nondescripts, 1951
Bengeo, 1875
Bentley Heath, 1920
Berkhamsted, 1875
Bishop's Stortford, 1825
Bovingdon, 1884
Boxmoor, 1857
Bramfield, 1952
Broxbourne, 1848
Buntingford, 1980
Bushey, 1864
Carpenters Arms, 1985
Cheshunt, 1860
Chipperfield Clarendon, 1844
Chorleywood, 1851
Cockfosters, 1873
County Hall (Herts.), 1936
Croxley Guild of Sport & Social, 2012
Datchworth, 1930
Dynamics Hatfield, 1923
Essendon, 1810
F.M.Arthur's XI, 1928
Flamstead, 1875
Frogmore, 1850
Full Tossers, 1988
Great Gaddesden, 1874
Greenwood Park, 1992
Harpenden, 1863
Harpenden Dolphins, 1944
Hatch End, 1933
Hatfield Hyde, 1889
Hemel Hempstead Town, 1850
Hertford, 1860
Hertingfordbury, 1890
Hitchin, 1866
Hockerill, 1878
Hoddesdon, 1882
Ickleford, 1947
Ivanhoe, 1916
Kimpton, 1880
Kings Langley, 1830
Knebworth Blues, 1969
Knebworth Park, 1871
Langleybury, 1950
Letchworth Garden City, 1905
Leverstock Green, 1920
Little Berkhamsted Sahibs, 1883
Little Gaddesden, 1890
Little Hadham, 1948

London Colney, 1858
Long Marston, 1867
Met.Police (Bushey), 1920
Monken Hadley, 1954
Myddelton House, 1879
North Mymms, 1861
Northchurch, 1885
Oak Hill, 1955
Offley & Stopsley, 1998
Old Albanian, 1930
Old Camdenians, 1931
Old Elizabethans, 1940
Old Finchleians, 1904
Old Fullerians, 1947
Old Haberdashers, 1947
Old Merchant Taylors, 1912
Old Owens, 1924
Outlaws, 1947
Pirton, 1964
Players & Jesters, 1975
Potten End, 1894
Potters Bar, 1862
Preston, 1882
Radlett, 1884
Redbourn, 1823
Reed, 1956
Rosslyn, 1922
Roving Reporters, 1973
Roxbourne, 1946
Saracens, 1929
Sarratt, 1889
Sawbridgeworth, 1862
Shenley Village, 1861
Southgate Compton, 1970
St. Albans, 1800
St. Margaretsbury, 1737
Stevenage, 1878
Totteridge Millhillians, 1881
Tring Park, 1836
Waltham Cross Rosedale, 1891
Watford Town, 1950
Watton-at-Stone, 1837
Welwyn Garden City, 1921
West Herts, 1891
Wheathampstead, 1824
Whitwell, 1955
Wormley, 1947

Kent

Bapchild, 1784
Bardhill, 1935
Beckenham, 1866
Bexley, 1805
Bexleyheath, 1870
Bickley Park, 1868
Bidborough, 1893
Blackheath, 1863
Blackheath Select XI, 1993
Blue Star, 1920
Borstal, 1885
Bromley, 1820
Bromley Common, 1889
Bromley Town & Old Bromleians, 1885
Burgess Park (Colts), 2000
Carlton Sports, 1928
Catford & Cyphers, 1890
Catford Wanderers, 1906
Chislehurst & West Kent, 1802
Crofton, 1986
Cudham Wyse, 1965
Dartford, 1727
Dulwich Wanderers, 1930
Earlswood Strollers, 1985
Farningham, 1857
Folkestone, 1856
Greenheath, 1951
Hayes, 1828
High Halstow, 1889
Holmesdale, 1840
Horton Kirby, 1882
L.E.S.S.A. Wanderers, 1987
Leigh (Tonbridge), 1700
Lettsom Eleven, 1982
Limpsfield Chart, 1900
Linden Park, 1876
Lordswood, 1966
Meopham, 1776
Nonington, 1878
OD Cuaco, 2001
Old Brockleians, 1928
Old Elthamians, 1935
Orpington, 1848
Pembury, 1872
R.A.C.S., 1920
Rainham, 1856
Ramsgate Corinthian, 1933
Rasra Eagles, 1924
Roan & Lambethan, 2002
Robinson Lakeside, 1991
Rodmersham, 1885
Sabina, 1964
Sandwich Town, 1880
Sevenoaks Vine, 1734
Shades, 1987
Southborough, 1800
St. Mary Cray, 1920

Statics, 1950
Ten-Em-Bee, 2014
The Mote, 1857
Tunbridge Wells, 1782
Waggoners, 1985
Walmer, 1860
Wickham Park, 1933
Wilmington, 1889
Wye, 1882

Middlesex

Acton, 1908
Agricola, 1973
AJ Sports, 1990
Alexandra Park, 1888
Arkley, 1932
Barnes, 1919
BBC Bushmen, 1943
Belmont & Edgware, 1974
Bessborough, 1904
Bohemians, 1979
Botany Bay, 1900
Brentham, 1908
British Airways, 1947
Brondesbury, 1887
C.R.S.Cardinals, 1931
Captain Scott XI, 1978
Chaseville, 1926
Chiswick & Whitton, 1999
Crane, 1990
Crouch End Calthorpe, 1874
Cypos, 1990
Darji, 1972
Ealing, 1870
Ealing Hanwellians, 1851
Eastcote, 1863
Edmonton, 1872
Elite, 2000
Elthorne, 1990
Enfield, 1856
Finchley, 1832
Fives, 1941
Fleet Street Strollers, 1976
Gaieties, 1937
Gentlemen of Hampstead, 1960
Golden Eleven, 1976
Goodwill Wanderers, 1991
Grace's, 1996
Grimsdyke, 1946
Gubbays, 1981
Hadley Wood Green Sports, 1996
Hampstead, 1865
Hampton Hill, 1855
Hampton Wick Royal, 1863
Harefield, 1938
Harlesden Wanderers, 1923
Harrow, 1888
Harrow St Mary's, 1881
Harrow Town, 1913
Harrow United, 1995
Harrow Weald, 1878
Harrowdene, 1927
Harrow-on-the-Hill, 1972
Hayes, 1797
Headstone St. George, 1928
Highgate, 1879
Highgate Irregulars, 1983
HLCC, 1975
Holtwhites Trinibis, 1889
Honourable Artillery Company, 1846
Hornsey, 1870
Ickenham, 1850
Iconoclasts, 1979
Indian Gymkhana, 1916
Inter-Varsity, 1973
J B, 2011
Kensington, 1973
Kenton, 1921
Kew, 1881
King's Bench Walk, 2000
LCR XI, 2011
London Erratics, 1974
London Maccabi Vale, 1956
London Theatres, 1958
London Tigers, 2007
Mayfield, 1925
Middlesex Tamil Sports & Social, 1989
N.P.L.Teddington, 2000
New Calypsonians, 1925
Nomads, 1903
North Harrow, 1954
North London Muslim, 1980
North Middlesex, 1875
North Two, 1982
Northampton Exiles, 1897
Northfields, 1920
Northwood, 1878
Northwood Town, 1937
Nu-Line, 2008
Octopus, 1947
Old Actonians, 1922
Old Citizens, 1893
Old Eastcotians, 1959
Old Isleworthians & Heston, 1998
Old Minchendenians, 1927
Pacific, 1983

Paddington, 1920
Paragon, 1977
Parkfield & Headstone, 1863
Perivale Phoenicians, 1940
Phoenix, 2005
Pinner, 1835
Priory Park, 1967
Queensbury, 1932
Rajput Samaj, 1981
Ramgahria, 1993
Red Sky, 2013
Richmond, 1740
Ruislip, 1960
Ruislip Victoria, 1947
Shepherds Bush, 1882
South Hampstead, 1875
South Harrow, 1931
Southall Dragons, 1994
Southgate, 1855
Southgate Adelaide, 1870
Southlands (formerly Southgate Synagogue), 1976
Spelthorne Melrose, 1929
St. John's Wood, 1951
Stage, 1930
Stanmore, 1853
Stanmore Jaffereys, 1986
Stanmore Warriors, 2012
Tabard Pilgrims, 1996
Teddington, 1827
Teddington Town, 1891
Thames Valley Gentlemen, 1967
Thames Valley Ramblers, 1921
The Cricket Society, 1945
The Windermere, 2008
Turnham Green and Polytechnic, 1853
Twickenham, 1833
U.C.S. Old Boys, 1896
Uxbridge, 1789
Uxbridge Casuals, 1922
Washington, 1973
Waxlow, 1957
Wealdstone Corinthians, 1932
Wembley, 1860
West Harrow, 1918
West London, 2006
White Swans, 1982
Whittington, 1990
Wilkinson Way, 1978
Willesden Community, 2010
Willesden Green, 1981
Winchmore Hill, 1880
Woodlands (Kingsbury), 1945
Woodlawn, 1937
Wycombe House, 1889
Yarl, 1992
Youth Wing, 1978

Norfolk

Norwich, 1999

Northamptonshire

Pimms Allsorts, 2013

Nottinghamshire

West Indian Cavaliers, 1980

Oxfordshire

Aston Rowant, 1881
Banbury, 1949
Bicester & North Oxford, 1995
Greys Green, 1873
Henley, 1886
Hetairoi, 1980
Horspath, 1892
Kidmore End, 1863
Oxford, 1994
Peppard Stoke Row, 1890

Surrey

54th OCA, 1954
Abinger, 1870
Actors Anonymous, 1986
Addiscombe, 1865
Albamorphics, 1983
Ashtead, 1887
Australia House, 1920
Badgers, 1959
Bank of England, 1908
Banstead, 1842
Barnes Common, 1976
Barnes Occasionals, 1984
Battersea Ironsides, 1943
Beddington, 1863
Beddington Village, 1925
Blackheath, 1878
Blues, 1948
Brook, 1923
Burgh Heath, 1898

Byfleet, 1876
Camberley, 1944
Carnegie, 1955
Caterham, 1873
Chadwick, 1980
Chaldon, 1921
Charing X Westminster Med.Sc.Staff, 1960
Cheam, 1864
Chertsey, 1737
Chessington, 1919
Chiddingfold, 1804
Chipstead-Coulsdon & Walcountians, 1874
Chobham, 1843
Chudley Ales, 1975
Churchleigh, 1947
Churt, 1875
Clapham Nomads, 1994
Clapham Old Xaverians, 1946
Cobham Avorians, 1928
Croydon, 2011
Deando Ruxley, 2002
Dorking, 1771
Downsiders, 1983
Dulwich, 1867
East Horsley, 1937
East Molesey, 1730
Economicals, 1952
Effingham, 1853
Egham, 1913
Englefield Green, 1879
Epsom, 1800
Epsom Methodist, 1986
Esher, 1863
Farnham, 1782
Felbridge & Sunnyside, 1893
Forest Green Estonia, 1895
Franklin Lewin, 1921
Frensham, 1899
Frimley, 1820
Frimley Green, 1982
Giltec, 1953
Godalming, 1767
Grouse and Label, 2006
Guildford, 1870
Ham & Petersham, 1815
Haslemere, 1827
Headley, 1893
Hook & Southborough, 1870
Horley, 1792
Horsley & Send, 1886
International Rescue, 1991
Jack Frost XI, 1961
Jesters, 1927
John Fisher, 1929
Kempton, 2003
Kings (Ashford), 1993
Kingston Methodist, 1904
Leatherhead (Sunday Strollers), 1850
Leigh, 1900
London Gymkhana, 2012
Long Ditton, 1959
Magdalen, 1944
Malden Wanderers, 1879
Maori Oxshott, 1896
Merrow, 1857
Merstham, 1864
Mitcham, 1685
Mogador Wanderers, 1949
Morden, 1891
Mostyn, 1967
Mpingwe, 1990
Mynthurst, 1998
Nasir, 2005
Nepotist, 1980
Normandy, 1895
Norwood Exiles, 1995
Nutfield, 1863
Nutley Hall, 1981
Ockham, 1900
Ockley, 1852
Old Ashfordians, 1928
Old Castletonians, 1963
Old Dorkinian, 1949
Old Emanuel, 1926
Old Freemens, 1955
Old Pauline, 1930
Old Rutlishians, 1909
Old Suttonians, 1959
Old Tenisonians, 1923
Old Whitgiftians, 1878
Old Wimbledonians, 1935
Old Woking, 1962
Oxted and Limpsfield, 1890
Park Hill, 1928
Pirbright, 1787
Pretenders, 1956
Putney, 1870
Puttenham & Wanborough, 1837
Pyrford, 1858
R.N.V.R., 1946
Raynes Park Former Pupils, 1947
Reigate Pilgrims, 1946
Reigate Priory, 1852
Richmond Nomads, 1946
Ripley, 1749
Riverbank Ramblers, 1989
Riverside, 1949
Roehampton, 1842

Sanderstead, 1881
Selsdon, 1927
Shamley Green, 1840
Shepperton, 1881
South Bank, 1892
South Park Manor, 2003
Southern Railway and Kenley, 2002
Spencer, 1872
St. James, 1986
St. Lukes, 1983
Sticky Wicket, 2009
Streatham & Marlborough, 1805
Sunbury, 1938
Surbiton Imperial, 1986
Surrey Cryptics, 1976
Surrey Gymkhana, 1999
Surrey Ovalites, 1981
Sutton, 1857
Tadworth, 1903
Temple Sheen Eccentrics, 1944
Thames Ditton, 1833
The Cricketers Cricket Club, 2013
Thorpe Manhattens, 1953
Tilford, 1886
Trafford (Croydon), 1990
Trinity (Oxley), 1948
Trinity Mid-Whitgiftian, 1908
Uplands, 1940
Valley End, 1895
Verdayne Green, 1982
Viscount, 1981
Vishwa, 1984
Wallington, 1921
Walton-on-Thames, 1898
Warlingham, 1856
West Indies United, 1960
Westfield, 1875
Weybridge, 1924
Weybridge Vandals, 1932
Wimbledon, 1854
Wimbledon United, 1920
Woking & Horsell, 1905
Woldingham Village, 1900
Wood Street Village, 1959
Woodmansterne, 1921
Woodpeckers, 1936
Worcester Park, 1920

East Sussex

Battle, 1738
Chiddingly, 1958
Crowborough, 1945
Ditchling, 1818
Fletching, 1912
Hailsham, 1884
Hellingly, 1758
Ringmer, 1755
Rottingdean, 1758
Wadhurst, 1758
Willingdon, 1890

West Sussex

Crawley, 1886
Findon, 1867
Horsham, 1771
Horsham Trinity, 1921
Keymer & Hassocks, 1905
Lindfield, 1747
Stirlands, 1936
Three Bridges, 1884

The following leagues are also affiliated to the CCC: Shepherd Neame Essex Cricket League, Shepherd Neame Kent Cricket League, Middlesex County Cricket League, The Surrey Championship, Home Counties Premier Cricket League, Saracens Hertfordshire Cricket League, Bedfordshire County Cricket League, BTCL (British Tamils Cricket League), Chess Valley Sunday League, Morant Chilterns Cricket League, East Sussex Cricket League, Elliott Davis London Cricket League, Essex County Cricket League, ETCL Premier Cricket League, Herts & Essex Cricket League, Jersey Cricket Board, Middlesex 1987 Cricket League, Middlesex Championship, Middlesex Premier Cricket League, T-Rippon Mid-Essex Cricket League, NCL (National Cricket League), South East Sunday Cricket League, South London Sunday Cricket League, Fullers Surrey County League, Surrey Cricket League, Telugu Association of London Cricket League, Morrant Thames Valley Cricket League, Thameside Sunday League, The Essex Sunday League, Three Counties Cricket League, Victoria Park Community Cricket League, West Sussex Invitation Cricket League